EFFECTIVE
ADVOCACY
IN SOCIAL WORK

JANE DALRYMPLE & JANE BOYLAN

This book forms part of the SAGE Social Work in Action series,
edited by Steven M. Shardlow.

EFFECTIVE ADVOCACY IN SOCIAL WORK

JANE DALRYMPLE & JANE BOYLAN

Los Angeles | London | New Delhi
Singapore | Washington DC

Los Angeles | London | New Delhi
Singapore | Washington DC

SAGE Publications Ltd
1 Oliver's Yard
55 City Road
London EC1Y 1SP

SAGE Publications Inc.
2455 Teller Road
Thousand Oaks, California 91320

SAGE Publications India Pvt Ltd
B 1/I 1 Mohan Cooperative Industrial Area
Mathura Road
New Delhi 110 044

SAGE Publications Asia-Pacific Pte Ltd
3 Church Street
#10-04 Samsung Hub
Singapore 049483

Editor: Kate Wharton
Assistant editor: Emma Milman
Production editor: Katie Forsythe
Copyeditor: Solveig Gardner Servian
Proofreader: Imogen Roome
Indexer: Avril Ehrlich
Marketing manager: Tamara Navaratnam
Cover design: Wendy Scott
Typeset by: C&M Digitals (P) Ltd, Chennai, India
Printed in Great Britain by Henry Ling Limited at
the Dorset Press, Dorchester, DT1 1HD

MIX
Paper from
responsible sources
FSC
www.fsc.org FSC® C013985

Library of Congress Control Number: 2013935593

British Library Cataloguing in Publication data

A catalogue record for this book is available from
the British Library

ISBN 978-1-4462-0149-7
ISBN 978-1-4462-0150-3 (pbk)

For Rosemary and Pam

Contents

About the Authors

Jane Boylan is Senior Lecturer in Social Work at the University of Keele, England. Her research interests include advocacy, looked after children and children and young people's rights. She has published widely in the field of children's rights and advocacy, including *Understanding Advocacy for Children and Young People* (Open University Press, 2009) with Jane Dalrymple.

Jane Dalrymple is a freelance trainer and consultant. She practiced as a social worker in children and family services for many years and ran a national advocacy service for five years. For the last 16 years she has worked as a senior lecturer on the social work course at the University of the West of England. She has published widely in the field of advocacy including *Understanding Advocacy for Children and Young People* (Open University Press, 2009) with Jane Boylan. Jane now works as an independent trainer across the UK and in Europe and assesses independent advocates.

Acknowledgements

We have been fortunate in undertaking this work to have had the support of colleagues, friends and our families. Special thanks are due to all those who have commented on draft chapters and given thoughtful advice and observations. Particular thanks go to John Pierson, Mo Ray, Pat Woolley, Kate Mercer and Beverley Burke who all read various chapters and gave very helpful feedback. We would also like to thank the students and practitioners for enthusiastically sharing their experiences which contributed to case material, in particular we would like to thank Nicola, Bev, Isobel, Michael and Becky. Special thanks to Emma Milman of SAGE for her patience and support throughout the writing process. Thanks are also due to Steven Shardlow who originally approached us to write the book. Finally, Paul and Ian for their tolerance, support and good food.

The authors and publisher would like to thank the following for permission to reproduce copyright material in the form of extracts, figures and tables:

Figure 1.4 reprinted by kind permission of the Welsh Government.

Various extracts in Chapter 2 reprinted by kind permission of Joyce Rimmer.

Photo 2.1 reprinted by kind permission of the archive of the Institute of Medical Social Workers, Modern Records Centre, University of Warwick.

Photo 2.2 reprinted by kind permission of the National Portrait Gallery, London.

Derek's story in Chapter 3 reprinted with kind permission of Derek James and Advocacy Matters.

The extract from the research report in Chapter 3, Local authority children's rights services in Scotland, reprinted with kind permission of Susan Elsley.

Material in the 'Motivation to be a social worker' case study in Chapter 3 reprinted with the kind permission of Guardian News and Media Ltd.

Introduction

Advocacy has traditionally been a key element of social work practice (Coulshed and Orme, 1998; Payne, 2000a; Trevithick, 2005, 2012; Boylan and Dalrymple, 2009). It was identified as a central skill by the Central Council for Education and Training in Social Work (CCETSW) in 1995, an essential part of the social work role identified by the British Association of Social Workers (1996), and a key skill for social workers identified in the National Occupational Standards for Social Work (relevant for social workers in Wales, Scotland and Northern Ireland) where Key Role 3 states that social workers should support individuals to represent their needs, views and circumstances. An aspect of this role is to advocate with, and on behalf of individuals, families, carers, groups and communities (TOPSS UK Partnership, 2002). The Professional Capabilities Framework (TCSW, 2012) for social workers in England requires social workers to recognise and promote individual's rights to autonomy and self-determination (2012: 2) and advance human rights and promote social justice (2012: 4), and therefore we can see that effective social work advocacy is fundamental. However, while social workers recognise advocacy as an important feature of contemporary practice, they may feel less sure about how to translate the concept into action. This partly reflects the nature of social work today, which over recent years has become constrained by bureaucracy and proceduralisation of services and resources.

The development of independent advocacy, particularly the provision of statutory advocacy, has also developed within the current climate of social work practice, and has contributed to the way social workers now view their advocacy role. Service users have fought vigorously over many years to have a voice in decisions concerning their lives and in how services are provided, and have been a significant force in promoting the development of independent advocacy services. As a consequence, advocacy in social work has been subsumed by independent advocacy, with debates between the independent advocacy sector and health and welfare professionals about what advocacy really is. We believe that independent advocacy has a crucial role to play in maintaining the participation rights of people using services. Service users and carers must have access to independent advocacy support when it is difficult, if not impossible, for social workers to take on an advocacy role. However, we also argue that social workers and other health and welfare professionals have a crucial role to play in promoting rights, participation and service user involvement, and that they should be reclaiming their advocacy role.

The changing landscape of social work practice provides new opportunities for social workers to appraise their role as advocates. The introduction of more personalised responsive social care is one mechanism for supporting this approach in adult services. In children's services, more integrated approaches to service delivery mean that social workers are expected to familiarise themselves with the role of independent advocacy within a culture of shared working and joint responsibility. Such changes provide possibilities for independent advocacy services to become 'partners' in promoting the rights and voices of service users and carers, while maintaining their independence from service providers. Within this rapidly changing context of practice we argue for a culture of advocacy within social work where practitioners develop a critical awareness of when and how to use their advocacy skills appropriately.

In this book we will contextualise the concept of advocacy through an examination of the changing social work role alongside legal and policy requirements for service user involvement and advocacy/representation in decision making. We will explore the challenges that social workers face as advocates through consideration of three broad approaches to thinking about advocacy theory and practice: acting as advocates; supporting self-advocacy; and facilitating access to independent advocacy. Theoretical frameworks that inform social work advocacy will be examined, and ways of working with service users in order to ensure that their needs and views are represented will be explored. This will enable social workers to develop a critical awareness of how and when they can intercede as advocates. Through the use of case studies we will also consider issues for social workers in assessing when and how they might work with an independent advocate. The rationale for this book emanates from messages from research about advocacy practice, the need for service users to have access to independent advocacy, and advocacy in social work. The traditional advocacy role of social workers is located alongside discourses of rights, participation and service user involvement. These will be examined alongside policy imperatives that promote independent advocacy.

We begin in Chapter 1 by considering definitions of advocacy and examine the various approaches to advocacy in order to promote critical awareness about the parameters and limitations of social work advocacy. This will entail discussion about definitions of advocacy, the relationship between advocacy and social justice, and exploration of the way in which social work advocacy can effect change. Readers will be encouraged to consider how they can draw on models of advocacy in order to develop their advocacy role as social workers.

In Chapter 2 we go on to contextualise social work advocacy, providing a historical backdrop in which to locate social work and advocacy. The traditional role of social workers is examined, and the development of practice from 'doing on behalf of' to working alongside service users and carers is considered. The chapter begins with consideration of the historical context of practice and the development of legislation to include service users and carers in decision making and rights to have access to independent advocacy. It includes a timeline which highlights some key developments in social work and advocacy.

Chapter 3 provides a critique of the reviews of social work roles undertaken in all four nations of the United Kingdom. The chapter explores some of the commonalities and differences between the reviews and the relationship between various discourses within the legal and policy context and how these ideas inform practice. This is followed in Chapter 4 by an examination of advocacy skills. The chapter focuses on the principles of advocacy and how they can be integrated into the process of assessment, planning, intervention and review.

We move on in Chapter 5 to consider the role of social work advocacy in promoting partnership and participation with service users and carers. The chapter will also consider the challenges of partnership working within inter-disciplinary teams where the professionals involved may have different perspectives about promoting service user voice. Chapter 6 goes on to look at advocacy across the life course. Within the changing context of social care practice various forms of advocacy practice have developed with different service user groups such as young people, vulnerable adults and older people in various situations including transitions, immigration and criminal justice. We will highlight the commonalities in promoting service user voice as well as considering different knowledge and skills needed in particular situations.

Research indicates that service users and carers have found complaints procedures inaccessible and difficult to use. This is reflected in the statutory right to independent advocacy in relation to representations and complaints procedures. In Chapter 7 we will therefore consider the tensions for social workers and services users when a complaint has been made. This will include discussion about accountability and creating open organisations through using complaints systems for improving practice. The historical use of advocates to support service users making a complaint will be examined as well as the impact this has had on the relationship between independent advocacy and social work practice.

Chapter 8 looks at legal and policy mandates for independent advocacy and the place of independent advocacy in social work practice. Finally, Chapter 9 draws on the arguments developed through the book to demonstrate that social work advocacy is an essential element of social work practice. Developing a culture of advocacy provides the opportunity for social workers to be activists: dynamic rather than reactive practitioners. Reclaiming advocacy in social work is a step towards ensuring that the experiences of service users and carers are valued, and form the bedrock of social work policy and practice which makes a difference in the lives of the people who need to use them.

1

What is Advocacy and How do we Use it in Social Work?

Overview

- Context of social work advocacy
- Defining advocacy in relation to professional practice
- Social work advocacy
- Models of advocacy
- Commentary
- Summary
- Discussion questions

Advocacy has been described as being 'at the heart of social work' (Sheafor and Horejsi, 2003: 57), a key function of social work practice in terms of helping service users and carers become independent from service providers and in the process developing the skills to advocate for themselves (Haynes and Mickleson, 1997) and an important element of social work practice (Payne, 2000a). Advocacy can be defined in many ways, but the following definition is a useful starting point. This definition is part of the guidance for Independent Mental Capacity Advocates introduced through the Mental Capacity Act 2005 in England. It relates to people who use mental health services and are deemed to lack capacity – a group who can struggle to have a voice in the systems and structures that impact on their lives:

Advocacy ... promotes equality, social justice and social inclusion. It can empower people to speak up for themselves. Advocacy can help people become more aware of their own rights, to exercise those rights and be involved in and influence decisions that are being made about their future. (Lee, 2007: 7)

We see here that advocacy involves ensuring that service users are able to have a voice in decisions that concern their lives – to make their views known and be heard. However, there is also a broader meaning to advocacy at the start of this definition which echoes social work values in relation to promoting equality, social justice and social inclusion.

The notion of advocacy as a mechanism to promote social justice is an element of other advocacy definitions from various sources. Social justice reflects the activism of advocacy and has been explained as 'an idea that mobilises people to act in order to bring about change' (Newman and Yeates, 2008: 2). While the concept of social justice is contested, the important element here is its 'mobilising' potential which has been fundamental in efforts to challenge inequality and injustice: for example, motivating social workers to engage in social action (Hare, 2004). Social justice has been defined as 'an ideal condition in which all members of a society have the same basic rights, protection, opportunities, obligations, and social benefits' (Reamer, 1998, cited in Hare, 2004: 416). Advocacy therefore works to ensure that service users and carers, who are often denied these basic rights and opportunities, are empowered not only to regain voice and agency but also to be recognised as citizens. This is reflected in a definition of advocacy by the Scottish Executive, which states that:

[Advocacy is] a crucial element in achieving social justice. It is a way to ensure that everyone matters and everyone is heard – including people who are at risk of exclusion and people who have particular difficulties in making their views known. (SIAA, 2010: 4)

Later in the chapter we will see that this principle is also fundamental to social work practice. However, before thinking about social work advocacy we will first consider models of advocacy more generally, going on to consider the origins of social work advocacy. Finally, the chapter will examine the role of advocacy within social work practice.

Models of advocacy

A way of understanding social work advocacy in contemporary practice is to consider a number of theoretical frameworks which have developed within generic advocacy practice. These are examined below.

Case (or issue-based) and systemic (or cause) advocacy

This model identifies two elements of advocacy:

- Case or issue-based advocacy (where work is focused with individuals or small groups such as families in a task-centred way).
- Systemic or cause advocacy (where knowledge from individual cases contributes to collective advocacy for systemic change to legislation, policy or practice).

For many social workers case advocacy is more likely to be part of their day-to-day practice. The empowering potential of advocacy can best be understood in terms of the relationship between case and systemic advocacy, which identifies how advocacy can contribute to changes at both individual (case) and structural (systemic) levels. However, advocacy at both levels are inevitably inter-related (Mickelson, 1995). Social work advocacy aims to promote change, and a model for understanding advocacy that links both case and systemic advocacy (see Figure 1.1) demonstrates the necessity of this inter-relationship since individual situations provide the information required to promote changes in systems, policy and legislation (Office of the Child Youth and Family Advocate, 2000).

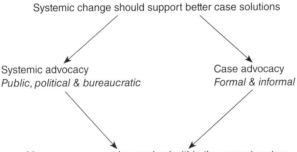

Root causes of many problems experienced by service users and carers are systemic

Systemic change should support better case solutions

Systemic advocacy
Public, political & bureaucratic

Case advocacy
Formal & informal

Many cases cannot be resolved within the current system
Case advocacy 'informs' our systemic advocacy and tells us what changes are needed

Figure 1.1   Framework for understanding advocacy

Case advocacy informing systemic advocacy

The UCAN independent advocacy project was set up in 1994 and worked closely with the local authority until 2005. The work of the project focused in the early days on children and young people involved in child protection and the project worked from the premise

(Continued)

(Continued)

that since many children and young people start being 'looked after' (Children Act 1989) through the child protection process, they needed to be able to experience 'a fair and just process at that stage, with opportunity to be heard, take part in decision making and have an understanding of their own protection needs' (Wyllie, 2002: 6).

In relation to child protection, one way of promoting systemic work was that every time a child or young person used UCAN they had the opportunity for their views and experiences about advocacy, and the processes/systems they found themselves in, to be recorded. With their permission, these views were used anonymously to influence the child protection and 'looked after' systems (that is, an ongoing, systematic process at the time that it is important to children and young people) (UCAN, 2001: 15). In this way the organisation was able to identify how advocacy became a tool for promoting change:

> Advocacy is a process for change, a process for learning. It stimulates respect for children's and young people's rights and promotes participation in the planning and challenging of the systems that impact on their lives. Acting on children's and young people's experiences and views, the advocacy extends beyond individual casework. (UCAN, 2005)

Combining the promotion of rights with changes in policy and practice required the advocacy project to:

- Listen to and hear the views of individual young people who had presented feedback about their experiences of case advocacy, the advocacy service and the systems they were involved in.
- Use the views of young people to inform cause or systemic advocacy.
- Liaise closely with the child protection co-ordinator, independent chairs of Child Protection Conferences and social work teams.
- Work together with project staff to facilitate practical ways of working towards greater participation of children and young people.
- Involve children and young people in this process.

These actions helped to shape a number of changes, such as an invitation letter sent to young people about their conference, minutes of the meeting sent to young people, and ensuring that young people had the opportunity to enter the conference room before any of the professionals.

Active and passive advocacy

Another way of understanding advocacy is in terms of active and passive approaches (Jenkins, 1995). The two approaches relate to perspectives of service users either as individuals requiring provision or protection or as citizens and active participants. Passive advocacy involves the advocate speaking up for someone else, and active advocacy is applied to speaking up for oneself. However, these approaches can also be seen as part of a continuum (Hodgson, 1995), since advocacy in practice is likely to combine both approaches. Furthermore, advocacy is contested, which means that it is difficult to identify what constitutes advocacy. For example, some independent advocates do not necessarily view social work advocacy as 'proper' advocacy or recognise social workers as having an advocacy role. Some argue that the advocacy role of social workers is only located at the passive end of the continuum. Hodgson also makes the distinction between case and systemic advocacy, and notes that these are all linked (see Figure 1.2).

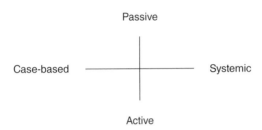

Figure 1.2   Hodgson's (1995) model of advocacy

Active and passive advocacy

CASE EXAMPLE

Mika (age 5) and Alec (age 7) have been living with foster carers for just over a week, having been brought into the care of the local authority because of concerns relating to emotional abuse and neglect. Their parents both have learning difficulties. There is a close bond between them and their children. Alec told the foster carer that he wanted to see his parents. He explained to the carer that he was worried that Mika was not well because he was normally very noisy and lively and he thought that this was because he missed his mother. Alec said that his mother was not well and that he understood that she could not look after them properly but that they needed to see their parents. The foster carer realised that while Alec had some understanding of the situation, Mika was finding it more difficult. The carer contacted the social worker and asked her to visit the children to explain what was happening and to arrange for them to see their parents as soon as possible. The social worker visited Alec and Mika and tried to explain to them why they were living away from their parents. In talking with the children she observed that Mika was very withdrawn as a result of not seeing his parents, and she listened to what Alec had to say about the situation. He said 'It's OK living here and we like it. But I'm worried about Mum and Dad 'cos they will be unhappy now. I used to help them and I love them very much. I want them to be OK too. It would be nice if they could live here.' At a review[1] of the placement the social worker represented Alec's views and felt that regular contact would be in the best interests of the two boys. However, the professionals

(Continued)

(Continued)

involved were not in agreement about what should happen. The social worker spent time with Alec to promote his involvement in the decision making by looking at ways he could present his views and ensure that they were heard at the next review meeting. The options included Alec attending all or part of the meeting, Alec drawing a picture or making a wishlist that either he or the social worker could present to the meeting, or the foster carer supporting him either to attend the meeting or by presenting his views. Alec wanted to go to the meeting with the social worker so that he could tell people what he wanted. He drew a picture which he took to the second review to explain how he felt. Before the meeting he practised what he wanted to say with the social worker and his foster carer.

In this situation both passive and active advocacy were used to support Alec and his brother:

- The foster carer advocated for Alec and Mika in asking the social worker to visit to explain what was happening.
- The social worker represented Alec's views at the first meeting.
- The social worker enabled Alec to have a more active role where he was supported to be engaged in the decision-making process and was encouraged to self-advocate.

External and internal advocacy

This model fits well with social work advocacy. 'External advocacy' refers to advocates working outside a system, while 'internal advocacy' relates to advocacy by social workers and other professionals working within a system. In the early development of advocacy theory, external advocacy was defined as 'an independent movement of consumers … and their allies to monitor and change human service agencies' (Bicklen, 1976: 310). Internal advocacy was described as 'a continuous and cooperative process of interactions' between service users and professionals guaranteeing the rights of service users to appropriate services. Internal advocacy has been identified as 'a critical component' of the partnership relationship that needs to exist between service users and social workers or other professionals (McLoughlin et al., 1979).

CASE EXAMPLE

External and internal advocacy

Parents for children and young people with specific needs will come into contact with a range of professionals and often find that they are the only people fighting for their children's rights. They also work with professionals to ensure that their children receive the services they need and that they are supported as carers. The co-operative process (internal advocacy) can sometimes be challenging for the professionals involved. It has been suggested, for example, that after a series of negative experiences with professionals, parents may be categorised as either 'resistant' (afraid of professionals and sceptical about procedures) or 'compliant' (agreeing with anything that professionals say, agreeing with decisions and letting professionals take the lead). The challenge for social workers in such situations is to defuse any resentment and defensiveness with those parents who may be finding it difficult to work with professionals and to encourage participation of parents who tend to follow the professional lead. Social workers without advocacy skills in such situations may 'drive the resistant parent to anger and the compliant parent home' (McLoughlin et al., 1979: 55). Figure 1.3 demonstrates patterns of interactions that may occur.

	Advocate behaviours		Non-advocate behaviours	
	Verbal	Non-verbal	Verbal	Non-verbal
'Resistant' type parents	'Please explain your concerns further.' 'How can we help?' 'Could I tell you what we've found?' 'Let's consider all the alternatives.' 'Let's look at the pluses and minuses of each alternative.'	Listens with no interruptions. Keeps eye contact. Sits next to a parent or at a round table.	'We know what's best ...' 'We have decided ...' 'The alternative is ... or else ...' 'Your child just won't respond ...'	Looks at papers, avoids eye or body contact with parent. Sits far away from parent, often has a physical barrier. Appears agitated or in a hurry, e.g. looking at a watch or clock.
'Compliant' type parents	Constantly asks questions about the child or young person concerned. 'Let's talk about the options/ recommendations – please tell me what you think.' 'What thoughts/ ideas do you have about what is best?'	As above. Takes as much time as necessary to ensure that parent's and children/young people's rights are respected. Does not show signs of impatience, e.g. watching clock.	'We have decided ...' Nothing else needs to be said because the parents want to get the process finished as soon as they can.	Avoids eye or body contact. Moves quickly through the process to get things finished.

Figure 1.3 Patterns of interactions of Social Worker and Parent (adapted from McLoughlin et al., 1979: 55)

Welsh model: advocacy jigsaw

The Welsh Government has developed a model for providing advocacy services for children and young people which recognises that there are different ways of providing advocacy and a range of people who can be advocates. In particular it identifies the advocacy role of professionals as a key part of an advocacy jigsaw – where all

ADVOCACY JIGSAW

There are many different ways of providing advocacy, and many people who can be advocates. However, there is a difference between Informal Advocacy, Formal Advocacy, Independent/Professional Advocacy and Peer Advocacy. The following jigsaw shows these differences and how they interlink.

Examples of related and interlinked services policy areas

14-19 learning pathways

Participation and Children's Rights

Personal Support

Education Inclusion

Social Services Guidance on Complaints

NHS Guidance on Complaints

Youth Support Services

School Counselling

Formal Advocacy

Sometimes you might prefer to ask for help to access your rights and entitlements through professionals who work with children and young people. These are usually people who are paid to help and advocate on behalf of children and young people i.e. youth workers, teachers, school nurses, play workers, care workers etc. They help you get information, find out about services, help you make decisions, find where to get more help if you need it, and make sure you have a say in decisions that affect you.

Peer Advocacy

Sometimes you might prefer to go to other children and young people for help and support to have something stopped, started or changed. Some children and young people are more confident than others and they would feel comfortable in putting your opinion over to others. In some cases, children and young people have received training on being a peer advocate and are part of a scheme or a project.

Informal Advocacy

Most of you get support to access your rights and entitlements from parents, carers, family members, friends, neighbours, friends' parents and so on. They help you to get your point across, help you say how you feel and make decisions. They are unpaid advocates.

Independent/Professional Advocacy

When you feel that you are not being listened to, or are unable or stopped from accessing your rights and entitlements, some of you may want to access independent professional advocacy. This usually involves trained people who are qualified to help you have your voice heard in any decision that affect you. They may deal with specific issues because you're not happy with the current situation and feel that you are not being listened to. They could come with you to meetings and make sure you understood what was happening at all times, and that your opinion was considered. They do not offer advice, but help you express your view regardless of their opinion.

An Advocate....
- *Supports you to make sure you have your say.*
- *Listens to you.*
- *Gives you confidence.*
- *Gives you information.*
- *Gives you Practical help.*
- *Negotiates on your behalf.*

ADVOCACY MAY INCLUDE

Information Giving	Navigating	Listening	Supporting	Disentangling	Representing	Empowering	Advising	Negotiating

Figure 1.4 Advocacy jigsaw (WAG, 2009)

Source: Welsh Assembly Government (2009) *A Guide to the Model of Delivering Advocacy Services to Children and Young People.* Cardiff: Welsh Assembly Government. Republished with kind permission of the Welsh Government.

parts of the jigsaw interlink. Professionals are recognised as 'formal advocates' who are paid to help children and young people – which includes advocacy. The advocacy role of key people in the lives of children and young people (such as parents, neighbours and friends) is also recognised as important but is identified as 'informal' advocacy'. The other two parts of the jigsaw are peer advocacy – which recognises that often children and young people prefer to talk to their friends rather than adults (Butler and Williamson, 1994; Hallett et al., 2003) – and independent professional advocacy.

This model clearly acknowledges the importance of all forms of advocacy and that the edges of the different parts of the jigsaw are blurred. It recognises that children and young people may need to use any or all parts of the jigsaw either separately or together. Importantly, it brings into focus the need for access to different forms of advocacy support and puts the advocacy role of professionals firmly in the mix. Furthermore, this is enhanced by statutory guidance produced to support the implementation of the model.

Social work advocacy

Advocacy in social work has its origins in the 'casework' element of professions and in the Mutual Aid movement. The former is based on an individual model of representing someone's interests. The term comes from the Latin word *advocatus*, which means the function of an advocate is to give evidence by supporting verbally or making arguments for a cause (Woodrow, 1997). It is historically allied to law, with lawyers advocating for their clients within the judicial system. While primarily case advocacy operates at an individual level, it also involves representing the wider interests of service user groups within the judicial systems. For social workers the advocacy role takes on some of the qualities that might be used by a lawyer, described as 'preparing the way' for a service user, 'arranging a deal' with another agency or profession or 'organising resources' for a service user (Payne, 2000b: 46). For Payne, advocacy involves careful and complete representation of the views of a service user or a carer in decision-making processes.

The Mutual Aid movement of the 1800s advanced social change and community action. Mutual Aid is fundamentally about self-help. The Mutual Aid movement developed to support people with low incomes to save regular amounts from their wages to cover expenses such as funerals. We might recognise the underpinning philosophy in credit unions, which enable people to save and borrow without having to pay massive rates of interest. If people cannot borrow money from the usual channels, Mutual Aid is an important safety net to protect individuals from loan sharks. Despite the individualist focus, Mutual Aid is also a collective method of mutual support. However, there are tensions in the concepts of individualist and collectivist approaches to society. While by definition they appear to be oppositional, there is an association between them that creates some tension and ambiguity in understanding Mutual Aid. In a similar way there are tensions in understanding the concept of advocacy. At an individual level, there are commentators who feel that the ultimate goal of any advocacy should be self-advocacy (Brandon, 1995), while for others systemic or cause advocacy (to change policy and practice to promote macro change) may be the ultimate goal of any advocacy work (see Box 1.2).

Box 1.2   Advocacy and promoting change

[A]dvocacy organisations attempt to change the status quo. (Young, 1992: 4)

Social work advocacy works to 'effect changes in policies, practices and laws that affect all people in a specific class or group'. (Litzelfelner and Petr, 1997: 393)

Advocacy is 'a political act with consequences for both individuals and the community as a whole, challenging inequality, opposing racism, preventing abuse, or even introducing someone to a new opportunity or social setting – all constituting steps towards a more civil and just society'. (Henderson and Pochin, 2001: 15)

To assist clients in upholding their rights to receive resources and services or to actively support causes to change programs and policies that have a negative effect on individual clients or client groups. (Sheafor and Horejsi, 2003: 57)

These two origins of social work advocacy mean that advocacy operates in what Adams (2002: 180) calls the 'contested space' between informal self-representation and professional help and support. In some instances social workers might be supporting service users or carers advocating for themselves, either individually or as a group. In other situations a social worker or other service professional may be advocating on behalf of a service user or group of users. In very specific circumstances it involves a professional advocate with specific knowledge and expertise. Such a person will be independent of any health or social service system. This independence is important in certain situations. For example, legislation to protect the rights of people using mental health services provides for Independent Mental Health Advocates (IMHA) to support some people within the remit of the Mental Health Act 2007 and Independent Mental Capacity Advocates (IMCA) to protect the rights of some people within the remit of the Mental Capacity Act 2005. These roles are discussed further in Chapter 8. There are also a number of other situations where independent advocacy services are important and necessary to support service users or carers to have a voice in decision making. The skills for social work advococates in such situations are to have the knowledge and understanding to work with and support independent advocacy.

Framing definitions of advocacy in social work practice

The international definition of social work (adopted by the British Association of Social Workers in 2002) is generally used as a starting point to consider what social work does. The definition states that:

> The social work profession promotes social change, problem solving in human relationships and the empowerment and liberation of people to enhance well-being. Utilising theories of human behaviour and social systems, social work intervenes at points where people interact with their environments. Principles of human rights and social justice are fundamental to social work. (IFSW and IASSW, 2001)

While we will use this definition to examine the advocacy role of social work, it is important to note that it should not be accepted uncritically. A number of commentators note that it is an essentially western and colonial perspective that does not take account of other cultures (for example, Coates et al 2006; Hutchins and Taylor, 2007) with concepts that are open to interpretation within and between countries and professional communities (Leung, 2007). Yet it has been argued that for western social workers the definition does not take account of their prescribed role within statutory settings (Asquith et al., 2005; Welbourn, 2011). Definitions are never static; they reflect debates, emerging discourses and varying contexts of practice. However, while social work cannot and should not be constrained by definitions, there is a need for social work to be clear about its identity (Rogowski, 2010) particularly, perhaps, for those who predominantly work in the statutory sector and are therefore under the scrutiny of the public gaze. In a critical analysis of the international definition from a relational approach, Folgheraiter (2012) recasts the definition above, while continuing to follow its structure. He also acknowledges the complexity of social work, recognising that, as a discipline, it cannot be reduced to an abstract statement. At the same time he notes the need to 'fix essential coordinates from which to approach and savour' (2012: 107) what he calls the 'mystery' of social work. He offers a very short definition as an example of portraying social work from a relational perspective which, since we will refer to the relational perspective throughout this book, we have found helpful:

> Social work is every professional activity whose ultimate purpose is to transform people's concerns about their lives into human energy to change them for the better. (2012: 105)

For the purposes of examining advocacy in social work in the UK we are using the original international definition, while mindful of its limitations, as it is widely used in understanding contemporary social work practice, and is a useful tool to consider this very particular aspect of social work practice.

Adams et al. (2009a) note that three dimensions of social work can be seen in the international definition, which also equate to Payne's (2006) account of approaches to social work:

- Promoting social change.
- Promoting problem solving.
- Empowerment and liberation.

Social work advocacy is weaved through these dimensions. The first dimension (social change) relates to transformational social work (see, for example, Allan, 2003; Adams et al., 2005, 2009b), whether with individuals, groups or communities. Principles underpinning approaches to critical social work theory and practice relate to this aspect of social work. At an individual level it involves advocacy on behalf of service users' and carers' needs within health and social care services. Social work advocacy also involves enabling people who use services to understand the oppression and disadvantage they face and to use this knowledge to promote change. In work with groups or communities, social work brings people together for mutual help and support to promote social transformation through changing structures and challenging inequality and injustice in society. This aspect of social work advocacy is less about direct advocacy and more about supporting self- or collective advocacy with service users and carers and attempts to mobilise people to challenge the impact of oppression in society (Payne, 2009b). Many definitions of advocacy refer to promoting change and transformation (see Box 1.2).

CASE EXAMPLE

Promoting social change

Rav worked as a social worker with a national voluntary organisation that provided services for older people. He had been working with older prisoners in two prisons in his local area and became aware that a number of the prisoners had serious health problems which were not being met by the National Health Service (NHS). Rav was aware from working in the prison that many of the prisoners seemed resigned to the fact that they had lost their rights by being in prison. He therefore set up a monthly meeting for them to which he invited guest speakers. Rav contacted a local Independent Complaints Advocacy Service (ICAS[2]) who specifically worked with people who wanted to make complaints in relation to the NHS. An ICAS advocate spoke to the men and explained what advocacy is. The advocate told them that while ICAS could not support them to challenge the prison system, prisoners do have rights about making a complaint if they feel that they are being failed in relation to their health care treatment. While the prisoners initially had to use the prison complaints system, the advocate explained that if they were not satisfied they had a right to an advocate to support them through the NHS complaints process. An independent advocacy service was set up to enable the men to make a free call to ICAS using their PIN card. Leaflets and posters about the advocacy service were put onto every wing. As a result one man, who had been in prison a long time and had felt unable to complain about his serious health problems, felt able to improve his situation.

The advocacy skills of Rav in this example involved promoting change in the prison system to:

- Promote the rights of prisoners.
- Ensure that older prisoners had access to information about their rights to health care.
- Ensure that prisoners had access to the independent advocacy service if they wanted to make a complaint in relation to the NHS.

Hutchins and Taylor (2007) note that promoting change is not always easy for social workers employed by the state. This is because of the tensions in the social control elements of social work which are particularly relevant for statutory social workers in the UK (Dickens, 2011). Inevitably, this highlights the tensions for social work advocacy in statutory social work. Social workers in non-governmental organisations (NGOs) can find it easier to challenge state decision making but may also be dependent on either local or national government structures for their funding (Boylan and Dalrymple, 2009; Pithouse and Parry, 2005). In Rav's case, he promoted change by establishing a group which was welcomed by the prison governor and linked into a service (ICAS) that the prisoners had a statutory right to access.

The second dimension (promoting problem solving) is the process of providing help, advice, support and packages of services to enable people to manage the difficulties they face in their lives. Social work advocacy here involves supporting service users and carers to participate in decision making and ensuring that their wishes and feelings are promoted within health and social services (Payne, 2009b). A number of advocacy definitions recognise that empowerment and voice in decision making are important elements of advocacy practice (see Box 1.3).

Box 1.3   Advocacy and voice

Advocacy means amplifying the voice. (Samuel, 2002: 9)

It is a way of enabling those who may have difficulty speaking up for themselves to do so and thus can be key to involvement in decision making. It generally means representing the view of a person or supporting them to exercise their rights. (Nua Research Services, 2001 in Weafer, 2003: 7)

Advocacy involves a person(s), either an individual or a group ... or their representative, pressing their case with influential others, about situations which affect them directly or, and more usually, trying to prevent proposed changes which will leave them worse off. (Brandon, 1995: 1)

Problem solving

Charlotte is a 19-year-old learning disabled black young woman. She lives with her parents, and attends college where she has a number of friends, some of whom she also went to school with. The college is quite near to where she lives and so normally one of her parents or her older sister will drop her off and pick her up afterwards. Recently Charlotte has found out that a number of her friends have a 'personal budget'[3] and have been telling her about going to regular activities they have been attending at a community centre in another area of the town. Charlotte is keen to join her friends but her parents are a little disconcerted by this and ask social services for more information. Her social worker, Denise, provided Charlotte and her family with accessible information about personal budgets and explained how she could help them. However, Denise also became aware that Charlotte's wishes were rather different to those of her parents, who felt that Charlotte did not have enough experience of going out alone. They were worried that she would be 'easily led' by other young people. While they understood how a personal budget could be used and felt that this could be helpful for Charlotte, they did not feel that she should be able to use it in this way and were concerned about the autonomy this would give her. They were especially worried that Charlotte felt that the money would help her to travel to the community centre by bus. They had identified that there were other leisure and social activities that they felt would be better for her which were nearer home.

In order to support Charlotte, Denise's advocacy role in this case involved:

- Developing a relationship with Charlotte to ensure that she was able to have a voice in the decision making.
- Talking with Charlotte and her parents about possible risks and how to manage risk.
- Negotiating with Charlotte's parents to help them manage their anxiety and recognise that Charlotte was at an age when she could start to make informed decisions for herself – even if she needed the support of her family and social worker to do this.
- Identifying that Charlotte had strong and supportive relationships with her friends at college.
- Enabling Charlotte's parents to understand how Charlotte needed to continue to feel secure within her social network. This would then help her to develop her confidence and become more independent.

The third dimension (empowerment and liberation) is about empowering therapeutic practice (see Box 1.4). It involves the use of relationships and interpersonal skills to help the personal growth of people who are having a particularly difficult time and may be disadvantaged. The aim here is to enable service users and carers to find ways of dealing with the situations they are experiencing.

Box 1.4   Advocacy and empowerment

When people are denied or unable to gain access to a fair share of what's on offer in society – when they are denied information or opportunities to take part in decisions concerning their lives – when they are dispossessed of insight, dignity, self confidence – then it becomes necessary in a caring society for more powerful people to act with integrity on their behalf or wherever possible to enable them to move to a point where they can retrieve control for themselves. (Advocacy in Action, 1990)

Advocacy involves a person(s), either a vulnerable individual or group or their agreed representative, effectively pressing their case with influential others, about situations which either affect them directly or, and more usually, trying to prevent proposed changes which will leave them worse off. Both the intent and the outcome of such advocacy should increase the individual's sense of power; help them to feel more confident, to become more assertive and to gain increased choices. (Brandon, 1995: 1)

Many people in society are disempowered by systems which have a significant effect on almost every aspect of their lives. These are people who are disempowered to such an extent that they are unlikely to be able to fulfil their basic human needs, or demand their basic human rights. A person's initial hopes and dreams can be severely limited by this. Independent advocacy can help to widen a person's horizons and enable them to become active members of society. (Advocacy 2000, 2002: 49)

Empowerment

Mr Evers was a white 76-year-old male who was admitted to hospital under Section 2 of the Mental Health Act 1982. He was diagnosed with late onset of Huntington's Disease. After three months on the ward Mr Evers' condition was being assisted with medication and he became an informal patient under Section 131 of the Mental Health Act 1983. Isla was a social worker who had known the family for some time. When Mr Evers was ready to be discharged from hospital his family felt that he could not return home. Huntington's Disease is a degenerative condition and Mr Evers' aggressive behaviour and lack of insight into his condition (manifestations of the disease) meant that his wife felt unable to care for him at home. Isla initially discussed with Mr Evers the concerns that had led to the decision that he could not return to the family home. She knew that he needed to be aware of the consequences of his situation even though he might lack the capacity to understand it. She then needed to find a placement that acknowledged Mr Evers' views and would

CASE EXAMPLE

(Continued)

(Continued)

also meet his specialist needs. It was also important to Mr Evers that wherever he lived he would be able to take part in meaningful activities. Finally, Isla had to present a request for funding to the Trust's Funding Approval Panel of placement options. She was aware that she would have to put a strong case to gain funding approval.

Key aspects of Isla's social work advocacy role involved:

- Talking to Mr Evers on the ward in order to obtain his thoughts on placement options and find out his needs and wishes.
- Liaising with his family to ascertain their views. All were agreed that they wanted a placement in an accessible location so that the family could visit regularly.
- Researching Huntington's Disease in order to understand how it develops, the impact this would have on Mr Evers' caring needs and the best options for placement.
- Researching a range of housing options, thinking about the risk that accompanied various options both to Mr Evers and to others. She arranged for providers to assess Mr Evers on the ward.
- Throughout the process Isla kept Mr Evers and his family informed about what she was doing as she liaised with the Huntington's Disease Association, ward staff, psychiatrists, residential and nursing home care staff in order to achieve a positive and informed outcome for Mr Evers.

While Isla initially identified her advocacy role as ensuring that Mr Evers' wishes and feelings were taken into account when planning provision, her advocacy role went beyond this in the process of finding appropriate accommodation. She also found that she had to challenge the responses of potential providers to 'labelling' Mr Evers. Mr Evers was declined by one residential home because of his mental health diagnosis. Another home would not even assess Mr Evers regardless of the fact that he was receiving medication, was in the early stages of Huntington's Disease and was therefore still quite independent. Isla felt that it was important to challenge such views as they could negatively influence the outcome.

Commentary

Definitions of advocacy incorporate many of the principles that underpin social work (see Figure 1.5). In this chapter we have considered the roles of social work and advocacy as a means of promoting voice and empowerment at a more individual level and challenging social injustice and promoting change at a systemic level. The process of seeking to define advocacy in the development of social work has been ongoing and has been criticised by Kutchins and Kutchins for appearing to expand the meaning of advocacy 'to encompass the full range of social action for worthy causes' (1978: 22). They go on to state that advocacy is merely a technique, even though it is a good technique, for promoting social, political and economic change.

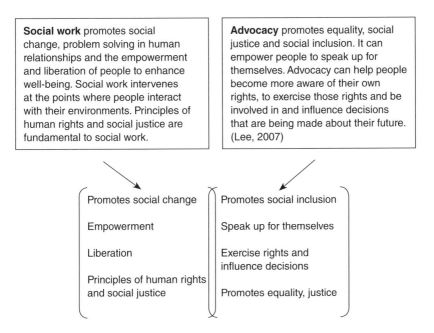

Figure 1.5   Social work and advocacy

At a systemic level advocacy should encompass 'a strategy aimed at changing social systems, institutions and structures' (Flekkoy, 1998: 246). Systemic advocacy has also been identified as 'people-centred advocacy', which is described as 'a set of organized actions aimed at influencing public policies, societal attitudes, and socio-political processes that enable and empower the marginalized to speak for themselves' (Samuel, 2002: 9). Social workers are in a unique position because they are able to advocate and challenge the systems from within. They may be influencing decision making by the way they are working with a service user or carer, but at a structural level they may be working to change and inform the system. This could mean advocating *for* the person but *against* the system they are located in. However, while definitions of systemic advocacy identify its potential to question the dominant and powerful position of providers of health and social services and policy makers, it is not always easy for social work advocates to confront the professional power of the organisations within which they are located. Nevertheless, while it may not make social workers popular either within their own agency or with other professionals, it has been argued that 'what is right is not always popular' (Dominelli, 2009: 57). In promoting the rights of service users within the institutions of health and social care practice, social workers may well need to prepare themselves for the possibility of unsupportive and hostile responses. Reflective social workers will critically analyse their work which may enable them able to promote structural change through using a 'critical reflexive lens' (Dominelli, 2009: 24).

In view of this it is perhaps unsurprising that within day-to-day practice 'social workers continue to focus on micro level interventions while forgetting the meso and macro levels because they seem out of reach. At the individual (micro) level, they can gain a sense of personal satisfaction and be appreciated by service users for practical help that eases their lives' (Beresford et al., 2006). The reality of practice is that while they focus on social work advocacy with individuals, and the daily priorities and demands of practice, they often have little time to address structural issues. Ultimately, this results in structural issues being left for others to address (or not, as the case may be) and service users and carers to struggle. Social work advocacy at an individual level can perhaps more easily be identified and integrated into the social work role. However, there are still tensions for social workers who may have to make decisions in the 'best interest' of a service user and will find it difficult to truly represent their views, or indeed go against what the service users or carers may want.

Michaela's reflections

CASE EXAMPLE

Michaela was a student social worker working in a local authority children and families team. She attended a meeting to discuss the placement of a baby, Noah, with substitute carers. The meeting was held at the hospital and was attended by his mother Carla (18) (who had just had Noah). Jed (23), Noah's father, had a history of violence and was also a Schedule 1 offender.[4]

Michaela reflects on the process:

> The balance of professionals against the couple felt wrong, the meeting was conducted efficiently and procedurally correct. However, in my opinion, the information went straight over Carla's head. I had worked closely with the couple before the baby was born, meeting with them three times a week. It appeared to me that Carla did not fully understand a lot of the decisions being made. However, as she was present at meetings that had been held prior to the birth of the baby, it was recorded that she had been given information and understood what was happening. Despite trying to advocate for Carla to be given the opportunity to keep Noah and to have her views considered in the decision-making process, I felt the case was progressing towards adoption without her fully comprehending the process, what her rights were or possible options open to her. Carla moved to a hostel at one point but without support she quickly left and returned to Jed. For me it felt that the outcome was determined regardless of Carla's efforts, and Noah was going to be placed for adoption. Reflecting on the case it seemed that following procedure was the most important thing and we were losing sight of the needs of a young mother.

On the other hand I was also very aware that there was a baby who needed protecting and I was committed to ensuring that I sought the best outcome, bearing in mind that the safety of Noah was the paramount consideration. But it did feel difficult. Reflecting back, I feel that Carla would have benefited from an independent advocate – someone neutral to talk to about letters, possible options, information about her rights and to provide relevant information so that she could understand what was happening. The outcome may have been the same, but Carla will have to deal with any decisions made long after Noah has been removed and I feel that we left her on her own. In the end I just did not feel that I could advocate for Carla but I knew that she needed someone to do that.

We can see from Michaela's reflections that social workers recognise their advocacy role as an integral element of their practice and are aware of the dilemmas this can present in practice. While acknowledging that social work as a profession is committed to inclusive practice, 'the concept of the social worker as expert purveyor and assessor of requisite services is in conflict with the concept of the social worker as advocate' (Timms, 1995: 135). We have seen that social work advocacy operates within competing and sometimes contradictory values. Essentially it can be understood as 'the exclusive and mutual representation of a client(s) or a cause in a forum attempting to systematically influence decision making in an unjust or unresponsive system(s)' (Schneider and Lester, 2000: 65). This brings together both case and systemic advocacy, although this is complex if social workers find themselves part of an unjust or unresponsive system. The challenge for effective social work advocacy is knowing when to act as an advocate and understanding the limitations of the social work advocacy role, and when to find other ways of supporting people through access to independent advocacy.

Summary

- Changes in the delivery of welfare services have had an impact on how far social workers feel able to directly act in the advocacy role.
- Social workers are rethinking their advocacy role as part of the process of ensuring that service users and carers have a voice in the planning and delivery of services.
- Advocacy works to ensure that service users and carers are empowered to regain control of their lives and to be recognised as citizens.
- Advocacy is about promoting change and challenging injustice at both individual level and systemic levels.
- Social workers need to be reflective and reflexive if they are to be effective advocates in social work.

Discussion questions

1 What do you feel is the purpose of advocacy in contemporary social work?
2 What are the benefits of social work advocacy for service users and carers?
3 Reflecting on the stories of Rav, Isla and Charlotte, identify ways in which they were able to promote change, enable voice and work in an empowering way.
4 Thinking about advocacy for Mika and Alec, how can social workers ensure that the views of younger children are fully represented in decision making?

Notes

1 Legislation requires that foster placements are regularly reviewed. The first review takes place within twenty days, the second is three months after the first review and thereafter at six-monthly intervals. The specified frequency of reviews is a minimum standard. A review should take place as often as the circumstances of the individual case require. Where there is a need for significant changes to the care plan, then the date of the review should be brought forward. No significant change to the care plan can be made unless it has been considered first at a review, unless this is not reasonably practicable (Department for Education, 2011: 88, para 4.5).
2 The Independent Complaints Advocacy Service (ICAS) supports patients and their carers wishing to pursue a complaint about their NHS treatment or care. This is a national statutory service which was launched in September 2003.
3 The Local Authority circular 'A vision for adult social care' (DH, 2010a) promoted the need for people to have more choice and flexibility in terms of services through the increased use of personal budgets.
4 Schedule 1 offenders are persons convicted of an offence listed in the first schedule of the Children and Young Persons Act 1933. The serious offences listed in Schedule 1 include murder, manslaughter, assault, cruelty and a number of sexual offences.

Further reading

Brandon, B. and Brandon, T. (2001) *Advocacy in Social Work*. Birmingham: Venture Press.
Schnieder, R. and Lester, L. (2001) *Social Work Advocacy: A New Framework for Action*. Belmont, CA: Brooks/Cole.
Wilks, T. (2012) *Advocacy and Social Work Practice*. Maidenhead: Open University Press.

2

Contextualising Social Work Advocacy

Overview

- Early days in social work advocacy
- Advocacy and social work education
- Advocating for change
- New challenges for social work advocacy
- Advocacy as a social movement
- Commentary
- Summary
- Discussion questions

Early days in social work advocacy

Brandon and Brandon remind us that far from being a new concept in social work, advocacy does in fact have an established tradition, noting that 'there is widespread delusion that advocacy in social care is of recent origin' (2001: 3). Early pioneers led the way in relation to what we now recognise as individual case advocacy and systemic advocacy or cause advocacy (Box 2.1). In order to understand the role of advocacy in practice it is helpful to consider the history of social work and its emergence through two approaches to working with people who lived in poverty in the mid 1800s: the work of the Charity Organisation Society (COS) which was set up in 1869 (social work as a profession is usually considered to have developed from then) and the development of the Settlement Movement twenty years later. In fact, the history of social work in Britain at this time has been described as

a remarkable story of courageous men and women who fought for the rights of people in distress. They established voluntary hospitals, schools and children's homes, many of the biggest voluntary organisations, for example the Salvation Army, were set up during this period. (Rimmer, 1980: 3)

We can only briefly touch on a few of their narratives in this chapter but hope that they will give a flavour of some of the achievements, as well as insight into why advocacy is such an essential element of social work practice.

Box 2.1   Early social work pioneers

Early pioneers of social work advocacy include people such as Sidney and Beatrice Webb, Josephine Butler, Octavia Hill, Samuel Barnet, Charles Loch, Helen Bosanquet, Edward Denison, Margaret Sewell, Jane Addams, Elizabeth Fry, Mary Richmond and Arnold Toynbee.

During the Industrial Revolution social problems resulted from the mass movement of rural populations to the urban centres, in which working conditions were difficult and living conditions poor. At the same time there was an increasing sense of moral responsibility for the poor by social reformers who felt they had to do something to alleviate the problems arising from industrialisation. Many charities were established and the purpose of the COS was to co-ordinate charities initially in London and then in other cities, including Birmingham, Liverpool, Oxford and Manchester. The organisation developed a way of working which involved providing poor relief as a way of leading by example. The process first involved establishing who was entitled to assistance. A system of family visitors was set up to assess families and make a judgement about whether or not they should receive poor relief. This in time became known as case work – the word 'case' indicating that a systematic process of investigation was taking place. From the 1890s the terminology of 'social work' also entered the vocabulary as a way of describing how visitors investigated, helped and supported the people who were identified to be 'deserving' of help (Pierson, 2011). However, the way in which the COS individualised social issues and adopted a condemnatory approach to the people they were working with has been criticised (Woodroofe, 1962), as have the principles underpinning the approach of COS. Volunteers and paid workers were often seen as 'rescuing' and blaming the poor for their own situation, while bringing a 'superior morality' to the working classes:

There can be no doubt that poverty of the working class is due, not to their circumstances (which are more favourable than those of any other working population in Europe), but to their improvident habits and thriftlessness. If they are ever to be more prosperous, it must be through self-denial, temperance and forethought. (Charity Organisation Society, 1881: 50)

Nevertheless, the local branches of the COS could and sometimes were more independent of London organisational thinking, where intellectuals and ideologues within the organisation functioned. At this point, it could be argued that there was a need for those people who were labelled as undeserving to have an advocate to fight for their rights. The work of Mary Stewart is an interesting example of how more careful analysis of the lives of people needing a service could negate the oppressive attitudes that prevailed at the time and demonstrates the potential for advocacy.

Mary Stewart

Mary Stewart, the first hospital Almoner (Medical Social Worker), was seconded from the COS in 1895 to the Royal Free Hospital in London. Her role involved home visiting, liaising with other organisations and, of course, with doctors. Her primary responsibility was to ensure that the outpatients system was not abused by people who could afford to pay for treatment. Mary Stewart undertook careful analysis of the poor she came into contact with at the Royal Free Hospital and became experienced in investigating and assessing need. In contrast to the COS's orthodox position which viewed people using hospital clinics and dispensaries as 'malingerers', work-shy and therefore not deserving of such services, Mary Stewart found that most were in fact very ill, often chronically. She established that very few people were attempting to abuse the system by trying to get a free service. The role of the almoner slowly became recognised by medical staff as useful and Mary Stewart made an important contribution to the establishment of advocacy as a key element of the social work role.

Photo 2.1   Mary Stewart. The original of this image is held in the archive of the Institute of Medical Social Workers (ref: MSS. MSS.378/IMSW/A/1/2/58)

The Settlement Movement (see Box 2.2), which developed in the late nineteenth century, also had its origins in a sense of moral responsibility felt by the middle and upper-middle classes. The difference between this movement and the COS was in the approach to poverty and its underlying causes. The first permanent Settlement House in England was Toynbee Hall, founded in 1884 in London by Samuel and Henrietta Barnett.

Samuel Barnett had lived and worked in deprived communities. The belief that it was important to both live and work in the local community was central to the Settlement Movement ethos. Barnett saw the work of the Settlement Movement as being part of a process of social reform and supporting

Photo 2.2 Samuel and Henrietta Barnett © National Portrait Gallery, London

the community to improve their conditions (Wilson et al., 2011). Houses were eventually established in England, Scotland and the USA, most being set up by churches, universities or colleges, with the exception of the Birmingham (1899) and Liverpool (1897) Women's Settlement Houses. The principle underpinning the Settlement Movement in contrast to the ideology of the COS was a fundamental belief in 'the value' of the individual, the family and the community:

> Settlements should act as centres for local activities, promote discussion of local and public issues and provide leadership when needed. (Rimmer, 1980: 8)

Box 2.2   Start of the Settlements

Rimmer's (1980) account of the Birmingham Settlement, founded by the National Union of Women's Workers to work with local women and children in need, describes the vision, enthusiasm and determination of the women at the Settlement House. Through an impressive range of work, the Settlement had contact with most of the women and children in the local community. Pioneering services and early examples of social work advocacy included:

- Setting up a 'Poor Man's Lawyer' service to provide free legal advice to men and women.
- The provision of 'clubs' for girls (who lacked privacy at home) which met in the evenings. Toys and games were bought to these sessions and children were given the opportunity to play. So successful were these activities that a waiting list operated and junior and senior 'clubs 'evolved which eventually led to the establishment of a Girl Guide group in the Settlement.
- Development of recreation activities for disabled children.
- Establishment of a 'Provident Society' – a savings scheme for local people.
- Providing loans for glasses, and organising convalescent holidays.
- Providing child care classes for mothers.
- Instigating after-care visiting, in 1904, which encouraged girls about to leave school to seek training for skilled work.

The aim was that people who lived in the Settlements – including those such as William Beveridge, who later wrote the Beveridge Report (1942), Clement Attlee and Jane Addams – would study social problems and seek reform. Clement Attlee, who went on to become Prime Minister, was very influenced by the time he spent with the Settlement Movement and in his 1920 text *The Social Worker* presented a clear view of social workers as advocates.

Box 2.3 The aims of the Birmingham Settlement

The Aims of the (Birmingham) Settlement, as published in 1903 in the Annual Report, gave prominence to the training of social workers.

Aim:

(1) To provide a centre for the Resident and non-Resident Workers for systematic study with reference to social work and industrial conditions.

(2) To promote the physical, intellectual and moral welfare particularly of the women and children in the neighbourhood.

Training of Workers: Students are given work, under experienced workers, which will afford them insight into present conditions. Arrangements are made for them to attend some committees, and for visits to educational, poor law and other institutions. They are advised as to a course of reading, and lectures and classes are arranged.

In 1908 the last two sentences were replaced by 'They are advised take the University Course of Social Study, and the Lectures are illustrated by visits to educational, Poor Law and other institutions etc. Supplementary Lectures are also arranged for those who do not take the full course'. (Rimmer, 1980: 49)

In 1924, Eileen Younghusband became involved in Settlement work in the East End of London. Her pioneering work on behalf of the poor and her lobbying for better conditions is a clear example of early social work systemic advocacy. Eileen Younghusband was acutely aware, through her work with the Settlement, of the dire circumstances and poor living conditions experienced by families and children and young people. Her work had an impact on early forms of community social work. Community work has notably embraced advocacy as a way of challenging discrimination and oppression at a collective level and to work with the individual service users.

Importantly, Eileen Younghusband's work in highlighting the impact of impoverished conditions led to her supporting the establishment of Citizens Advice Bureaux, which provided what we would now recognise as forms of case and systemic advocacy. In 1935 the Government recognised that there needed to be information services alongside newly developing welfare services. The prospect of a war in 1938 led the National Council of Social Services to set up a group to explore ways in which civilians could be supported during a war. In September 1939, when war was declared, the first 200 Citizens Advice Bureaux opened and were run by volunteers from public buildings and private houses with financial support from local councils. The advisers dealt with a range of issues from homelessness (as a result of wartime raids), problems relating to missing documents such as ration books, funeral insurance claims and providing debt advice. Locating relatives missing as a consequence of the war meant that the Citizens Advice Bureaux worked with other agencies such as the Red Cross. An indication of the continuing importance of Citizens Advice Bureaux can be seen in a comment by Lord Beveridge in 1948 (Brasnett, 1964), who described the volunteers of Citizens Advice Bureaux as having a major impact on the lives of people in distress through giving their time, knowledge and friendship.

Advocacy and social work education

Eileen Younghusband also had a significant impact on the development of social work education and training through her teaching at the London School of Economics from 1929 to 1957. She advocated for radical changes in social work education and organisation in the UK after the Second World War and played a significant role in the International Association of Schools of Social Work (IASSW). Younghusband is also associated with a number of key government reports and with the establishment of the National Institute of Social Work in London. A significant report looked at the role and function of social work. The publication of the Younghusband Report (1959) resulted in the Council for Training in Social Work to be set up and a social work certificate.

Social work education was initially influenced by both the COS and the Settlement Movement. The COS recognised the imperative to train the 'visitors' while the aims of the Settlement Movement highlighted the importance of training social workers (Box 2.3). The two came together to establish the School of Sociology in 1912, which in time became incorporated into the London School of Economics. This means that the two perspectives on social work – the individual liberal approach of the COS and the social justice ideals underpinning the Settlement Movement – also became incorporated into social work education and practice. It has been argued that the subsequent 'compromise and mutual toleration that existed' in early social work education with its 'uneasy relationship between the two positions' (Lynn, 1999: 42) is still apparent in social work today.

Arguably, this also explains differing views and practice concerning the role of advocacy in social work. Classic texts in social work theory and practice have continually identified the social work advocacy role (for example, Coulshed, 1991; Davies, 1994; Payne, 1997; Trevithick, 2012). However, advocacy became less of a focus within social work education in the 1960s as the professional expertise of welfare professionals and interpersonal work with service users drew on psychological therapeutic interventions as the focus of study (Payne, 2000b).

Social work education enabled social work to begin to develop an identity as a profession. However, this also contributed in some part to negating the advocacy role of social workers. Social workers wanted to be viewed as expert professionals – the fact that they had been trained and qualified through higher education was part of the justification for this. The knowledge and skills acquired through education meant that they were in a position as qualified experts to identify need and provide an appropriate response. In some instances this required them to form a judgement: for example, in situations where there was a conflict between individual and social needs. The problem, however, was that within this view of the social work role there was no space for the views of service users. Service users were viewed as either not having the expertise, or being too vulnerable or too overwhelmed by their own difficulties to be able to make a meaningful contribution. In some instances, when the reason for social work intervention was due to the fact that a person's behaviour was judged to be unacceptable in some way, then that person was not allowed the right to a view. This meant that service users were regarded as passive recipients of care, *done to* by powerful public service professionals. There was no place for advocacy.

Changes in social work education and theory in the 1960s brought social work advocacy back on the agenda. Influential theories included systems theory and radical theories. Systems theory encouraged social workers to work with other organisations (systems), recognising that the system to be targeted was not necessarily the service user or their family. This meant that case advocacy was again used as a strategy for practice rather than theories informing psychological and therapeutic interventions which concentrated on changing individual behaviour.

Radical theories emphasised inequality and disadvantage, with a greater concentration on structural inequalities and informed thinking about social action in social work. They emerged as a response to critiques of individual casework. Radical social workers aimed, among other things, to widen benefits available to claimants and rejected the casework approach (Pierson, 2011). Radical social work practice set out to transform social institutions and the way social problems are created by capitalist societies through forms of case and systemic advocacy which supported service users, professional activity and political action (Dalrymple and Burke, 2006; Payne, 2005).

From these roots a number of critical approaches to social work emerged which informed the development of theory and practice, including structural social work, feminist approaches, black perspectives and anti-racist social work, and critical social work and anti-oppressive practice. At the same time service user movements developed, emphasising the rights of service users to participate in decision making and in the planning and delivery of services. The consequent debates and discourses accompanying such developments inevitably had an impact on understanding service user and carer perspectives and experiences and contributed to the move away from *doing to* to *working alongside* service users and carers.

Advocating for change

Towards the end of the 1960s, pressure groups, voluntary organisations and academic research highlighted the fact that, despite the existence of the Welfare State, poverty and inequality remained and groups such as older people, people who were mentally ill and children in poverty were suffering (Donnison, 2009). Independent advocacy and self-advocacy organisations began to emerge. The people who had been passive recipients of care, alongside the people who were in effect being controlled by professional intervention strategies, no longer felt the need to 'gratefully' accept inadequate services.

Pressure groups such as the Child Poverty Action Group (1965) and Shelter (1966) offered advice and support to individuals, families and communities as well as campaigning both locally and nationally for systemic change. They also started to influence social work thinking about the needs of individuals in such circumstances and provided a valuable resource to social work practitioners. Groups of service users whose needs had not been acknowledged started to fight for their rights: for example, survivors of domestic violence, lone parents, asylum seekers, pensioners, gay and lesbian people, disabled people, and people living in specific deprived neighbourhoods. Needs that had previously been hidden where also articulated, such as the health needs of black and minority ethnic groups or people with HIV or Aids. Increasingly their voices sought recognition and services as service users challenged the model of professional expertise and demonstrated that advocacy through collective action and self-help groups could be successful (Miller, 2004; Donnison, 2009).

Child Poverty Action Group today

JB v Oxford City Council and SSWP (JSA) [2011] UKUT 96 (AAC) File no CIS/1936/2010 – meaning of 'sheltered' accommodation

The Child Poverty Action Group campaigns for the abolition of child poverty in the UK and for a better deal for low-income families and children. One way of achieving this is through 'test cases' in the Courts. This combines case and systemic advocacy.

The case above concerns the meaning of the concept of 'sheltered' accommodation for the purposes of the housing benefit regulations. Service charges for fuel are ineligible to be met by housing benefit, unless they are in respect of services for communal areas (Paragraph 5 Schedule 1). 'Communal areas' mean areas of common access in sheltered accommodation (Paragraph 8).

In this case the claimant, who had severe learning difficulties, was a housing association tenant who lived in a property with four other tenants, all with learning difficulties. They each had their own bedroom and shared a kitchen, bathroom, two toilets, two sitting rooms and one other room. Care, support and supervision were provided twenty-four hours a day, with a room reserved exclusively for staff.

The local authority held that because the claimant was not in 'sheltered accommodation' the part of the rent that was for service charges for fuel and cleaning relating to communal rooms could not be included in the claimant's Housing Benefit.

The claimant's appeal was allowed by the Upper Tribunal. It was held that there was no statutory definition of 'sheltered accommodation'; it was to be given a meaning consistent with the underlying purpose of the scheme, which was about financial assistance to enable people to be or remain in their accommodation and it was not to be given a narrow or technical meaning. The local authority applied for permission to appeal to the Court of Appeal.

(From CPAG web site: www.cpag.org.uk/cro/test.htm)

In the 1970s and 1980s, welfare rights services rapidly developed as people realised that poverty had not been eradicated and that there was discrimination within the systems of income maintenance. Both case and systemic advocacy are key elements of welfare rights services which became important and popular services both independently and as part of social work in the 1970s. Welfare rights workers would advise individuals about benefits (case advocacy), run publicity campaigns about welfare benefits and contribute to debates about policy (systemic advocacy). Welfare rights advocacy became recognised as a key skill for social workers trying to provide practical services for people in poverty and alleviate its effect on individuals and families. It was recognised that advocating to obtain money for people, particularly when they have been refused it by the system, can make a big impact on people living in poverty. We can see from the case study relating to the Child Poverty Action Group that welfare rights issues remain a concern today, and as such one that requires social work advocacy skills.

The policies of the Thatcher government to reduce the costs of the welfare state began to take effect in the 1980s, and case and cause advocacy in this context became increasingly important. Social workers were involved in 'take up' campaigns to ensure that service users received the benefits they were entitled to and may have been unaware of. 'Principled advocacy' (Bateman, 1995) developed as a way of social workers obtaining as much as possible for service users without colluding with the oppressive elements of the system (Payne, 2000a).

The Barclay Report and advocacy

The Barclay Committee was established in 1980 'to review the role and tasks of social workers in local authority social services departments and related voluntary agencies in England and Wales and to make recommendations' (Barclay, 1982: vii). The Barclay Report, published in 1982, identified an important advocacy role for social work, stating that Social Workers would be

failing in their duty if they did not speak out in the light of the personal knowledge and the evidence amassed from contact with such (poor and disadvantaged) people, challenging policy decisions or the way resources are allocated.
(1982: 9)

The need for social worker intervention to take account of service users' views in
decisions about service delivery and to recognise and value their right to self-
determination was highlighted by Barclay. However, the report added to the confusion in defining advocacy in social work, as outlined in Chapter 1, through
using the terms 'advice', 'advocacy', 'brokerage', 'mediation' and 'negotiation'
interchangeably (Bull, 1989).

New challenges for social work advocacy

The neo-liberal ideology of the Thatcher government during the 1980s emphasised
family responsibilities in the provision of care and the use of voluntary and informal networks. In the 1990s, voluntary and private sector organisations were
encouraged to compete for contracts in a new market economy; services were
purchased by the local authority and *provided* by a range of organisations.
This purchaser–provider split meant that the social work role became one of
commissioning services and care management. Within adult social work the implementation of the care management process included assessment, care planning,
monitoring and review of individualised packages of care. Ostensibly this provided
opportunities for innovative social work advocates to work alongside service users
(as consumers of services) to promote increased consultation and involvement in
the assessment and decision-making process, to maximise choice and to promote
user control. However, concerns regarding community care policy and the care
management process include the potential for professionals to dominate the process, control resource allocation and deny service users the opportunity to be
involved in the assessment process. This led to a recognition of the limitations of
the social work advocacy role and the need for service users and carers to have
access to independent advocacy.

   In 1997 the Labour government initiated a modernisation agenda which, despite
being promoted as an agenda for change, essentially continued to control public
spending, increase private sector involvement in public services and to regulate,
inspect and control both social work and social workers. New Labour stated a
commitment to equality, autonomy, community and democracy, with the driver
for change being the need to improve services that were not 'providing the support
that people should expect' set out in *Modernising Social Services* (DH, 1998: 5).
For many practitioners the reality of the New Labour agenda was that legalism
became a feature of practice. Arguments by commentators that statutory mandates
could promote and encourage good practice (Brayne and Broadbent, 2002) were

countered by others who argued that social workers were drawn into being part of a controlling process that supported repressive legislation. Nevertheless, the development of contracting and regulating services means that there is now a network of provision organised to meet local needs that provides a range of services across public, private and voluntary providers. User involvement, consultation and partnership are key elements of commissioning plans. More recent developments in relation to the 'personalisation' of services puts service users at the centre of the process of choosing support for their needs as they define them. This means that relationships with service users have changed and social care now includes brokerage, providing advice, information and advocacy to support service users to understand what services are available and to make choices in relation to those services (Carr, 2012).

Policy and legislative developments reflect the importance of service user and carer involvement in service provision, and acknowledgement of the legal and human rights of service user groups have led to government recognition of the need for some service user groups to have access to independent advocacy (see timeline in Box 2.4).

Developments in all four nations of the UK indicate that independent advocacy is now taken seriously. Examples in each country include:

- **Wales:** In 2010 a National Independent Advocacy Board was set up in relation to services for children and young people. This Board took an independent strategic overview of the development of advocacy services for children and young people in Wales and made recommendations to Welsh Ministers on various matters relating to advocacy.
- **Scotland:** In January 2001 the Scottish Executive published *Independent Advocacy: A Guide For Commissioners*, which provides practical suggestions on commissioning independent advocacy.
- **Northern Ireland:** In June 2011 the Department of Health, Social Services and Public Safety published a draft document for consultation, *Developing Advocacy Services – A Guide for Commissioners*, and set up a working group to help develop a policy on advocacy services in a health and social care setting.
- **England:** In 2009 the Office for Disability Issues produced a report *Access to Independent Advocacy: An Evidence Review*. (Townsley et al., 2009)

Clearly, the recognition and development of independent advocacy services has had an impact on social work advocacy. However, far from taking over from social work advocacy, we would argue the need for social workers to reclaim their advocacy role. It is as important now to develop knowledge and understanding about the practice of advocacy as it was in the days of Mary Stewart or Samuel and Henrietta Barnet. What is exciting is that independent advocacy is also available to support service users and carers as an additional safeguard to ensuring that their voices are heard and their rights are not violated.

Advocacy as a social movement

The emergence of the service user movement has been an important driver in the development of independent advocacy. There are many examples of attempts to advocate and lobby for greater self-determination and control. Within the disability rights movement, advocacy to enable disabled people to control their own lives began in the USA and Sweden in the 1960s (Williams and Shoultz, 1982). At a conference organised by the Cerebral Palsy Association, parents and carers expressed a concern that became a major theme of the conference, namely 'What will happen to my child when I'm gone?'. As a consequence, Wolfensberger and O'Brien (1977) worked with parents of children with cerebral palsy and developed the concept of the citizen advocate.

The adoption by the UN of two United Nations Declarations[1] in 1971 reinforced the concept of advocacy. Central to both were the principles of equality, individual rights, including rights to needs led service provision and, importantly, legal protection from abuse. Underpinning both declarations was the belief that these principles could be attained through personal self-advocacy. This was seen as a means of ensuring that these principles were met and that individuals had a way of ensuring their voices were heard. For those who were unable to advocate on their own behalf, assistance from other citizens in the community was seen as the way forward. Following these declarations the first citizen advocacy project was established in the USA in 1971.

In the 1970s, advocacy developments in Europe included a system of internally funded advocacy in Dutch psychiatric hospitals. However, due to potential conflict of interests this was later replaced by a system of paid independent advocates, echoing Wolfensberger's (1974: 56) assertion that advocates should not be 'tied financially or organisationally' to service providers. Other groups within mental health have had a campaigning and advocacy role: for example, the National Association of Mental Health, which in 1972 became MIND. This organisation has a long and impressive history in lobbying the rights of people experiencing mental ill health. Successful campaigns included highlighting the need for appropriate services and for service users to have greater control over decision making.

We can see from the overview in this chapter that advocacy is closely associated with rights and justice. Participation choice and user involvement have become central to social policy and public legislation and different forms of formal and informal advocacy have evolved, which have the potential to challenge and can act as pathway for change. Independent advocacy and social worker advocacy are now viewed as important vehicles for facilitating service user and carers' rights. Advocacy also has a central role for those who wish to challenge or seek to redress the power imbalance that exists between users and providers of social welfare services.

Commentary

Within the history of social work there have been influential and effective advocates, arguing for the rights of individuals and communities to have a decent standard of living and opportunities to lead safe and fulfilling lives. The Settlement Movement is testimony to the way that early social work recognised the need to target services to local neighbourhoods, which they then went on to organise and deliver, including early forms of family support and preventative work. These initiatives from a twenty-first century point of view may seem only partial forms of social work advocacy, but relative to the times in which they were developed we would argue they certainly qualify as such.

However, over the last two decades there has been less scope for social workers to translate the concept into action. In both social work practice and education there has been an emphasis on the role of the social worker as someone who brings together people and services and as a manager of care packages. As a consequence it has become increasingly difficult for social workers to act as advocates (Payne, 1991; Boylan and Dalrymple, 2009) and to adhere to Herbert and Mould's vision of advocacy involving

> the constant vigilance of social workers regarding whether policies, procedures and practices, (within their own organisation and within other child-serving organisations and agencies) are meeting the needs of children on their caseloads. (1992: 119)

Since much social work is primarily situated within local authorities, the negotiation of the different accountabilities between employers, professional values, professional self, service users and the public is a continual issue for practitioners. Furthermore, social workers may fear the consequences of challenging the policy and practice of their employing authority (Kennedy, 1990: 32). Rather than let the bureaucratic processes dominate, the challenge for practitioners has been to balance advocacy for the rights and needs for service users and carers with agency policies and procedures. This involves negotiating practice in a way that is not oppressive, when the functions of social work include social control and management of constrained resources, when the social work force is depleted and quality assurance mechanisms or performance indicators make any flexible response difficult if not impossible (Braye and Preston-Shoot, 2009b; Payne, 2009b). Advocacy is and should be a skill in the social work repertoire (Boylan and Dalrymple, 2009; Topss, 2002). At the same time, there will be occasions when it is not possible for a social worker to advocate and the skill then is to support service users and carers when they need access to an independent advocate.

Box 2.4   Timeline for advocacy and social work 1800–2011

This identifies some key points in social work history but is by no means comprehensive. The aim is to give a flavour of some relevant historical moments.

Date	Activity	Development of advocacy
1803–1876	John Perceval	**Pioneer and activist** of the mental health advocacy movement, founded the Alleged Lunatics Friend Society in 1845. Exposing poor treatment and abuse of mental health patients. He argued for greater rights for patients' involvement in decisions concerning their treatment.
1869	Charity Organisation Society founded (COS)	**Organisation** that developed the casework method; the origin of social work investigation and assessment stems from their work. Ideas were in direct contrast to the Fabian Society and Quaker movement. COS criticised for not helping those deemed as 'undeserving' who had to rely on harsh Poor Law provision. The COS was the first organisation to use the term 'social work'.
1884	NSPCC established	**Organisation** that promoted the need for the protection of children; raised public awareness of neglect and ill treatment for children and campaigned for legal reform. Set up to act as an independent voice for children and young people.
	Fabian Society founded: early members included George Bernard Shaw, Beatrice and Sidney Webb, Emmeline Pankhurst	**Organisation** committed to social reform and collective action. Founder of the Labour Party and joined with other movements such as the Society of Friends (Quakers).
	First Settlement in England opened in 1884 at Toynbee Hall	**Settlements** promoted self-help, campaigned for better housing conditions for the poor. Reaction to constraints of COS. Early example of social work as a form of social and community action.
1889	Prevention of Cruelty to Children Act	**Legislation** passed after campaigning by Benjamin Waugh (a secretary of the NSPCC) and his supporters took place over a period of five years before this Act was passed.
1891	Poor man's lawyer scheme	**A scheme** providing legal advice which began at the Mansfield Settlement but spread to other settlements.

Date	Activity	Development of advocacy
1895	Mary Stewart appointed as first hospital Almoner (Medical Social Worker)	**Pioneer** whose work established advocacy as part of the social work role.
1896	National Association for Promoting the Welfare of the Feeble Minded	**Organisation** that preceded MENCAP.
1903	First training course for social workers Hospital Almoners Committee established	Started to establish social work as a profession with standards and codes. Forerunner of the British Association of Social Workers (BASW).
1909	The work of the Children's Care Committees began in London	Started to consider the needs of children more explicitly, recognising that the poor law provisions were unsuitable and inhospitable for children.
1913	Mental Deficiencies Act	**Legislation** provided for guardianship of learning disabled people to allow individuals to remain in the community, rather than placed in institutions or colonies.
1913	The Brighton Guardianship Society founded	Set up to further the guardianship for learning disabled people. Pioneered a different care system, progressive arguing against segregation and institutionalisation – the stated policy of segregation, that took away any notion of citizenship.
1920	Clement Attlee wrote the textbook *The Social Worker*	Highlighted the advocacy role of the social worker in addressing social injustice.
1930's	Emergence of the Rank and File radical social work movement; Bertha Reynolds, an early social worker, argued that a good social worker had to be radical	Wanted to empower those who were discriminated against and fight for social change.
1939	First Citizen's Advice Bureau opened	Advisers helped people with a range of problems that often involved advocacy.
1942	Beveridge Report published	**Report** that social workers, who had found themselves trying to fill gaps in the provision of welfare, contributed to and was the basis of substantial changes in social care and welfare and the establishment of the welfare state.
1946	MIND established – an organisation that campaigns for people with mental health issues	**Organisation** with roots in self-advocacy by people who had experienced mental health hospitals.

(Continued)

(Continued)

Date	Activity	Development of advocacy
	Judy Fryd, a mother of a child with a learning disability, formed The National Society of Parents of Backward Children (later to become MENCAP)	An example of carers taking their own action and campaigning for the rights of their children.
1947	Report on the Employment and Training of Social Workers	This was the first Younghusband **Report** and shaped the direction of social work education.
1960's	Pressure groups such as Child Poverty Action Group (CPAG) and Shelter developed	Campaigning **organisations** publicising injustice and promoting rights.
1961	Amnesty International set up	A campaigning **organisation** set up to protect people when they are denied justice, fairness, freedom and truth. Their work involves case and systemic advocacy.
1966	Citizen advocacy became established	Developed as a way of working in partnership with people who have a learning disability. **Advocacy** was identified as part of the process of protecting vulnerable people.
1968	First welfare rights officer appointed	Recognised that **advocacy** on social security issues was an important role.
1968	Seebohm Committee commissioned to review the organisation and responsibilities of social services in England and Wales	**Report** produced that envisaged greater service user involvement in the planning and delivery of social services.
1972	*Case Con* Manifesto published by a group of radical social workers	Emphasis on community/neighbourhood participation. Emergence of community social work; advocates included Barbara Kahan and Bob Holman. Believed that social workers should organise independently of the state and in the interest of the working class.
1975	Children Act	**Legislation** provided the establishment of panels of guardian ad Litem (now Children's Guardian) in care proceedings with an overriding duty to safeguard and promote the interest of the child.

Date	Activity	Development of advocacy
1979	National Association of Young People in Care (NAYPIC) founded	**Organisation** run by and for looked after children and young people, to promote the rights and views of looked after children, campaigned for greater involvement in decision making, advocated for a rights and representation service. Influenced social work policy and practice in relation to children and young people. Submitted evidence to enquiries into the abuse of children in residential care.
1982	Barclay Report published; the report was commissioned to review the role and tasks of social workers	**Report** envisaged important advocacy role for social workers, negotiating on behalf of service users and acting as broker.
1983	Mental Health Act	**Legislation together with the code of practice** which emphasised the rights of mental health patients, including their right to information and representation.
1984	People First established following an international conference on self-advocacy	First formal **self-advocacy** group in the UK, although self-advocacy had been developing since the 1970s. Self-advocacy groups continued to develop both in the UK and worldwide.
1986	Disabled Person's Act	**Legislation** that identified the need for disabled people to have access to an independent advocate.
	Charity SANE founded	Aims to raise awareness of mental illness and support those experiencing mental health.
1987	Mike Lindsay appointed as the First Children's Rights Officer in Leicestershire	Specific responsibilities to promote the rights of children in care.
1988	Griffiths Report on Community Care	Report recommended that social workers become brokers and care managers with introduction of purchaser/provider split.
1989	Children Act	**Legislation which together with related guidance** emphasised the participation of children and young people in decision making and the need to work in partnership with children and young people and their parents. This provided a fresh impetus for the advocacy role in ascertaining their wishes and feelings and promoting their meaningful involvement in decision making. Introduced representation and complaints procedures.

(Continued)

(Continued)

Date	Activity	Development of advocacy
1990	NHS and Community Care Act	**Legislation and guidance** which together required local authorities to consult with voluntary organisations representing the interests of service users and carers with objectives that included the need to promote choice and self-determination for service users.
	Policy Guidance: Community Care and the Next Decade and Beyond	
	Diploma in Social Work replaced previous certificate qualification	The guidance also recognised the need to be aware of possible role conflict for service providers acting as advocates.
		Qualifying social workers expected, among other things, to have a knowledge and understanding of empowerment and anti-oppressive practice.
1991	Mental Illness Specific Grant	Provided **funding** to develop social care services for people who needed mental health services. This led to the development of advocacy groups and rapid growth of local survivors groups.
1992	Children's Rights Officers and Advocates (CROA) established	Set up as a **forum** for professionals engaged in children's rights and promoted the development of independent advocacy services for children and young people.
1996	Community Care (Direct Payments Act)	**Legislation** gave local authorities the power to make payments to people age 18–65; this was the first piece of legislation relating to the 'personalisation' agenda that also led to debates about the role of social work – in particular enabling social workers to move away from care management and back to more traditional casework.
1997	Utting Report	**Report** recognised importance of independent advocacy services to support young people making a complaint.
1998	'Quality Protects' (England) and 'Children First' (Wales) published	**Initiatives to improve services for children in need** which introduced funding to improve services including financially supporting the development of independent advocacy and children's rights services
	White Paper 'Modernising Social Services' published	Vision by the New Labour Government of personalised social services.

Date	Activity	Development of advocacy
	Human Rights Act	**Legislation** that European Convention on Human Rights incorporated into British legislation which is intended to prevent discrimination and unfair treatment, echoing the ideals of advocacy.
2000	Waterhouse Report	**Report on abuse of Children in Wales** highlighted the need to improve complaints procedures and independent advocacy support for young people who wanted to make a complaint.
	Care Standards Act 2000	**National Minimum Standards for Care Homes** recognised the role of independent advocacy and recommended use of visiting advocates to homes and access to independent advocacy for people living in residential care.
2001	Valuing People: A New Strategy for Learning Disability in the 21st Century	**White paper outlining Government plan to improve the lives of people with learning disabilities (in England).** Promotes the need for advocacy with an objective being 'to enable people with learning disabilities to have as much choice and control as possible over their lives through advocacy and a person-centred approach to planning the services they need' (DH, 2001b: 26).
		It states the need to 'give people with learning disabilities more choice and control by developing advocacy, extending direct payments and introducing a national framework for promoting a person centred approach to planning' (DH, 2001b: 27).
		The Government said that it would invest £1.3 million per annum for the next three years to establish a National Citizen Advocacy Network and promote self-advocacy, in partnership with the voluntary sector.

(Continued)

(Continued)

Date	Activity	Development of advocacy
2002	Patient Advice and Liaison Services (PALS) established	**Service to help people using the NHS.** Plans for the introduction of PALS were announced in the Government's 'NHS Plan' of 2000, which said:
		'Patients are the most important people in the health service. It doesn't always appear that way. Too many patients feel talked at, rather than listened to. This has to change.'
		'Patients need an identifiable person they can turn to if they have a problem or need information while they are using hospital and other NHS services ... PALS will act as an independent facilitator to handle patient and family concerns, with direct access to the chief executive and the power to negotiate immediate solutions.'
	Adoption and Children Act	**Legislation that amended the Children Act 1989 by inserting into it a new section 26A,** which imposes on local authorities the duty to make arrangements for the provision of advocacy services for care leavers making or intending to make representations under section 24D of the Act, and for children making or intending to make representations under section 26. When a child or young person indicates that they have a concern or problem that is not being resolved and a complaint is likely to be made, local authorities should ensure that children or young people have access to advocacy support.
	Get it Sorted	**Guidance** that together with the Adoption and Children Act makes the point that advocacy support should be available for any child or young person considering making a complaint about any aspect of their care.
	National Standards for the Provision of Children's Advocacy Services (England)	**Standards** setting out the core principles that children and young people can expect from professionals providing advocacy services in England. There are ten standards.

Date	Activity	Development of advocacy
2003	Independent Complaints Advocacy Service (ICAS) launched by the Department of Health	**ICAS** delivers a free and professional support service to clients wishing to pursue a complaint about the NHS:
	National Minimum Standards for Care Homes	14.3 Service users and their relatives and friends are informed of how to contact external agents (e.g. advocates), who will act in their interests.
		17.2 Where service users lack capacity, the registered person facilitates access to available advocacy services.
	National Standards for the Provision of Children's Advocacy Services (Wales)	**Standards** setting out the core principles that children and young people can expect from professionals providing advocacy services in Wales. These are the same as the standards for England.
	Mental Health (Care and Treatment) (Scotland) Act	**Legislation** introducing right of access to independent advocacy in Scotland.
2005	Mental Capacity Act 2005	**Legislation** that gives a person who lacks capacity the right to an Independent Mental Capacity Advocate when a decision is to be made on their behalf. The role of the Advocate is to support and represent the person who lacks capacity. Any information or reports the independent mental capacity advocate has is to be taken into account as part of the decision-making process in order to ensure that the decision is in the person's best interests. Similar legislation exists in Scotland.
	Independence, Wellbeing and Choice	**Green Paper** setting out a vision for adult social care over the next 10–15 years and how this might be realised. Recognises that with respect to direct payments 'Support services and local advocacy services may be well placed to participate in the circle of support/trust arrangement for managing the payment' (DH, 2005: 85).

(Continued)

(Continued)

Date	Activity	Development of advocacy
2006	Our Health, Our Care, Our Say	**White paper** setting out vision to provide good quality local social care and health services.
2007	Mental Health Act	**Legislation** that places a duty on the appropriate authority to make arrangements for help to be provided by independent mental health advocates. Patients qualify for an advocate if: they are liable to compulsory treatment under the powers of the Act, except in certain emergency situations; they are on supervised community treatment; they are informal patients who are discussing the possibility of treatment to which S57 or S58A applies (neurosurgery for mental disorder or ECT for patient under 18 years).
	Putting People First: a shared commitment and vision for the provision of adult social care	A **protocol** setting out and supporting the commitment of the government to independent living and outlining the aims and values guiding the transformation of adult social care. The proposals include the need for 'a universal information, advice and advocacy service for people needing services and their carers, irrespective of their eligibility for public funding' (DH, 2007a: 3).
	No Secrets	No secrets **statutory guidance** (DH/HO, 2000) set out the first comprehensive policy framework on adult safeguarding. Calling for coherent partnership work, it gave local authorities the lead role in developing local policies and procedures on adult safeguarding.
		No Secrets set out some basic principles of empowerment, confidentiality, information, advocacy and rights, to be balanced with risks to the self and others. It stated that outcomes should be audited routinely so that problems can be learned from and **practice** improved.

Date	Activity	Development of advocacy
2008	Service Framework for the Future provision of Advocacy for Children in Wales	**Measure** introduced by the Welsh Assembly government 'strengthen the voice of children and young people in the provision of public services in Wales. The Government intends to put in place a New Service Framework for the Future Provision of Advocacy Service in Wales. The new framework will be implemented over the next two years' (WAG, 2008).
	Independent Living Strategy	**A cross-government strategy** to improve disabled people's experiences and life chances recognising the need for a focus on 'the role of advocacy, support and brokerage services as assessment and care management systems develop to take account of the personalisation agenda; how to promote choice and control for older people in, or about to move into, residential and nursing care; and the need for advocacy support amongst people who are particularly vulnerable to losing choice and control' (DH 2008: 40).
	Mental Health Act	**Legislation** giving people (who qualify under the act) the right Independent Mental Health Advocacy.
2009	SSIA Code of Practice for Independent Advocacy Review of 'No Secrets'	**Principles and Standards** for independent advocacy in Scotland. In 2007 the Department of Health (2009c) announced a **review** of No Secrets. The consultation received responses from 12,000 people. Most challenged the term 'vulnerable adult', and as a result the report used the term 'adult'. A key message from the consultation was the central role of empowerment or 'listening to the victim's voice' (p. 5). Some groups, in particular people from black and minority ethnic backgrounds, and the older generation, had less understanding of what abuse meant and how to get help. Participants expressed concern that the balance of choice and risk flagged up in No Secrets is still undetermined, and the need to clarify this given the personalisation agenda.

(Continued)

(Continued)

Date	Activity	Development of advocacy
2010	Prioritising need in the context of Putting People First: A whole system approach to eligibility for social care – Guidance on Eligibility Criteria for Adult Social Care, England	**Guidance to** assist councils with adult social services responsibilities to determine eligibility for adult social care in a fair, transparent and consistent way. 'Targeted interventions might include information and advice to support people and their carers in making decisions and access to advocacy and brokerage to assess their care options. If people are supported to make informed choices at an early stage, the risk of needs escalating in the future may be reduced' (DH 2010b: 14).
	Improving Dementia Services in Northern Ireland – A Regional Strategy	**A draft report** which states that 'Independent information, support, and advocacy should be offered at the point of diagnosis' and that 'Independent advocacy should be available to people with dementia in order to support them in decision making …'.
	Mental Health (Wales) measure	**A measure** that widens the scope of Independent Mental Health Advocacy in Wales.
	Equality Act	**Legislation** that brought together nine separate pieces of legislation into one single Act, simplifying the law and strengthening it to help tackle discrimination and inequality.
2011	Patient Rights (Scotland) Act	**Established a Patient Advice and Support Service** (PASS) to provide information and help patients and members of the public to know and understand their rights and responsibilities when using health services. Where necessary, PASS has a duty to direct people to other types of support, such as advocacy or communication support services.

Summary

- Early forms of social work advocacy can be identified in the work of the Settlement Movement.
- The development of the service user movement has been significant in ensuring that service users are involved in the planning and delivery of services and have informed social work education.
- Independent advocacy has evolved in recognition of the marginalisation of service users.
- Social workers now have to use their advocacy skills within a market economy of service provision and understand the of independent advocacy services within this.

Discussion questions

1 How important was social work advocacy in the Settlement Movement?
2 Look at the list of social work pioneers at the beginning of this chapter and identify their advocacy role.
3 Consider the role of the workers in the Settlement Movement and think about the challenges they faced as they advocated for the people in the local community.
4 What do you consider the advocacy role to be in the context of the disability rights movement, children's rights and radical social work?
5 How is advocacy viewed in your practice?

Note

1 Declaration on the Rights of the Mentally Retarded Persons, 1971 and the UN Declaration on the Rights of Disabled Persons, 2009.

Further reading

Brandon, D. and Brandon, T. (2001). *Advocacy in Social Work*. Birmingham: Venture Press.
Pierson, J. (2011). *Understanding Social Work*. Maidenhead: Open University Press.
Whelan, R. (2001). *Helping the Poor: Friendly Visiting, Dole Charities and Dole Queues*. London: Civitas.
Wilson, K., Ruch, G., Lymbery, M. and Cooper, A. (2011) *Social Work: An Introduction to Contemporary Practice* (2nd edition). Harlow: Pearson Education. Chapter 4 provides a useful historical account of social work.
Younghusband, E. (1978). *Social Work in Britain, 1950–1975*. London: George Allen and Unwin.

3

Reclaiming Advocacy in Contemporary Social Work

Overview

- Purpose of social work – current debates
- Commentary
- Summary
- Discussion questions

Social workers practice in situations where societal and individual problems are complex. Current social work practice is underpinned by a business model: achieving targets, managing risk and organising packages of care. Alongside this the development of independent advocacy services (both as a result of activism by user movements and through legislation) has unintentionally led to the advocacy role being seen by many as a separate way of working rather than a core element of social work.

In all four nations of the UK, the last decade has seen scrutiny of social work practice which has led to reviews of the social work profession (DfES and DH, 2006; Scottish Executive, 2006; Bogues, 2008; Health Care Board, 2012). In this process there appears to have been a move away from consideration of social work practice in terms of its values. Values-based definitions of social work (such as the IASSW definition discussed in Chapter 1) can be criticised for being ambiguous about what social work actually does. The IASSW definition, for example, has been described as too generalist, 'grand and bland' (Dickens, 2011: 8). The reviews of social work have moved away from this ambiguity and returned to consideration of social work in terms of its role and tasks. In this chapter we will consider the main elements of the reviews and discuss the significance of these for reclaiming and practicing effective social work advocacy.

Current debates about the purpose and direction of social work

The social, political and economic contexts of practice differ within the four nations of the UK. Since devolution, when some powers were transferred by statute from the Parliament of the United Kingdom to the Scottish Parliament, the National Assembly for Wales and the Northern Ireland Assembly (1999), each country has had greater autonomy in the development and provision of services. This has provided opportunities for services to develop that are more relevant to the needs of people in each of the four nations (see Box 3.1).

The review process provided an opportunity for social workers, social work educators, service users and carers and politicians to contribute their perspectives and understanding about social work practice. The completed reviews can now be used as a tool with which to interrogate practice through debating what social work is, what social workers do and what social work has to offer society (Bogues, 2008). Analysis of the reviews also enables us to consider the place of advocacy in social work.

Box 3.1 Reviews of social work in the four nations of the UK

2005 *Social Work in Wales: A Profession to Value* (ADSS Cymru)

2006 *Changing Lives:* Report of the 21st Century Social Work Review (Scottish Executive)

2006 England: Review of Social Care Workforce *Options for Excellence* (DfES and DH)

2008 *Social Work at Its Best: A Statement of Social Work Roles and Tasks for the 21st Century* (General Social Care Council)

2008 Review of the Roles and Tasks of Social Work in Northern Ireland, (Northern Ireland Social Care Council)

2009 England: Report of Task Force *Building a Safe, Confident Future*

2010 The Role of Social Work in Adult Social Services in England (Department of Health, Directors of Adult Social Services)

2012 Report from Northern Ireland (Department of Health, Social Services and Public Safety)

England

In England a review of the social care workforce was undertaken between 2005 and 2006. The subsequent report, *Options for Excellence* (DfES and DH, 2006), states that

Social work is a problem-solving activity, carried out by the worker through relationships with the individual, family and community. Social work is usually needed when individuals, families or groups are facing a major and often life-changing problem or challenge. Social workers help individuals and families to achieve the outcomes they want in the ways they prefer. (2006: 49)

Significantly, the description of what social workers actually do, at the start of this report, states that 'Social workers carry out a variety of tasks, including casework, acting as an advocate, risk assessment and working as a care manager' (2006: 9) (see Box 3.2).

Here advocacy is a stated element of contemporary social work practice, although there are tensions between the elements of casework and advocacy and those of risk assessment and care management. The concepts of participation and the protection of dignity, rights and choice are recognised in the review as important factors underpinning social work practice. The advocacy role of social work here therefore involves promoting participation and ensuring that dignity, rights and choices are not disregarded.

Box 3.2   The focus of social work

- Promoting people's ability to maximise their own capabilities and life options, including participation in education, training, employment social and leisure activities.
- Developing people's ability to form positive relationships within their family and social network.
- Helping people to create and maintain independence, and, when this is not possible, to benefit from alternative forms of support that protect their dignity, rights and choices.
- Protecting people's human rights, and promoting the exercise of their rights and responsibilities as citizens.

(Department for Education and Skills and Department of Health, 2006: 49)

Following the death in 2007 of a seventeen-month-old baby, Peter Connolly, the Department of Health and Department for Skills and Families undertook a comprehensive review of social work in England. The Social Work Task Force was set up in 2008, producing an interim report in July 2009 and the final report *Building a Safe, Confident Future* in December 2009. A radical package of recommendations was put forward with the aim of transforming both the social work profession and public understanding of social work. However, the subsequent public definition of social work (Box 3.3) they produced, while easy to understand, has been criticised for over-simplifying the task (Dickens, 2011).

Box 3.3   Public description of social work

Social work helps adults and children to be safe so they can cope and take control of their lives again.

Social workers [can] make life better for people in crisis who are struggling to cope, feel alone and cannot sort out their problems unaided.

How social workers do this depends on the circumstances. Usually they work in partnership with the people they are supporting – check out what they need, find what will help them, build their confidence, and open doors to other services.

Sometimes, in extreme situations such as where people are at risk of harm or in danger of hurting others, social workers have to take stronger action to protect them – they have the legal powers and duties to do this.

You may think you already do this for your friends and family but social workers have specialist training in fully analysing problems and unmet needs, in how people develop and relate to each other, in understanding the challenging circumstances some people face, and in how best to help them cope and make progress. They are qualified to tell when people are in danger of being harmed or harming others and know when and how to use their legal powers and responsibilities in these situations.

You may think that you'll never need a social worker but there is a wide range of situations where you or your family might need one, such as:

- caring for family members;
- having problems with family relationships and conflict;
- struggling with the challenges of growing old;
- suffering serious personal troubles and mental distress;
- having drug and alcohol problems;
- facing difficulties as a result of disability;
- being isolated within the community; or
- having practical problems with money or housing.

Source: DCSF (2009: 67)

Further definitions of social work specifically in relation to services for children and families and services for adults have followed. In 2009 a definition of social work for children by the Children's Workforce Development Council (CWDC) clearly indicates inherent tensions for the social work advocacy role and relationship-based social work in statutory settings:

No other profession has to manage such close relationships whilst making judgements and exercising powers with potentially serious consequences for the child and the family. (CWDC, 2009: para 14)

In relation to adult services it has been argued that while assessment, care planning and review remain part of social work practice, there is also a role for therapeutic practice, advocacy and community development work (DH, 2010b). In a statement about *The Future of Social Work and Adult Services in England*, social work is said to have a 'distinct contribution' in relation to personalising services and safeguarding human rights (see also Box 3.4).

Box 3.4   The role of social work in adult services

- Building professional relationships and empowering people as individuals in the their families and communities.
- Working through conflict and supporting people to manage their own risks.
- Knowing and applying legislation.
- Accessing practical support and services.
- Working with other professionals to achieve best outcomes for people.

(DH, 2010b: 2)

Following the Task Force report, a Social Work Reform Board was set up which developed an overarching standards framework – the *Professional Capabilities Framework for Social Workers in England* – to support and inform the national career structure. The components of this framework comprise:

> [p]rofessionalism, values and ethics, diversity, rights, justice and economic wellbeing, knowledge, critical reflection and analysis, intervention and skills, contexts and organisations, professional leadership. (TCSW, 2012)

Within this framework the advocacy role of social work is implied in the need for partnership working (which will be discussed further in Chapter 5). Social workers are expected to be able to challenge appropriately when service users experience oppression and marginalisation; principles of anti-oppressive practice and understanding the impact of power relations are also critical elements of effective advocacy practice. Specifically, advocacy is important in relation to the expectations that social workers will advance human rights and promote justice and economic wellbeing. It identifies the need for social workers to be skilled advocates in engaging with individuals, families, groups and communities. Finally, when working within organisations, there is an expectation that social workers are 'pro-actively responsive' to the challenges of contemporary practice. This indicates the wider role for systemic social work advocacy (see Figure 1.5).

Motivation to be a social worker

The material in this case study is reprinted with the kind permission of Guardian News and Media Ltd.

It wasn't until leaving secondary school that I decided I wanted to work with vulnerable people. In fact after leaving school, and during college, my career choices lingered around going into teaching, social care, youth work or psychology.

During school I had gone through a pretty rough time when I was a teenager, where I found myself receiving mental health support and had what was called an 'inclusion worker' from the local youth service. In fact my school days took a sour turn when my head teacher called my parents to tell them that the school had concerns about me; mainly around disengaging from education, self-harming and substance misuse.

I found myself consuming copious amounts of alcohol on a daily basis, missing school or simply walking out, getting suspended on a regular basis, experimenting with harder substances and getting into trouble with just about anyone I came into contact with.

This is no X Factor sob story, and wouldn't want it to be interpreted as such, but with the benefit of hindsight what these experiences taught me was that people can lose control over their destiny, and climbing back up the slippery slope can be incredibly hard.

When a close friend of mine sadly passed away from cancer, I became the 16-year-old that was looking for answers. Amongst the grief, I suddenly found the ability to question everything about us as human beings, the communities we live in, our responses to life events, and how we as people interact with the systems we have around us.

My enthusiasm for social care really grew when I started college. Out of nowhere I was answering some of my own questions, but more importantly my questions started to develop and have a greater sense of meaning. Studying social care, I was surrounded by people who shared the same interests as me.

Being introduced to the health and social care sector was the 'light bulb' moment for me. I realised that not only could I help people, but actually I could really make a positive contribution to the profession I went on to study. Tackling oppression, campaigning for equality, and upholding rights became the driving force behind my choice of studying social work at university.

The course seemed to combine all of my then interests and appeared to want to further fine tune my desire to know more. I remember working really hard to try and better my grades, trying different techniques with essays and revision, and delving into the world of research and the process of evidence-based practice. Every minute of it, even the frustrating times, was fascinating.

Social care is made up of a number of careers, and the people that fulfil the roles should represent the diversity of the communities we aim to serve. It consists of professions that are rooted in values and ethics, and sadly at times we have to fight the

(Continued)

3

(Continued)

very systems we work within in order to successfully enable people to regain control and power over their lives.

(www.guardian.co.uk/social-care-network/social-life-blog/2012/mar/16/social-work-climb-slippery-slope?INTCMP=ILCNETTXT3487, accessed 3.4.12)

Wales

In 2004/5, a review of social work in Wales resulted in the report *Social Work in Wales: A Profession to Value*. This focused on the statutory tasks of social work and identified six key roles and responsibilities:

- assessing needs of service users and their carers holistically where packages of care are negotiated, monitored and reviewed;
- assessing risk to service users and others which are balanced in a way that promotes independence of service and carers;
- making decisions about allocation of scarce resources;
- promoting social inclusion;
- collaborating with other agencies;
- ensuring accountability through effective recording. (ADSS [Cymru], 2005).

The only specific reference to advocacy in the report relates to ensuring that service users have access to independent advocacy when making a complaint (see Chapter 7 for further discussion about this).

Arguably this is a disappointing review in comparison to *Options for Excellence* (DfES and DH, 2006) in England, and it is difficult to find a way of using it to reclaim social work advocacy. However, a later document *Fulfilled Lives, Supportive Communities: A Strategy for Social Service in Wales over the Next Decade* identifies the 'defining feature' (Welsh Assembly Government, 2007: 2) of social work as being the balance between care and control and empowerment. This was further strengthened in 2010 following an Independent Commission on Social Services (and a number of other reviews on the workforce and on safeguarding). A report on the future of Social Services and Social Care *Sustainable Social Services for Wales: A Framework for Action* (Welsh Assembly Government, 2007) put emphasis on responsive citizen-centred services. In particular, the vision and principles articulated in the document (see Box 3.5) clearly promote the importance of strengthening the voices of service users and carers underpinned by the values that are enshrined in the Children Act 1989, The United Nations Convention on the Rights of the Child and the United Nations Principles for Older People. The principles start with a commitment to a 'strong voice' and the vision acknowledges that there are times when service users and carers need help to have their voice heard. It looks to developing interdependency within families, groups and communities, recognising that public service are critical elements of communities and that as citizens everyone has a right to receive those services.

Box 3.5   Principles: sustainable social service in Wales

We will work to the following principles:

• *A strong voice and real control*

We all expect to make our own decisions and control our own lives. Children and young people have a right to be heard and to have a significant say in matters that affect them. We will support and strengthen people's ability to contribute as individuals within their own networks and communities. We will provide help to make people's voices strong and clear. We will actively listen and act on what we have heard.

• *Supporting each other*

We will work to support, strengthen and build on people's desire to help each other, especially at times of difficulty.

• *Safety*

We all, whether young or older, have a right to be protected from avoidable harm and from neglect.

• *Respect*

We all expect that, when we use services, we are treated with dignity and respect. We will treat individuals as responsible people and enable them to make balanced decisions about the risks that they are prepared to take.

• *Recovery and restoration*

When we face a difficulty, whether as children, young people or adults, we very often look for support that enables us to return to living in the way that we choose.

• *Adjusting to new circumstances*

Sometimes we find that our circumstances have changed more permanently. We expect to be supported in adjusting to our new situation.

• *Stability*

We all need stability to grow and develop, and this is especially true of children. Any support we provide must therefore maximise this.

• *Simplicity*

We all need to know how to find out about getting help in the most straight-forward way possible.

• *Professionalism*

We all expect professionals who work with us to be competent, confident and safe.

Source: Welsh Assembly Government (2007: 9)

With the emphasis on stronger user and carer voice it is easier to see how social work advocacy can be reclaimed. The report also recognises the need for independent advocacy in some situations and indicates, for example, that the effects of institutionalisation for people living in care homes can be ameliorated by embedding independent advocacy in support services. The report is therefore clearly aware of the importance of advocacy as a safeguarding function, noting that there has been progress in developing advocacy services for older people and making a commitment to putting a business case for more coherent delivery of independent advocacy services. Similarly, there have been a number of reports and initiatives relating to the provision of independent advocacy for children and young people. The Welsh Assembly Government has issued a model for providing independent advocacy for children and young people, which is to be underpinned by statutory guidance. It also set up a National Independent Advocacy Board to discuss and advise ministers on issues concerning advocacy services for children and young people. This Board plays an important role in monitoring the implementation of the model alongside a quality assurance role in relation to the provision of advocacy services, although to date it has not been implemented. While a report by the Children's Commissioner for Wales (Towler, 2012) indicates that there is a long way to go, since many vulnerable young people are unaware of their right to advocacy, it is fair to say that the Welsh Government is forward-thinking in promoting the principles and values of advocacy. This can also be seen in the fact that the Government has also considerably extended the remit of independent advocacy for people using mental health services. Clearly the Welsh Assembly Government recognises that all service users should have access to independent advocacy, and that this should be supported. The social work advocacy role, then, is to be aware that service users can and should have access to independent advocacy.

CASE EXAMPLE

Social worker promotes independent advocacy

Derek's Story

I first found out about Advocacy Matters (Wales) from my social worker in November 2005 when I moved back to Cardiff from Tamworth in Staffordshire a little while after my father passed away. I moved back because I felt I was being treated very unfairly by my uncle up in Tamworth. My uncle was trustee for me but didn't like me spending any of the money in the trust. My dad's will said that I could use the money for my care and well-being but that whatever was left after me would go to my uncle and his family anyway.

When I got back to Cardiff I was lucky enough to have the help of my auntie Sue and an old friend of mine Paul, who is her nephew, and I have been living with my friend, not far from my auntie who helps me a lot as well since I came back to Cardiff. What my advocate, Huw, has helped me to do is to have my trust transferred to another organisation down here (the Friendly Trust), away from my uncle and his family, so that I can use it like I was meant to use it to help me to buy a house where I can live my life without worrying.

I am very grateful to Huw and Advocacy Matters (Wales) that they have been able to help me to speak, to write letters, get my debts and benefits sorted and support which we think, with the help of my social worker, we can also get.

Advocacy Matters (Wales) has helped me enormously to deal with difficult situations in my life. In the last two years I just couldn't manage on my own. Now I can see everything in my life improving because of everyone who has helped me here, but especially because I have had an advocate to help me deal with everyone and everything I have needed to deal with. Things are now almost all sorted out and I should be moving into my own place quite soon where I can relax and enjoy my life with all the support I need. That would have been very difficult, maybe some things would have been impossible, if I hadn't had an advocate to help me.

I wanted to write this story and have written it with the help of my advocate to try to show how much advocacy is needed for people who cannot deal with so many things that other people can deal with. This is my way of saying 'thank you' and hoping that Advocacy Matters (Wales) stay around for a very long time to come so that lots of other people can use their help, which they are happy to give. They know how to do a lot of things that lots of people don't really know how to go about doing.

Huw has told me that when our work is finished he will have to leave to work with someone else who needs help. I'll miss him but I know I'll get invites to the summer BBQ and Christmas disco as well as the AGM, and I have been to all of these in the last couple of years, so we'll keep in touch that way. I know if I have problems in the future I only have to ring Advocacy Matters (Wales) and they will get me an advocate to help me as soon as they can.

Source: Advocacy Matters (2012) Derek's Story. Available at: www.advocacymatterswales.co.uk/learning-disability-services/dereks-story/. Republished with kind permission of Derek James and Advocacy Matters.

Scotland

The Scottish Executive commissioned a review of social work in 2004 and a number of consultation events and reports were also commissioned as part of this process with a final document *Changing Lives: Report of the 21st Century Social Work Review* published in 2006. A core part of the review was to

> define and clarify the distinctive contribution of the social worker in an environment increasingly focused on integrated teamwork. (Scottish Executive, 2006: 26)

Within the review it was recognised that the challenge for social work was to promote integrated approaches while also keeping and continuing to develop the social work role. Following this, in February 2006, Scottish ministers accepted the recommendations of the report with a commitment to act on them. As a result, five change programmes were established as mechanisms to implement the change agenda and deliver key strategic pieces of work. The completion and publication of these 'core products' took place in March 2011.

In terms of thinking about social work advocacy, this review identified six core roles (Box 3.6) which, as in the reports for England and Wales, also reflect the tensions in practice that social workers have to embrace. The caseworker role of the social worker at the top of the list highlights the importance of the use of relationship. This is based on specific research commissioned as part of the review research (McNeill et al., 2005; Kerr et al., 2005), which identified that the quality of the therapeutic relationship was central to achieving positive outcomes for service users in the context of working with both voluntary and involuntary service users.

Box 3.6   Six core social work roles needed to deliver the functions of social work

1 **Case worker** working with individuals to help them address personal issues.
2 **Advocate** on behalf of the poor and socially excluded.
3 **Partner** working together with disadvantaged or disempowered individuals and groups.
4 **Assessor** of risk or need for a number of client groups; also associated with surveillance.
5 **Care manager** who arranges services for users in a mixed economy of care, but may have little direct client contact.
6 **Agent of social control** who helps to maintain the social system against the demands of individuals whose behaviour is problematic.

(Scottish Executive, 2006: 28)

The second role identified for social workers was that of advocate. Unfortunately, the reference to advocacy 'on behalf of' rather than advocacy 'with' or 'alongside' people negates, to some degree, its empowering potential. However, this is mitigated by the description of the social worker's partnership role, which is underpinned by the need for relationship. While the roles appear to be disconnected in the way that they are presented in this document, we would argue that there is a connection to be made since partnership is an element of any meaningful advocacy relationship. Nonetheless, there are clear distinctions between these first three roles and the following three, which focus on the surveillance and control aspects of social work. The report notes that the 'combination and priority' (Scottish Executive, 2006: 28) of the roles will vary depending on the circumstances of a particular situation and arguably reflect the complexity and dilemmas of social work practice.

Commentators have noted that the report essentially views social workers as a limited resource having a principle role in statutory tasks, particularly in relation to safeguarding vulnerable adults and children. The danger of such a narrow focus is that it will be more difficult for social workers to practice in an empowering way, respond to need and embrace the wider advocacy role and challenge social injustice (Ritchie and Woodward, 2009). However, the Government in Scotland has had a strong commitment to ensuring access to independent advocacy and promoting service user voice as a key part of the provision of services. This is reiterated in *Independent Advocacy: A Guide for Commissioners* (Scottish Executive, 2001), *Independent Advocacy: A Guide for Commissioners* (Scottish Independent Advocacy Alliance, 2010) and *Principles and Standards for Independent Advocacy* (SIAA, 2008):

> The Scottish Government's policy is, and will remain, that Independent advocacy should be available to all who need it. No-one should need to ask for an advocate. Health professionals should recognise when someone could benefit from advocacy and ensure that they have access to it. (Shona Robinson, Minister for Public Health, SIAA Launch Party for the *Principles and Standards for Independent Advocacy*, May 2008)

Local authority children's rights services in Scotland – extract from research report

Local authorities have a strategic role in providing advocacy support for children and young people. They do this through commissioning services from independent organisations as well as providing advocacy themselves.

The study found that local authorities can provide advocacy through the ongoing delivery of its children's services and in line with policy and practice areas such as Getting it Right for Every Child (GIRFEC). Local authority mangers, social workers, teachers and youth workers can provide advocacy as part of their ongoing role. This contribution to advocacy support is difficult to quantify, but was acknowledged to be a valuable resource by many in this study. In addition, local authorities may run participation and consultation activities for children and young people which can be described as collective or group advocacy.

Under half of local authorities directly employ children's rights officers with in-service children's rights officer posts. There are differing levels of resources in local authorities which have these posts, with the majority of children's rights officers being singleton posts, either full- or part-time. A small number of local authorities such as Aberdeenshire, Edinburgh, Glasgow and South Lanarkshire have more than

(Continued)

(Continued)

one children's rights officer post to provide services to a wider group of children and young people.

...

There was some variance in the remits of children's rights officers. It is hard, therefore, to compare the details of different services across Scotland. Children's rights services in local authorities predominantly focus on children and young people looked after away from home in residential or foster care. Some local authorities also cover other areas including the rights of disabled children, education issues and unaccompanied and separated children and young people.

Children's rights officers provided advocacy support to individual children and young people. They also had other roles such as providing feedback on the quality of services, consultation with groups of children and young people, and providing input to policy and practice. Many had a role in contributing to strategy and policy development and providing expert advice on children's rights to their local authority.

(Elsley, 2010)

Northern Ireland

In 2008 the Northern Ireland Social Care Council was commissioned to carry out a review of the roles and tasks of social work. A consultation for this review with service users, practitioners, managers and educators culminated in the report *People Work not just Paperwork* (Bogues, 2008). The title of the report signposts a dynamic approach to thinking about social work, and thoughtfully examines the social work advocacy role.

Box 3.7   Roles and tasks of social work

Ways in which social work contributes to society:

- Mediator
- Co-ordinator
- Service broker
- Advocacy
- Community developer
- Assessor
- Working with risk

Source: Bogues (2008: 12)

Service users in workshops contributing to this consultation were able to describe how social workers had advocated on their behalf and felt that this was important.

However, some 'queried' the advocacy role in contemporary social work practice. At the same time service users and carers argued for increased social work advocacy, holding a view that social workers are well placed to argue with their employers and with central government. A quotation from a service user underlines this point: 'Social workers need to stop fighting against us and start fighting with us' (Bogues, 2008: 7).

Service users and carers emphasized the importance of sharing power, partnership working and supporting the voice of services users and carers. In listing the roles and tasks of social work, a number ways in which social work contributes to society are identified (Box 3.7). Advocacy is clearly identified as a specific role with the acknowledgement that 'the social work advocacy role has been weakened' (Bogues, 2008: 13) and therefore needs to be strengthened. The report identifies a 'strong sense' in responses of people in the consultation that such an advocacy role is strongly associated with a rights-based approach to social work. There are two other roles that are compatible with and enhance the advocacy role. First, the role of 'rights promoter' makes the commitment to rights a 'more central component of effective social work practice' (2008: 15). While acknowledging the challenge for social workers in balancing the promotion of rights with the consequences of risk, the report notes that the establishment of rights within legislation now provides social work with a firm base to promote the rights of service users and carers. The second role that is significant is that of promoter of choice and independence, which is described as a 'core element' (2008: 15) of social work. This requires social workers to use their advocacy skills when enabling people to make decisions through the provision of information and possible options.

In April 2012 a strategy for social work in Northern Ireland was published (Health Care Board, 2012). This outlines ten strategic priorities for building a foundation for social work under three key headings:

- Strengthening the capacity of the workforce.
- Improving social work services.
- Building leadership and trust.

From an advocacy perspective this is disappointing after the strong emphasis in the consultation document. The vision for social work in Northern Ireland focuses on social wellbeing and the principles underpinning this do resonate with social work advocacy values:

Social workers will work to improve and safeguard the social wellbeing of individuals, families and communities by promoting their independence, supporting their social inclusion and participation in society, empowering them to take control of their lives and helping them to keep safe. (Health Care Board, 2012: 3)

Five key social work roles are identified in Box 3.8 which paint a rather different picture of social work to that outlined in Box 3.7, and it is clearly difficult to find a similar emphasis on advocacy to that put forward in the consultation document.

> ## Box 3.8   Five key social work roles
>
> 1 Prevention: Empowerment
> 2 Support: Early intervention
> 3 Intervention: Person-centred social work practice
> 4 Protection: Investigation and management of risk
> 5 Control: Restriction of the exercise of rights or liberty
>
> (Bogues, 2008: 17)

The outcomes for social work (Box 3.9) do, however, strike a balance between improving and safeguarding wellbeing and recognise the importance of enabling service users and carers to be able to participate in decision making, with their rights respected. A continuum of social work practice is envisaged, with the promotion of

> ## Box 3.9   Outcomes for social work
>
> Improving and safeguarding social wellbeing involves social workers working with people in pursuance of the following outcomes:
>
> • Keeping well and healthy and safe from harm.
> • Having a home where they feel safe and have a sense of belonging.
> • Having access to income and resources sufficient to meet their fundamental needs.
> • Having supportive and trusting close relationships, including with family and friends.
> • Having opportunities to enjoy positive life experiences, including engagement in social and community activities.
> • Having opportunities to make a positive contribution, including participation in education, training, work or other purposeful activity.
> • Exercising choice and control about their live and how they live it.
> • Having the resilience and ability to cope when things change or go wrong.
> • Having a sense of self-worth and self-efficacy.
> • Living a fulfilling life where their individual rights and personal dignity are respected.
>
> *Source:* Bogues (2008)

rights and independence being at the forefront of practice and seen as the major part of the picture, and the professional role to safeguard and protect being presented at the end of the continuum. While the limitations of such a presentation of social work are acknowledged, it does reflect the social work role as empowering and promoting the self-determination and rights of people who are using services alongside safeguarding and protect people who are vulnerable.

Despite this, it is possible to find some nuggets in the plan and vision for social work for the advocacy role of social workers. Interestingly, the social work role in relation to systemic advocacy is articulated in strategic priority number ten, which states that

> [t]hose who deliver social work services and those who receive them have important roles in informing and influencing policy decisions as well as contributing to service improvements and practice developments. (NISCC, 2008)

Furthermore the Department for Health, Social Service and Public Safety has published draft guidelines for commissioners of advocacy services. As the extract below indicates, this does recognise that independent advocacy is needed to support vulnerable people:

> By empowering and helping to safeguard people who are at risk of exclusion or being discriminated against, advocacy has a significant role to play in promoting human rights and tackling inequalities in health and social care. (DHSSP, 2011 para 6.1)

Investing in independent advocacy

CASE EXAMPLE

What are the benefits of investing in independent advocacy services? Extract from draft policy for developing advocacy services.

5.25 Investing in independent advocacy services means that people who may be at risk of exclusion or being discriminated against have a vehicle through which they can, where possible, express their views or wishes, access information to help them make informed choices about their health and well-being and take control over their own lives. Advocacy empowers people to have their voice heard and helps to safeguard those who, for whatever reason, are unable to express their own views.

5.26 However, investing in advocacy services not only benefits the person needing support. It can also benefit commissioners and providers of health

(Continued)

(Continued)

and social care services. For example, advocacy can help prevent crises arising in a person's life which otherwise may result in an intervention that has much greater resource implications. It can also enhance capacity building at a community and individual level which can ultimately serve to reduce dependency on other health and social care services.

5.27 By giving those most at risk a vehicle through which they can have their voice heard, advocacy services can also help commissioners and service providers gain a better understanding of the needs of this important group. They can act as a valuable channel for seeking ideas and views on how current health and social care services can be improved to better meet those needs and to inform planning for future needs and service re-design.

(DHSSP, 2011: www.dhsspsni.gov.uk/a-draft-policy-for-developing-advocacy-services.pdf, accessed 24.04.12)

Commentary

Reviews of the roles and tasks of social work have taken place within a culture which appears to be focused on performance, targets and management of risk. The business agenda that drives the provision of social services, and hence of social work, has radically altered the social work profession. Furthermore, it has been argued that effective change needs to address more fundamental causes of what has been described as the current crisis in social work. That change cannot take place without a critical analysis of how far the new directions in social work are compatible with the business agenda. An examination of the four reviews provides a starting point for that analysis and also offers an opportunity to reclaim social work advocacy. Indeed arguably social work advocacy can also contribute to critiquing the business culture, using advocacy skills underpinned by social work values to support that process.

Three of the four reviews specifically locate advocacy as one of the roles of social work. The difficulty is that the other roles inevitably cause tensions for practice in so far as they do, to some extent, fit more with the business/risk management culture than one which promotes relationship-based practice. However, balancing care, control and empowerment has been a constant debate throughout the history of social work and the changing social, political and economic contexts of practice. The overall picture that emerges from these documents is that the social work task is underpinned by values which are about safeguarding rights, challenging oppression and injustice and promoting dignity and choice. Skills that have a particular resonance with advocacy – participation and partnership skills – are also identified. The vision of ensuring that service users and carers have a voice is particularly strong in the Welsh implementation document, which states that it will provide help to make people's voices strong and clear and will actively listen and act on what is heard.

However, the specific mention of advocacy as one of the social work roles in the other reviews of itself means that there is a commitment to promoting service user and carer voice.

It is apposite to reclaim the advocacy role that is clearly set out in all the reviews. Service users value the range of approaches that social workers use, including the social work advocacy role and an approach which promotes their rights and needs (Beresford, 2007). In any situation where a social worker is assessing risk, care managing or acting as an agent of social control there may be opportunities for effective social work advocacy. This is illustrated in the case of Martha, a social worker who is working with Charlotte and her children.

Charlotte and Martha

Charlotte is a single parent with four children, three of whom are living with foster carers on full care orders (Children Act 1989; Children (Scotland) Act 1995; Children (Northern Ireland) Order 1995).[1] Charlotte had been known to social services since early childhood and her own experiences of parenting had been negative and abusive. She has had a series of violent partners and she had spent considerable amounts of time with the children at a women's refuge. Charlotte has limited networks within the community and no family support (having been sexually abused by family members over a number of years). She continues to struggle to form relationships.

However, Martha has a good relationship with Charlotte and understands the situation, the family history and the family dynamics and the impact this has on her personally and, more importantly, her capacity to parent and her ability to meet her children's needs. Martha is aware of not wanting to fall into a 'mother blaming' culture, but both Martha and Charlotte recognise Charlotte's limitations. One of the challenges for Martha has been balancing the tension between the rights of Charlotte and her children to family life and the rights of the children to protection.

Charlotte is now expecting another child, and following a pre-birth assessment the decision has been made to make an application for an interim care order with respect to the new baby. This effectively means that the baby will be received into care when he or she is born and immediately placed with foster carers. Martha enabled Charlotte to understand the process and the decision making and ensured that Charlotte had access to legal redress to challenge those decisions. In a report for a child protection conference Martha strongly represented the views of Charlotte and of the older children (who were happy and settled in their placement). Martha wanted to continue to work with Charlotte and drew on the work that they had done together to put forward her views. However, she also put forward her own view about the safety of the newborn baby: while recognising the positive elements of Charlotte's parenting, she was also very clear that despite this her professional assessment was that the threshold of risk to the baby was too high to justify recommending that the child remained with Charlotte.

(Continued)

(Continued)

Martha's advocacy skill in this situation was to:

- ensure that throughout the process Charlotte understood what was happening;
- ensure that she was aware that she could challenge the local authority position;
- remind Charlotte that she did have the right to access to a solicitor and should do so; and
- maintain the relationship with Charlotte throughout this process.

Martha's story illustrates the importance of casework, partnership and advocacy practice. As an assessor of risk, Martha faced dilemmas that many social workers face within the context of safeguarding children.

Summary

- Social work has been scrutinised in all four nations of the UK in order to interrogate the social work role.
- The views of people who use services are shaping social work practice.
- Social work is complex and tensions remain between what have been called the 'care' and 'control' roles of social worker.
- The importance of independent advocacy as an element of service provision is now recognised.
- Reference to a relational approach to practice and to advocacy as an element of the role of the social worker provides an opportunity to reclaim social work advocacy.

Discussion questions

1 How far do the reviews contribute to enabling social workers to reclaim their advocacy role?
2 Is the re-emergence of relationship-based social work a realistic role for social work in contemporary practice?
3 What are the key challenges a social worker might face in a similar situation to Martha? Compare this situation to that of Michaela in Chapter 1.
4 What opportunities are there for you to strengthen your advocacy role?

Note

1   Legislation that requires the state to take responsibility for the care of children who cannot be looked after by their birth parents.

Further reading

Boylan, J. and Dalrymple, J. (2011) 'Advocacy, social justice and children's rights', *Practice: Social Work in Action*, 23 (1): 19–30.

Dickens, J. (2012) 'The definition of social work in the United Kingdon 2000–2010', *International Journal of Social Welfare*, 21: 34–43.

Folgheraiter, F. (2012) *The Mystery of Social Work: A Critical Analysis of the Global Definition and New Suggestions According to the Relational Theory*. Trento: Edizioni Erickson.

Jordon, B. (2004) 'Emancipatory social work? Opportunity or oxymoron?', *British Journal of Social Work*, 34 (1): 5–19.

Pierson, J. (2011) *Understanding Social Work*. Maidenhead: Open University Press.

4

Advocacy Skills

Good practice in social work involves the integration of knowledge, skills and values. While this book aims to be primarily a theoretical consideration of social work advocacy and seeks to reclaim advocacy in practice, it is impossible to think about advocacy without also exploring the skill base. Thompson (2000) notes that knowledge underpins practice, skills put the knowledge into practice and values are the ethical principles that ensure good practice. We saw in Chapter 1 that the key features or principles of advocacy are:

- Promoting equality, justice and social inclusion.
- Empowering people to speak up for themselves or to have their voices heard in the systems.
- Helping people to become aware of their rights and exercise those rights.
- Enabling people to be involved in and influence decisions being made about their future.

All four of these principles are reflected in the knowledge base required for social work outlined in the Professional Capability v Framework for England and the National Occupational Standards for Social work in the rest of the UK. They also link back to discussion in earlier chapters about the definition of social work and reflect the value base of social work. In this chapter we will therefore consider the social work process of assessment, planning, intervention and review. Case studies will be used to explore social work advocacy skills in each part of the process, with a commentary on the key features of advocacy as outlined above. But first we will consider the place of relationship within social work.

Relational social work

It has been argued that the core of social work practice is relational (Wilson et al., 2011); that is, social work is about relationships with both service users and other professionals. These relationships also extend to the organisational and policy contexts of practice as well as involving ourselves and inevitably inter-relate and influence each other. Wilson and colleagues analyse accounts of service users' views about social work skills over several decades. From this they identify that a key concern for service users is that social workers are able to develop good relational skills with people they are working with and respond to them sensitively and respectfully. Advocacy skills are also highlighted. Work by Rees and Wallace in 1982 noted that both advocacy and negotiation skills were important to service users, while over twenty years later Davis (2008) identified that service users want social workers to advocate for them in respect of their needs. This is further reiterated by service users in the consultation for the review of social work in Northern Ireland (Bogues, 2008) (see Chapter 3). Effective social work advocacy involves supporting and enabling service users to determine their lives through choice and involvement in decision making. Central to achieving this is the establishment of a meaningful relationship. Such a relationship is based on working with and for people within a partnership. The skills of effective partnership working mean that practitioners need to develop a relationship based on trust, respect, honesty and sharing risk (Allison, 2005). It requires social work advocates to be critical of anti-oppressive practitioners who recognise differential power relations, to be committed to listening to the people they are working with and to be able to reflect and appraise possible ways forward (Taylor et al., 2008).

It is perhaps useful at this point to briefly examine casework as part of the social work role, since this traditional social work approach involved, among other things, building a supportive relationship with 'clients'. Casework involves

work on cases guided by certain principles and the use of knowledge and human relation skills with the object of fulfilling the function of a particular agency. (Timms, 1964: 7)

The traditional casework relationship is described as:

> The dynamic interaction of attitudes and emotions between the caseworker and the client, with the purpose of helping a client achieve a better adjustment between [him]self and his environment, (Biestek, 1961: 12)

We saw in Chapter 2 that casework emerged as a way of working through the work of the Charity Organisation Society (COS). For the social worker this involved building a supportive relationship, offering guidance, understanding the situation of the family concerned and sometimes providing material assistance. However, this approach could also be described in terms of middle-class caseworkers *doing to* poor families rather than *working with* them.

Psychodynamic perspectives influenced casework from 1920 to 1960 when the emphasis was on family relationships, the nature of the relationship between the social worker and people they were working with, and the service users' experiences of childhood. The approach was in generally used in the 1950s and 1960s when social work was considered to be therapeutic and the problems encountered by service users were seen to be open to the influence of the social worker. External factors such as inadequate housing and unemployment were not regarded as important in the resolution of difficulties service users were encountering. This omission of structural considerations led to a major critique of this approach that resonates today (Pierson, 2011).

This critique was led by radical social work in the 1970s and criticised the casework approach because it focused on individual failure rather than wider social causes. The task of the social worker through the professional relationship was challenged as it meant doing nothing more than helping service users come to terms with their problems. This meant that service users were discouraged from gaining insight into the structural issues affecting their lives. As practitioners began to recognise the significance of structural issues – such as poverty – on the lives of service users, social work practice started to extend to include the social and structural aspects impacting on the lives of individuals and families. By the 1970s the emergence of other social work methods, including group work and community work, meant that casework became one of a range of possible social work approaches.

A return to the language of 'casework' in a number of the reviews considered in Chapter 3 is interesting. Arguably, it reflects contemporary literature on 'relationship based practice' (Ruch, 2005; Ruch et al., 2010; Ferguson, 2011; Folgheraiter, 2004, 2007). While the emphasis of casework is on one-to-one work with individuals or families, it has also been described as a 'nurturing relationship over time' (Davies, 2000: 45). Davies points out that while the critique of casework suggests that people were to be held responsible for their problems, an alternative perspective recognises that with the support of a social worker, individuals, families or groups have the capacity to resolve their problems and are responsible for their own decisions. Ferguson's call for a return to a 'relational approach' takes account of the critique of casework. He indicates that in contemporary practice:

Relationship based practice seeks to reach a deep understanding of the complexity of human beings, the uniqueness of the person, the problems at hand and what is happening in this case/encounter. It is a 'psycho-social' approach, which focuses on the interaction between the external factors that influence people's life chances and the social conditions they live in and their internal emotional worlds. (Ferguson, 2011: 8)

This clearly addresses some of the earlier critiques of casework. For Ferguson the approach explores structural factors such as power and inequalities since they are 'apparent and experienced in and through relationships' (2011: 8). The importance of the social work relationship is also highlighted in social work literature and government reports. For example, a comment from a service user network in the report *Social Work at Its Best: A Statement of Social Work Roles and Tasks for the 21st Century* (GSCC, 2008) indicates that there are three things that services users value most:

- social work's social approach;
- the social work relationship; and
- the positive personal qualities they associate with social workers. (Shaping Our Lives, 2007 cited in GSCC, 2008)

Munro, in her review of child protection, notes that work needs to be 'done *in a relationship* with children and family members' (2011: 20, italics original). Service users also identify importance of relationship (Box 4.1). Relationship-based practice has its roots in psychosocial approaches to practice and the psychodynamic base of casework (Wilson et al., 2011). In developing an understanding of the centrality of relationship with in social work, Wilson and colleagues (2011) identify two elements of relationship based practice. First, it uses the relationship between the social worker and the service user to understand the circumstances of the person or people they are working with. Second, the social worker and the service user relationship then becomes a source of information for providing help and intervention. They believe that effective and ethical social work practice combines good professional relationships with reflective practice.

Applying principles of relationship practice to work with children and families, the advocacy skills of social workers would involve: recognising the child within themselves, which influences how they understand families and their own values within the professional relationship; listening to the voice of the child in order to gain insight into the child's world; recognising strengths and weaknesses of families as way of safeguarding children and promoting their interests; acknowledging power and purpose through partnership working; empowering parents and children to enable them to engage positively with the social work process and in understanding the purpose of the intervention (Smeeton, 2012).

> **Box 4.1   What service users say about social work advocacy skills**
>
> Social workers are in a good position to speak up for people, both with their employers and at the Assembly. (Bogues, 2008: 7)
>
> [Children] said they value an ongoing relationship with their worker, that their needs and rights to protection should be at the heart of practice, that they should have a voice and be listened to. (Munro, 2011: 25)
>
> I was looking forward to her coming as a friend, I felt I could talk to her about anything, I wouldn't need to watch my tongue … I had complete confidence in her, complete confidence. (Older, white European bereaved woman) (Beresford et al., 2006: 3)

The assumption that underpins the concept of advocacy is that there are people who require support to manage their relationships with organisations and professionals when they are using health, welfare and other services. People often feel that they lack power as users of services, and there is a feeling of inevitability about the unequal power relations that exist between service users and organisations providing services (Wilson et al., 2011). The social work advocacy role can be an opportunity to provide a space to hear service user perspectives and establish the parameters of a more democratic relationship from an early point. If relationships are to be meaningful, the starting point has to be to invest time in developing a relationship with the service user. In this context the social worker will be drawing on core social work skills including preparing well for the first meeting, using active listening skills, allocating enough time, working at the service user's pace, and thinking about body language – what the social worker may be communicating to the service user and what their body language is telling the social worker. This usually starts when the social worker commences the assessment process.

Assessment

Assessment has always been a key element of social work and in contemporary practice is part of the legislative framework governing statutory assessment processes. The Professional Capabilities Framework in England states that social workers should be able to 'select and use appropriate frameworks to assess, give meaning to, plan, implement and review effective interventions and evaluate the outcomes, in partnership with service users' (TCSW, 2012: 7.5) while the *Standards of Proficiency* in social work expect that social workers should 'be able to assess a situation, determine its nature and severity and call upon the required knowledge and experience to deal with it' (HCPC, 2012: 4.1). For social workers in the rest of the UK, Key Role 1 states that they should be able to 'prepare for, and work with individuals, families, carers, groups and communities to assess their needs and circumstances' (Topss UK, 2002). Social workers and other professionals make decisions daily that relate to the lives of service users and inevitably have consequences for them. While a systematic review of texts and frameworks for assessment failed to find clarity with respect to a definition of assessment (Crisp et al., 2005), there are key components that a social work advocate has to consider in all assessment processes. Some assessments may be quite short, while others comprise a longer process which involve a number of contacts with a service user and/or carer. Essentially it is the first in a series of steps which involve answering two questions:

- What is the problem? (This includes consideration of other questions such as how long has it been a problem? Who is it a problem for? Are we the best organisation to assist with this problem?)
- What is happening to create the problem and why? (This involves analysing the situation in order to make sense of what is happening). (Wilson et al., 2011)

Smale and colleagues (2000) have identified three models of assessment that enable practitioners to critically reflect on their practice. In the *questioning model* the social worker is the expert who obtains and analyses the information to make a decision. The *procedural model* is one where the social worker assesses whether the service user is eligible to receive identified services. The *exchange model* assumes that service users are experts themselves and the assessment process involves an exchange of information between the service user and the social worker. The expertise of the social worker is in working in partnership with service users, enabling people to articulate their needs and have an active role in the assessment process.

In the following case example we consider the difficult situations that statutory social workers face when they are working in teams providing services for refugees and asylum seekers. Working with and for people when also engaged in a procedural process that is experienced as oppressive and disempowering by the service user requires particular skills and can make it difficult to see quite where advocacy skills come in. Here the importance of relationship and honesty from the start about the professional role of the social worker is crucial. The social worker has to be transparent about the nature of the relationship and, where necessary, the statutory responsibilities that they have. Developing critical reflective skills can help to ensure that the four features of advocacy remain as objectives for the social work advocate, who can then consider what skills are needed to make those objectives a reality.

Jude's advocacy skills

Jude works in a local authority asylum team and has recently undertaken a Human Rights Assessment as part of her duty to ascertain whether the local authority is breaching the human rights of Edith, a woman whose application for refugee status has failed. Edith has three children. Her eldest son is not a UK citizen. However, her other two children, who have a different father, are UK citizens. Both fathers live in the UK. Edith's youngest child is 3 months old, and Edith appears to be suffering from post-natal depression.

Jude's assessment was that the local authority were not breaching Edith's human rights under the Human Rights Act 1998. As part of this assessment Jude had researched information about Edith's country of origin from the UK Border Agency and the Refugee Council. Jude had to meet with Edith to explain the assessment to her. Jude was in a powerful position here and felt uncomfortable about having to give Edith news that was clearly going to be upsetting. This procedural part of the process, however, was ameliorated to some extent by her knowledge of the exchange model of assessment (Smale et al., 2000) where possible. Jude was mindful that as far as possible she wanted to work alongside Edith, and Jude had tried to balance the power dynamics in their relationship throughout the assessment process. She had given Edith as much information as she could about practical help that she could access and talked with her about available options and choices, particularly in relation to Edith's concerns about her depression and her financial situation. She had also been very clear about possible outcomes. These were limited, as there was a possibility that Edith might have to return to her country of origin (which would separate her children from their fathers). Jude had talked to Edith about ways of keeping contact if this happened. She also discussed the difference between returning on a voluntary basis and deportation. Jude was also aware that the children were entitled to services under the Children Act 1989, since if support was withdrawn they could become homeless. While therefore there was no duty for the Local Authority to support Edith under the Nationality, Immigration and Asylum Act 2002, the Children Act 1989 provided a legislative framework to safeguard the children if they became homeless.

On an initial reading it can be difficult to identify Jude's advocacy skills in this situation. However, if we look at the four key features of advocacy then we can see that:

- Jude used her skills to ensure that Edith was treated fairly in a system that felt unfair.
- Jude ensured that Edith understood the process, had the time and space to ask questions and clarify any issues that she was unsure about, and made sure that she listened and responded to Edith's worries and concerns.
- During the course of the conversation Edith mentioned that she had seen her General Practitioner (GP) for depression but that he had not given her time and told her to see her Health Visitor. Edith felt that there was no point in contacting the Health Visitor, but Jude explained that Health Visitors can complete

assessments for depression and can also provide extended visits for new mothers like Edith who appear to be depressed. In this way Jude assisted her to become aware of the rights that she did have at that point.

- Jude offered to contact the Health Visitor but Edith said that she felt confident about doing this herself now that she understood what she was entitled to. Jude also signposted Edith to organisations that could offer practical support.

While Edith's story is a very specific situation in relation to asylum, social workers need to be aware of the impact of legislative requirements in any assessment. Tensions may often exist between the requirements of legislation, the professional judgement of the social worker and the views of service users. Understanding the importance of relational social work and using pointers for anti-oppressive assessments to inform a meaningful dialogue between social workers and service users or carers informs the development of advocacy skills in order to develop empowerment practice (see Box 4.2).

Box 4.2　Pointers for anti-oppressive assessment

The right to a full assessment – there should be full and easy access to assessment for all groups

> If you have English as a second or third language and your child is disabled, how do you know your entitlement? (Member of Blackburn Asian Blind Association)

The need for flexible services

> In our culture, we do not really have appointments; we came from a place where you would just turn up if you wanted to see an official. (Member of Iranian Community Group)

Avoiding stigma of requesting help

> People here are from a generation who would not ask for help ... I said I would look after my wife through sickness and in health, I don't see myself as a carer, I am a husband. (Member of Bolton Dementia Carers Support Group)

Social workers should be well prepared – by researching the general culture or condition of the group/community/individual prior to the assessment

(Continued)

(Continued)

> They should tell you all the information you might find useful about rights, finances about social facilities and groups like ours. (Member of Manchester People First)

Social workers should be honest (and accurate) in their assessments

> It was full of false praise like 'she brushes her hair lovely, she dresses very well' – it wasn't realistic because some days I don't bother getting dressed! (Member of African Caribbean Mental Health Group)

Social workers should speak to service users and carers independently

> You can't complain about being exhausted in front of them [the person you are caring for]. (Member of Bolton Dementia Carers Support Group)

> The social worker didn't even talk to me; she spoke to my mum and then went. (Member of Learning Disabled People's Group)

Social workers should write records of assessments jointly with service users and carers

Social workers should make arrangements for trained interpreters and independent advocates to be part of the assessment process

Social workers should not have low expectations of people

> I have a degree, but because I am visually impaired, they always want me to go for jobs in call centres – they need to show us opportunities to improve our lives. (Member of Asian Disability Group)

(Shardlow et al., 2005: 35)

Planning

Social workers in England are expected to be able to 'use a planned and structured approach, informed by social work methods, models and tools, to promote positive change and independence and to prevent harm' (TCSW, 2012: 7.2), while in the rest of the UK similarly social workers need to be able to plan their work (Topss UK, 2002: Key Role 2). Planning is now a part of the language of social work practice and has moved beyond merely being the link between assessment and intervention to being an essential skill for practitioners (Holloway, 2005). Policy and legislation requires social workers to make plans in a number of specific circumstance. These include, for example: care plans for adults, transition planning, care plans for looked after children, plans in relation to children in need, child protection plans and pathway plans for young care leavers. Plans need to be informed by the views of service users and carers if their needs are to be met and indicates the importance of good planning

> if service are to be developed to meet the needs of children, young people, and families, if resources, assets and the workforce are to be deployed to the best effect, and if all partners are to focus on achieving the best possible local outcomes. (DfES, 2005: 4)

While most social work activity tends to be at the micro level with individuals and families, it is important to remember the macro advocacy role of social workers. Critical practice involves engaging people who require services and their carers. When services users, groups and communities participate in identifying and mapping needs, this can have an impact on planning and the way in which resources are allocated, and is more likely to alleviate the conditions that contribute to social problems. Service user and carer participation in the planning of services results in a shift of emphasis towards the needs of the service user rather than the needs of the organisation. There a number of reasons for planning (Preston-Shoot and Wigley 2005):

• Obtaining better services.
• Obtaining better outcomes for service users.
• Focus on business planning.
• Managing finite resources.
• Providing information to the public.

Parker and Bradley (2010) suggest that one way of thinking about the planning process is through the analogy of an architect's plan. This outlines what is needed to reach the desired outcome (for example, a new building). So effectively the plan is a map or picture of what the outcome will look like, based on conversations and relationships between the architect and the client. They also add to the analogy the notion of 'planning permission' – so this involves thinking about the players and reaching agreement on an effective plan. People not involved in this process may well ignore or attempt to jeopardise the plan, or be disappointed by it and fail to engage. Central to all these dynamics is the relationship between all parties. The observation by President D. Eisenhower that 'Plans are nothing; planning is everything' is perhaps apposite here.

Planning is therefore a skilled activity that requires social workers to use a range of communication, analytical and relational skills. Effective plans will provide a comprehensive picture of the current situation and identify other professionals or agencies that might be involved. In addition it will identify what action is likely to be taken, how, by whom and what the key issues are (Parker and Bradley, 2010). Planning has to take account of the changing nature of people's lives and must be fluid and responsive rather than inflexible. Things do not always go according to plan and there needs to be both contingency plans and regular reviews of plans to incorporate changing circumstances and new information. This enables plans to be developed or modified as necessary, and they become meaningful and dynamic documents. Plans do need to be thorough, but not overly complicated: 'Everything should be made as simple as possible, but not simpler' (Einstein). The tension for social workers is what could be seen as the dual purpose of plans: to ensure that the needs of the service users are met as well as meeting the management imperatives that inevitably impact on practice (Dalrymple and Burke, 2006). This is where the social work advocacy role may come into play in trying to meet the needs of the service user, which may be constrained by agency policies and resources.

CASE EXAMPLE

Rajinder's story

Rajinder is a 20-year-old man with learning difficulties who lives in his own flat in a supported living project where there is 24-hour support. He has a good relationship with his social worker, who he has known for a number of years. Rajinder has developed good support networks in the housing project and gets on well with most of the other tenants. However, he constantly feels under surveillance, and while he has the privacy of his own flat he does not really feel as independent as he would like. He felt inhibited by some of the routines, such as times when he was able to use the communal laundry facilities. He also stated that he would not necessarily choose to socialise with a number of the other tenants in the building. Rajinder has a good relationship with his parents but becomes frustrated at times as he feels they interfere too much in his life. Over the last year he has been developing a relationship with Leone, who is also a tenant, and they want to move into their own flat away from the project. Rajinder has discussed this with his parents but met with resistance, and they suggested that he discussed this with everyone at his next review meeting.

Rajinder's parents have always attended review meetings concerning future planning and decision making, but he now feels that as an adult that he would prefer that they did not attend his reviews. The last couple of reviews have been difficult and have resulted in some conflict between Rajinder and his parents. Rajinder's social worker helped him to understand his rights. She gave Rajinder information from the British Institute of Learning Disabilities (BILD, n.d.), who have produced a useful guide to the Human Rights Act which includes:

- I should be able to say what I like as long as I respect other people, and expect other people to listen to me. (Article 10)
- I should have my rights respected. (Article 6)
- I can speak out and complain if something is wrong. (Article 10)
- I should be safe at home and have time for myself. (Article 8)
- I can get married and have children. (Article 12)

A review is due at which Rajinder wants to formally to discuss his plans to move. As part of the planning for a review, his social worker would always meet with him to prepare for the meeting and explore the issues he wanted to raise. Rajinder spoke with his social worker about not wanting his parents to attend and his anxiety about not wanting to upset them. The social worker listened carefully to what he had to say and explored possible reactions from his parents and how Rajinder might feel about that. Rajinder did not feel confident to speak with his parents directly about this and asked the social worker to negotiate with them on his behalf. She suggested that a possible compromise would be that they received the minutes of the reviews. Rajinder liked this proposal as he knew that they would want to know what had been talked about and any decisions that had been made. He was happy for them to know this, but did not want them to be part of the decision-making process. For Rajinder a reflection of his growing independence was to have the autonomy to attend the meeting without parental support and the right to choose who attended his reviews.

Rajinder's social worker successfully negotiated this arrangement. She then worked with Rajinder to plan his agenda and rehearse what he wanted to say in the meeting. They considered together what might happen if Rajinder felt unable to articulate his views in the meeting at any point. Since Rajinder at this point did not feel confident they agreed to write down his views, wishes and feelings so that if needed his words could be presented to the meeting. However, he developed confidence through rehearsing and, as his parents were not present, his anxieties dissipated and he was able to present his views with the support of his social worker.

The social worker's advocacy skills here are easier to identify than in Edith's case:

- Rajinder's social worker helped him to be treated fairly within the review process and ensured that he was treated equally as an adult with views and opinions.
- Preparing people for decision-making meetings is an important aspect of the social work advocacy role, and the process empowered Rajinder to feel able to explore and raise his issues in a supportive environment.
- The social worker used her relationship with Rajinder and with his parents to skilfully manage the potential conflict that may have occurred in enabling him to assert his need for independence and autonomy.
- The social worker was able to work with Rajinder's parents to enable them to feel positive about the future for their son and continue to play an important part in his life – which he valued and would need.

Rajinder's social worker also used her macro advocacy skills to consider the issues raised by Rajinder in relation to his experiences in the supported living project. She was concerned about his experiences of being under surveillance and discussed these with her line manager. As a result of this she brought the matter to a team meeting where colleagues had heard similar feedback from service users or relatives. As a result, the team agreed that the manager would talk to the home and they could offer to work together to explore this further.

This cause or systemic advocacy validates the individual experiences of service users and can lead to positive change for them. Rajinder's social worker was committed to supervision and had positive experiences of this process with her line manager. This enabled her to advocate at a more systemic level.

Intervention

While intervention is considered to be a distinct stage in the social work process for the critical reflective practitioner, the very word 'intervention must give pause for thought. Horner notes that the medical definition of intervention is 'the act or fact of interfering so as to modify' (2009: 244). Arguably no one really wants to 'interfere' in anyone's life, and the oppressive connotations of the term cannot be ignored as it does indicate the moral and political authority of the social worker to invade 'the social territories' of social workers (Payne, 1996b: 43). This means that social workers have to balance the difficult elements of their role when taking action that is not in line with the wishes of the individual. Nevertheless, it is equally important to remember that interventions can be positive, affirming and creative (Coles and Connors, 2008: 199), and Trevithick (2012) notes that service users do look for and find supportive and helpful social work interventions. Furthermore, part of the professional duty of a social worker is to intervene at a more macro level in challenging the unfair and unjust conditions experienced by people who require social work support. Advocacy skills are important here to challenge discrimination and promote a more fair and just society. A number of authors describe intervention at three levels: micro (focus on individual or family members), mezzo (focus on community and neighbourhood – bringing people together) and macro (focus on policy and procedures) (Trevithick, 2012). Interventions at each of the three points involve ensuring that service users are heard through the use of both case and systemic advocacy and ensuring that structural problems which disadvantage service users are addressed. A useful definition of intervention is provided by Trevithick, who suggests that intervention refers to

> [t]he purposeful actions we undertake as professionals in a given situation, based on the knowledge and understanding we have acquired, the skills we have learned and the values we adopt. (2012: 159)

The assessment and planning processes that precede intervention provide a starting point for thinking about what intervention might look like in a given context. Through the assessment process answers to the questions identified by Wilson and colleagues (2011) above provide a framework that takes the practitioner on to another set of questions in relation to intervention:

- Do I have to do anything?
- Do I wish to do something?
- What is to be gained by doing nothing?
- What is to be gained by doing something?

- What are the likely outcomes of any of my interventions/actions?
- Who decides what interventions I can offer?
- How do I know which ones are effective? (Horner, 2009: 247)

Peter's story

Peter is a 78-year-old man who lives alone following his wife Olga's move to a nursing home six months ago. He has recently moved to live closer to his daughter so that she can support him and help him with his daily tasks. Peter is partially sighted, is showing signs of dementia and has arthritis in his hip. Peter and Olga have been together for nearly fifty years and he misses her. Peter feels lonely and depressed even though he sees his daughter every day. Since moving he has realised that he would rather see his wife every day and recognises that his daughter is doing her best and he understands that she is not able to take him as often as he would like. His daughter, Mary (52), realises that her father is lonely and feels that he needs more support than she can give. She has also noticed some change in the living conditions at her father's house with rubbish accumulating in the back garden and worries that this will attract vermin. He is fiercely independent and a very private man, so when Mary mentions her concerns about the rubbish or getting help through social services he insists that he can manage. His health appears to be deteriorating and he is becoming increasingly confused. Mary works part-time and is starting to feel depressed about the situation to the extent that she has recently taken some time off work because she felt she could not cope. While she loves her father his needs are increasing and combining visits to her mother with everything else is beginning to feel too much. Mary has tried to talk to her father about her feelings but he becomes angry and upset. Mary decides to contact the social services department for advice. Pat is allocated as their social worker and during subsequent visits undertakes a community care assessment.

Pat has considered the situation in a holistic way. Two main considerations inform her thinking: first, that it is important for Peter to retain as much independence as possible; and second, that Mary is supported to ensure her physical and mental wellbeing and reduce the risk that the relationship between Peter and his daughter breaks down. Pat feels that an early referral to his GP is essential to assess Peter's medical needs. While for Pat it is important to work with an understanding of the social model of disability, she is also aware that there is a place for the medical model (Oliver and Sapey, 1999). Pat feels that the issues about his physical health need to be addressed: he could be in pain with his arthritis, which might mean that he is not sleeping well; lack of sleep will increase both his confusion and contribute to his depression. Pain relief could therefore help him to feel calmer and less confused. The GP might also decide to refer Peter for an assessment for dementia. However, it could be that he has a urinary tract infection. Depression is often a part of dementia, so the depression may be part of the dementia or could be because Peter is grieving the

(Continued)

(Continued)

loss of Olga and his former home. If Peter is diagnosed with a form of dementia, then it might be appropriate to prescribe medication and possibly refer him to a memory clinic. Pat is aware that due to his poor eyesight Peter is vulnerable to falls, and so a referral to the optician is a consideration as well as a referral to the falls clinic for a risk assessment. Pat feels that it is important not only for Peter but in terms of the wider community, and that resources for such a referral is also a preventive strategy to reduce pressure on the NHS. She takes the following action:

- Pat carefully talks with Peter about a possible diagnosis of dementia. Pat needs to use her skills at this point to ensure that Peter and Mary are provided with as much information as possible and are aware of their rights to services. She appreciates that a diagnosis of dementia is likely to be upsetting but also tries to be reassuring and supportive, explaining that should this be the case help can be provided to enable Peter to live as independently as possible.
- At present Peter does have the capacity to make his own decisions. Helping him to be involved in and influence decisions about his future should he lack capacity is another skilled part of Pat's work. It is important that Peter feels empowered to make as many decisions as possible about his situation and future while he has capacity. Pat talks to him about a will and also explains to him how a living will can enable his wishes and feelings to contribute to decision making in the future.
- Pat discusses with Peter whether he feels that living with his daughter is a possible option should he be unable to look after himself. Peter acknowledges that his daughter would be unlikely to be able to cope should he need more care in the future. Furthermore, he felt that he would not want her to have to do that. This provides Pat with the opportunity to sensitively talk together about other options, including the possibility of residential care. Peter is happy with the care that is provided for Olga and there is a part of him that would like to be with her.

Personalisation acknowledges that service users have insights into their needs (see Box 4.3). The development of the personalisation agenda places individuals at the centre of the processes of planning, intervention and review, particularly in relation to the allocation of resources. Pat therefore works with Peter to identify his support needs, the support he has at the moment and any paid support he might need, rather than intervening in his life to provide services. This means that Pat's practice is based on working with Peter as a person with rights and entitlements as a citizen (Warren, 2007). Her role in this respect is to undertake

> a common assessment of individual social care needs, emphasising the importance of self-assessment. The role of the social workers will be focussed on advocacy and brokerage rather than assessment and gatekeeping. (DH, 2010b: 1, para 17)

> ## Box 4.3   The meaning of 'personalisation'
>
> - Tailoring support to people's individual needs.
> - Ensuring that people have access to information, advocacy and advice to make informed decisions about their care and support.
> - Finding new collaborative ways of working (sometimes known as 'co-production') that support people to actively engage in the design, delivery and evaluation of services.
> - Developing local partnerships to co-produce a range of services for people to choose from and opportunities for social inclusion and community development.
> - Developing the right leadership and organisational systems to enable staff to work in creative, person-centred ways embedding early intervention, reablement and prevention so that people are supported early on and in a way that's right for them, recognising and supporting carers in their role, while enabling them to maintain a life beyond their caring responsibilities, ensuring that all citizens have access to universal community services and resources – a total system response.
>
> (Carr, 2012: 3)

There are some tricky issues for Pat in connection to thinking about the relationship between risk and independence and also taking into account the perspectives of both Mary and Peter. Working with Mary is important but also adds to the complexity of working in partnership with Peter. Mary will be part of the process of agreeing how Peter is supported in terms of a direct payment (Community Care (Direct Payments) Act 1996) or personal budget. A personal budget, for example, could be looked at in terms of using it for transport for Peter to visit his wife, which would take pressure off Mary. Mary can also be offered a carer's assessment and may be linked into a carer's support group. The challenge for Pat's advocacy role is to ensure that both feel that they are treated fairly and able to speak up for themselves, particularly for Peter while he has capacity. She was able to make Peter aware of his rights as a citizen and to support him to exercise those rights and maximise his influence on decision both now and for the future.

Evaluation and review

The social work process has been described as 'one human event made up of a variety of elements' (Payne, 2009a: 168). We have already considered some of these elements (assessment, planning and intervention), but there is also a need to ensure that practice is effective, efficient, positive and constructive. This requires a systematic approach, being research-minded and embedding review and evaluation within practice (Thompson, 2000; Payne, 2009a). The importance of review and evaluation comes from our accountability to service users and carers, agencies and ourselves, as well as policy makers and funders (see Chapter 7) who will want to know if service users achieve their goals and if so whether that is as a result of social work interventions. Evaluation therefore requires social workers to find the space to listen and hear what service users say about their interactions with social workers and experiences of services. Space is also needed to read, reflect and evaluate practice.

For Fook (2002) the process of critical reflection can be a way of evaluating practice (by systematically scrutinising our practice) and as a research of practice (by documenting practice that provides the data identifying how practice may be changed). She argues that engagement with the process of critical reflection through evaluation and research enables the development of practice theory and knowledge. Reflection has been described as the ability of the worker to 'pattern or make sense of information, in whatever form, including the impact of her own behaviour or that of her organisation on others' (Smale et al., 2000: 220). At the start of a piece of work the social worker will research potential interventions to decide with the service user what is likely to be the most effective way of working together. Combining this with critical reflection after completing a piece of work facilitates evaluation, including the effect it has had on the service user. Fook (2002) demonstrates the way in which critical reflection highlights how reflective practice can reveal power relations and question dominant power relations.

CASE EXAMPLE

Fabio's experience

Fabio works in an agency supporting young people who use substances. He has been allocated to work with a fifteen-year-old young person, Jack, who has been referred by the GP. He writes to Jack to offer him an appointment and on their first meeting everything seems to go well. Fabio agrees a plan with the young person for them to meet weekly. Jack fails to attend the next appointment and Fabio is perplexed by this. He phones the young man and speaks to his mother, who is unable to shed any light on this. Fabio therefore writes a friendly letter to Jack offering another appointment and reminding him about their agreement. However, he fails to make the appointment. It is the policy of the agency not to visit service users at home, and to close cases where service users fail to respond. Fabio is reluctant to do this and reflects on possible options open to him at this stage. He agrees with his line manager to do a one-off visit and deliver the letter by hand. However, before visiting he reflects on his experience of the first visit. He also reflects on the feedback he is getting from Jack in this instance. He considers the possible reasons for Jack's apparent reluctance to engage with him and with the service. It could be that contacting Jack by text rather than letter is more effective. Fabio also considers that the policy to conduct visits in the office means that the power relations are stacked against Jack. There is also the possible stigma of visiting the office as it is easily identified as a service for young substance users. Fabio is aware from his reading and research that stereotypes can be attributed to particular agencies (Carnwell and Buchannan, 2009) and that Jack may not be ready to identify as a person who requires this service.

- We can see here that while there is no formal feedback from Jack about the service, the skilled practitioner will look for more nuanced feedback such as that provided in this case.
- The skill of the advocate is in ensuring that Jack's 'voice' is heard.
- Fabio's advocacy skills might subsequently be used in a number of ways to evaluate and improve the delivery of the service for young men like Jack.

Fabio identified that in contemporary practice there are other ways of communicating with service users than the more traditional methods of letter and telephone. Although e-participation is a relatively recent development, there are now many forms of electronic or e-participation which have a potentially important role in facilitating social work advocacy and alternative forms of communication. For example, in consulting with service users and carers, providing and exchanging information with and between service users and carers, eliciting service user views in relation to specific issues, facilitating broader participation strategies and informing commissioners of service delivery and influencing service planning. It can also be understood more broadly as a way of ensuring that governments, policy makers and service providers are aware of service users' perspectives from a 'bottom up' rather than a 'top down' approach. Macintosh describes e-participation as

> [t]he use of information and communication technologies to broaden and deepen political participation by enabling citizens to connect with one another and with their elected representatives. (2004: 2)

E-participation networks such as the *Participation Works* online gateway for children and young people's participation are an example of how technology is having an impact on practice. This is 'a hub for information, resources, news and networking on the involvement of young people in dialogue, decision making and influence across a wide range of settings' (www.participationworks.org.uk). E-participation can therefore be seen as a mechanism to promote the voice of service users, provide information, reduce isolation and increase visibility. Service users and social workers can use the technology to conduct research, identify research, share information and build and develop existing collaboration and networks. Other online tools can also be used both for case and systemic advocacy (for example, blogs or electronic newsletters), while Facebook and Twitter followers can participate in discussions.

Social work knowledge is contested, interactive and changing (Thompson, 2000) and derives from many sources including service user and carer experiences, practice wisdom (practitioners experiences), theory and policy/procedures. Social workers also use research to inform their knowledge base, and being research-minded is an element of reviewing and evaluating practice. Research is one form of knowledge which should be viewed alongside other knowledge; using research effectively requires that practitioners are willing to 'listen' to the messages from research (Sneddon, 2012). This involves keeping up to date and being confident about using research evidence in practice. Key role six of the National Occupational Standards for social work (for social workers in Wales, Scotland and Northern Ireland) expects that social workers are able to 'research, analyse, evaluate, and use current knowledge of best social work practice' (Topss UK, 2002). The Professional Capabilities Framework for social work for social workers in England also recognises the importance of research, requiring social workers to 'demonstrate a critical understanding of the application to social work of research' (TCSW, 2012: 5.1). The Health and Care Professions Council Standards of Proficiency for social workers in England also states that practitioners should 'recognise the value of research and analysis and be able to evaluate such evidence to inform their own practice' (HCPC, 2012: 4.6). The importance of using research in social work and social care has been highlighted by the Making Research Count initiative, established in 1998, by a group of social work academics (Box 4.4), and the establishment of the Social Care Institute for Excellence (SCIE) set up in 2001 by the Government. Other initiatives such as the Research in Practice (a charity established in 1996 within the Social Justice programme of Dartington Hall Trust) aim to create new knowledge and skills for specific user groups – in this instance to improve outcomes for children, young people and their families.

Box 4.4   Making research count

Aim: To improve social work and social care services through the extension of a knowledge-based approach.

Objectives:

- Strengthen the research skills and confidence of social work and social care practitioners.
- Disseminate research findings.
- Implement research findings into policy and practice.
- Involve managers and practitioners in setting research agendas.
- Incorporate service users' views.
- Encourage networking among professionals. (Humphreys et al., 2003)

If we consider Pat's work with Peter, the evidence base that she might consider includes research and evidence relating to direct payments and personal budgets. Such research has been identified as useful to increase choice and control for service users and influencing power relations between service users and carers and the state (Glasby and Littlechild, 2009). As part of her social work advocacy role, Pat is mindful of the features of advocacy that support service users' rights and therefore uses this research to inform empowerment practice. Pat is also aware that there has been increasing understanding of the needs of carers as a result of research about informal care and the nature of caring relationships (for example, Phillips et al., 2002; Ray and Chambers, 2009; Carers UK and Sheffield Hallam University, 2005; Carers UK, 2007). She is also mindful that Chambers and Phillips have commented that 'carers concerns are not embedded in mainstream thinking' (2009: 98) but recognises the dilemmas in trying to meet the needs of both Peter and Mary.

Since practice is a continuous process, social workers generally review and evaluate what they are doing before, during and after their work with service users and carers. This enables practitioners to be clear about what is to be achieved, how it is to be achieved, and knowing whether or not the work is successful (Thompson, 2000). For Parker and Bradley it is important

> that all social workers are educated in ways of reviewing their work and reflecting on outcomes so that practice can be continually improved, which enhances personal development and contributes to securing the best outcomes for people using social work services. (2010: 120)

Reviews of practice are necessary because situations and circumstances of service users and carers change over time – which requires a reflexive approach to practice in terms of assessment, planning and interventions. Reviews are part of a continuous process that considers what has been achieved from the planning stage and revises or refines plans accordingly. Reviews usually occur once social workers and service users and carers have started to work together, but planning the review needs to be at the start of the process so that everyone has clear objectives and know what they are working towards.

Reviews are important for a number of reasons. First and foremost there is an ethical imperative to share with the service users' understanding of the way in which intervention has had an impact or may have an impact on their lives (Payne, 2009a). Service users, carers and practitioners need to understand how practice has had an impact, and whether this has been appropriate and safe. Payne (1995: 215) suggests that for practitioners, reviews are approached in a dynamic way through consideration of a number of questions:

- What has been achieved for the service user?
- What is the right direction now?
- How have the views and attitudes among those involved changed?
- What are their views and wishes, especially those of service users and carers now?

For example, Rajnder's social worker would consider what had been achieved for him as a result of and following the review; what was the right way to continue working with Rajnder's parents to ensure that his relationship with them was not jeopardised; what were the attitudes of his parents and other professionals to Rajnder's situation; and what were the wishes and feelings of Rajnder and his parents following the review.

Rajinder and his social worker were planning for his life as part of a formal review process. There are formal requirements for reviews for service users in many situations, partly to ensure 'value for money' by public services. In the provision of services for adults, formal requirements are relatively more recent than in child care. Reviewing was introduced in the NHS and Community Care Act 1990, and as Payne notes, the 'lack of periodic review in many adults' cases meant that they drifted with very little strategic thought about "what next"' (1995: 213).

However, reviews are now a key element of care management (SSI/SWSG, 1991) in order to assess the outcomes of services provided and to identify any gaps in service provision. The model of self-directed support also requires review and provides an opportunity for the service user to think about whether the outcomes identified in the support plan have been achieved – and therefore whether the plan is working. This means that the social worker has a process by which to record progress against identified goals. In Peter's case, if he decided that he would like to use direct payments to meet his needs, then the review would focus on his strengths and provide an opportunity to make any improvements in his life. Pat would be able to consider how the money was spent and what impact this had on his life. Pat would also be able to ensure that Peter remained in control of his support.

Commentary

The principles of advocacy outlined at the start of this chapter are essentially principles that inform anti-oppressive practice. In many ways advocacy is a tool for anti-oppressive practice and enables social workers to recognise and challenge oppression in the lives of service users, both individually and structurally. This requires social workers to be reflective and reflexive. Critical *reflective* practice means going beyond simply reflecting to a more critical approach that questions the 'taken for granted' in order to achieve change. Many social workers find opportunities to work creatively within the context of managing resources by reinterpreting agency policies and using evidence from research or legislative mandates to counteract some of the managerial and bureaucratic dominance that they encounter. Lymbery (2004) comments that social workers need to identify ways of developing empowering reflective practice that involves challenging the imposition of bureaucratic structures and processes. *Reflexivity* means that social workers have to be self aware: understanding their identity as practitioners, the impact that they have on service users and that service users have on them. Parton (2000) describes reflexivity as a way of responding to the uniqueness of each individual. This means that within the context of promoting equality, justice and social inclusion, the social work advocate is working in a dynamic way.

The skills required to advocate within the systems that social workers are operating are underpinned by a knowledge of the law, research and practice experience. Through ongoing evaluation practitioners refine their advocacy skills, develop theory, seek out knowledge, and interrogate their own values. This means that continual self-analysis is needed in order to develop the skills to critically analyse practice. We saw that Fabio reflected on his work with Jack and reframed his practice to improve the interaction between them. Figure 4.1 demonstrates the inter-related nature of advocacy principles and advocacy skills which enables the social worker to act as an advocate, promote the rights of service users and carers, and develop a culture of advocacy (which is explored further in Chapter 9).

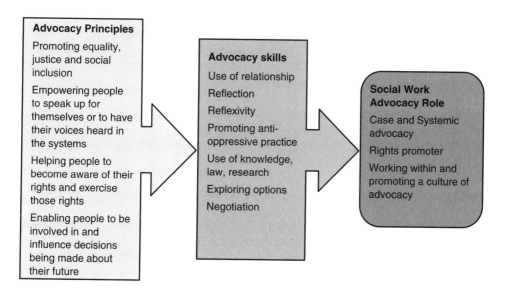

Figure 4.1

Summary

- A key advocacy skill is to enable service users and carers to influence decision making.
- Advocacy skills have been identified by service users as an important element of social work practice.
- The importance of relational social work has gained ascendancy in contemporary social work practice.
- Effective social work advocates are able to listen to service users, reflect and find possible ways forward together.
- Assessment, planning, intervention and review afford opportunities for social work advocacy.
- Skills in critical reflection are an essential part of the repertoire of skills for social workers who are committed to promoting advocacy.

Discussion questions

1 What personal and professional factors shape and inform the relationships you establish with service users and carers?
2 In what ways do you feel that your advocacy practice has been informed by:
   (a) research evidence?
   (b) service user and carer perspectives?
3 In your practice how do you evaluate the impact of service user involvement in your work whilst undertaking assessments and planning?
4 What do you feel have been the tangible outcomes as a result of using your social work advocacy skills?
5 Consider why service users feel that social workers are in a good position to speak up for them.

Further reading

Bateman, N. (2000) *Advocacy Skills for Health and Social Care Professionals*. London: Jessica Kingsley.

Dalrymple, J. and Burke, B. (2009) 'Critical intervention', in R. Adams, L. Dominelli, and M. Payne (eds), *Social Work: Themes, Issues and Critical Debates*. Basingstoke: Palgrave Macmillan.

Wilks, T. (2012) *Advocacy and Social Work Practice*. Maidenhead: Open University Press.

5

Participation and Partnership

Overview

- Participation
- Models of participation
- Partnership working
- Working in interdisciplinary teams
- Commentary
- Summary
- Discussion Questions

We saw in Chapter 2 that historically social work has tended to 'do to' rather than work alongside service users. As the social work profession has developed, however, the balance has shifted and there is now an increased awareness of the need for social work practitioners to work in partnership *with* service users and carers and with other professionals. Part of this change can be attributed to the role of social work advocacy in promoting participatory practice. This has in part been due to an awareness of how the concept of power, principles of participation and the rights agenda have shaped and informed social work policy, legislation and practice. It has also been a result of active work by practitioners committed to finding ways and means of working more collaboratively and fairly. As a profession, social work seeks to understand oppression, marginalisation and exclusion and to use approaches that counter oppression through inclusive, participative and empowering practice. Understanding the interplay between these ideas and social work advocacy goes some way to help understand service user experiences and identify opportunities for

promoting or enhancing participation. In this chapter we will begin with consideration of the terminology of partnership and participation in the context of working
with service users and carers. We will then go on to discuss working in partnership
with other professionals and organisations.

The concepts of involvement, collaboration, participation and partnership are all
used in relation to working with service users and carers in decision making. These
four concepts can be used interchangeably, but Cahill's (1996) concept analysis of
patient participation is a helpful way to think about how the terms are related. She
suggests that involvement and collaboration should be seen as the starting point of
a process that works towards partnership (see Figure 5.1). She argues that as players
in the partnership relationship become more involved with each other they begin to
collaborate, and as a result a greater sense of meaningful participation is likely to
emerge. Carnwell and Buchanan note that 'this sense of involvement can ultimately
result in sufficient trust, respect, and willingness on the part of different parties to
develop' (2009: 7).

Involvement      Partnership

Figure 5.1   A continuum of involvement (after Carnwell and Buchanan 2009: 17)

In thinking about social work advocacy, the concepts of participation and partnership are the two that we will focus on in this chapter.

Participation

The practice of advocacy is informed by theories of participation. This stems
from the historical roots of advocacy and the campaigns of service users mentioned in Chapter 2. The service user movement – particularly the disability
movement and the service user/survivor movement in relation to mental health –
has lobbied for many years to challenge the marginalisation of service users as
passive receivers of services and fought for status as citizens who have a voice. A
key aspect of these movements has been the way that service users have spoken
out about their experiences, both individually and collectively, in order to challenge their exclusion from full participation and involvement in society (Campbell
and Oliver, 1996; Oliver and Sapey, 2006; Sayce, 2000). Self-advocacy and collective advocacy groups have emerged through this process, as has the development of participatory practice. As independent advocacy organisations have
become established, participation has therefore developed as a central element of
advocacy practice.

Participation is an active and dynamic concept, which draws attention to the social
processes that social workers need to understand and respond to – such as upholding

service users and carers rights, promoting involvement/inclusion and challenging exclusion and marginalisation. Understanding discourses of participation involves consideration of the inter-relationship between participation, rights and justice. See Box 5.1 for helpful definitions of participation.

> ## Box 5.1 Definitions of participation
>
> The process of sharing decisions which affect one's life and the life of the community in which one lives. (Hart, 1992: 5)
>
> Participation involves 'taking part in, influencing processes, decisions, and activities that affect then in order to achieve greater respect for their rights'. (Lansdown, 2005: 273)
>
> Participation operates at many levels; it can range from individual control over day-to-day decisions about what to wear, what to eat and how to spend one's time, to collective decisions about service governance or commissioning (Mordey and Crutchfield, 2004). (Moriarty et al., 2007)
>
> We use the term participation not simply to mean 'taking part' or 'being present' but as having some influence over decisions and action. We also use the term 'involve' (passive verb) and 'participate' (active verb) interchangeably. (Kirby et al., 2003: 5)
>
> The right to participation, unlike others, such as the right to freedom or survival, almost invariably exists in the absence of another right, that of the right to self determination, and could therefore be described as a 'cosmetic' or 'compensatory' right. (Murray and Hallett, 2000: 15)

Participation is a contested concept, but is generally understood as meaning active involvement of service users and carers in decision making (Box 5.1). Hart's definition emphasises the 'process' of participation which, he argues, should be embedded in the daily life and relationships of individuals and their community. This is epitomised, for example, by the title of a government report on a strategy for learning disability, *Nothing About Us Without Us* (DH, 2001a), which was strongly influenced by a service users advisory group. Authors such as Lansdown (2005) and Kirby et al. (2003) highlight the importance of impact and influence. Murray and Hallett (2000) remind us that participation rights have developed for service users and carers because the right to self-determination has been marginalised. Their commentary is presented in relation to young people but is equally relevant to working with families and with vulnerable adults. They suggest that the right to participation is generally used in the context of service users' lack of power in society. This is picked up in social work literature where the concepts of participation and empowerment go hand in hand and are often used interchangeably. Informed by principles of anti-oppressive practice, the social worker needs to be aware, however, that while participation may allow for the possibility of empowerment, it is not intrinsically empowering. The case study of Michael later in this chapter demonstrates that a negative participatory experience is far from empowering, and it would possibly have been better for Michael not to have participated at all in his review.

The drivers for participation can be located in three mandates: legal and policy mandates, professional mandates and service user mandates (Braye, 2000). In the past twenty years participation has become a fundamental principle underpinning social care legislation and policy. Two key pieces of legislation, the Children Act 1989 and the Health and Community Care Act 1990, referred to the need to consult and involve service users. The New Labour government went on to publish a vision in *Modernising Social Services* (DH, 1998), which aimed to ensure the centrality of service users and carers in the provision of social services. Since then there has been increasing emphasis on inclusion, participatory practice, service user and carer involvement and partnership working in policy (which provides a framework for participation) and legislation (which is the legal mandate according 'rights' to participation). The Human Rights Act 1998 was another important milestone providing an opportunity for service users to challenge decisions made without their participation (Braye, 2000) and is a useful tool for social work advocates in ensuring that the rights of service users are not violated in the provision of services.

CASE EXAMPLE

Project to re-assess the needs of people with profound complex needs

A project team has been set up to work in a participatory way with a range of people who have profound complex needs and live in a range of settings. The work of the team has two broad strands. The first strand involves conducting a re-assessment of people's needs – recognising that needs can change over time. The second strand of work for the team is to assess the quality of services being delivered. Each person's needs are reviewed by a project worker in partnership with the Community Team they are attached to. On occasions this means drawing a multi-disciplinary team together to re-visit any previous assessment. Key to the process is that the assessment is person-centred and undertaken in partnership with everyone concerned, in order to ensure that the right judgements are made. This case example, based on work of the team, demonstrates how services are finding ways to improve their participatory practice and partnership working.

Ruth is a young woman who has a profound learning disability and is supported to live independently. She is unable to communicate using speech. The project social worker, Frances, is aware that Ruth is very likely to have something to say about where she lives, even though she may not communicate by talking to people. For Frances the primary consideration is to ensure that the re-assessment of Ruth's needs is person centred and that Ruth's voice is heard in the process. Part of Frances's motivation for working in this project is because she is aware that once people with a learning difficulty are in 'the system', it is really hard for either the person concerned or their parents to get their voices heard. She is also aware of the tensions in this process, since her role means that she has to balance Ruth's needs and what she would like with the resources available (through the Fair Access to Care (FACS) 2010 criteria (SCIE, 2010)).

Frances feels the responsibility and the importance of making sound judgements as the social worker leading the assessment. As part of the re-assessment process she works with the two provider services who are currently working with the Ruth and with Ruth's parents. Ruth's parents play a key role in supporting her as an independent adult. This helps Frances to assess the benefits of the service currently being offered. Frances's strategy is to try to enable everyone involved in Ruth's life to step back and think about what they are doing to support Ruth. This means asking questions such as whether the support is comparable with Ruth's non-disabled peer group. Frances recognises that assumptions can be made about what Ruth would like, based on judgements about what other people think that she would like.

In order to ensure that Ruth's voice is heard, Frances draws on the Mental Capacity Act 2005: she checks if there has been an assessment of capacity. She also tries to ascertain whether information has been presented to Ruth in a way that can help her to make a decision. She finds ways of assessing Ruth's non-verbal responses through devising activities, talking to everyone who spends time with her in different situations and spending time herself observing Ruth directly, so that she can see her actions and reactions over a period of time.

In trying to make a sound judgement about the quality of the service being offered to Ruth, Frances draws on evidence-based research to inform her thinking. This helps her to ask the right questions and also make a judgement about when not to ask questions. Frances finds this particularly helpful when grappling with the sticky question of considering what is a good quality service and thinking about what it is she is benchmarking against. As a critical practitioner she needs to be able raise any concerns, but Frances is aware that she also needs to work productively with Ruth and with everyone involved in her life in order to raise and maintain standards. Frances finds the Human Rights Act 1998 helpful in trying to ensure that the basic human rights of the people she is working with are not violated. She finds that one way of trying to hear the voices of service users is to sit and feel what it is like for a person to live in a particular setting. Frances has read research about residential care and observed situations where a culture has developed where carers have been so caught up in doing the everyday tasks that the subtleties of people's diverse communications have been missed. Frances views her advocacy role as helping staff to see what is happening – recognising that as she is not absorbed in the daily tasks she has time to consider the situation in more detail. This in turn enables her to ask questions about why things are done in a particular way and support carers to stop and think about their work as carers.

Frances uses her knowledge and advocacy skills to enable Ruth to participate in the process through:

(Continued)

(Continued)

- having a sound value base which is based on a person-centred approach to her practice;
- recognising that Ruth does have wishes and feelings even though she does not communicate using speech;
- ensuring that she uses a range of approaches to communicate with Ruth and to work with other people in Ruth's life to enable an accurate and fair assessment;
- a commitment to case and systemic advocacy;
- giving time to the process and relating with Ruth and the key people in her life;
- developing a culture of participation so that service users, carers and other key people in their lives are committed to working with service users in a way that enables them to have a voice in decision making about their lives.

In practice the law and policy in relation to participation is complex, but it can be used positively to promote the rights of service users and protect them from any unfair treatment or abuse of their rights (Dalrymple and Burke, 2006). Part of the advocacy role of the social worker is to be familiar with the law and to embrace it with confidence and enthusiasm. This may include, for example:

- Referencing the Human Rights Act 1998 and, for children specifically, the United Nations Convention on the Rights of the Child (UNCRC) 1989, in reports and decision-making meetings where necessary.
- Using the Children Act 1989 (England and Wales), the Children Scotland Act 1995 or the Children Northern Ireland Order 1995 to ensure that the wishes and feelings of children and young people are taken into account.
- Using *The Single Assessment Process: Guidance for Local Implementation* (DH, 2002) to ensure that the perspectives of older service users are centre stage in assessment and care planning.
- Using the Carers (Recognition and Services) Act 1995 to inform carers about their rights to an assessment.
- Using the Equality Act 2010 to ensure that a patient who has a medical problem of a personal nature that only affects men or women is able to have an interpreter of the same sex.

CASE EXAMPLE

Michael's review

Michael is seventeen years old and the subject of a care order (which expires on his eighteenth birthday in two months' time). For the past two years he has lived in a foster home with the aim of preparing him to live independently. He does not have any contact with his parents or other family members. Michael has recently had a statutory review to discuss his plan for leaving care. This took place at the foster home.

Michael attended his meeting but distanced himself by sitting at the far end of the room with this head in his hands, looking away from everyone else. Also present were the reviewing officer, social worker and foster carer. A member of the leaving care team was unable to attend because of the need to attend a compulsory training day on safeguarding. An independent visitor was involved, but also unable to attend.

The independent reviewing officer (IRO) noted that the review documentation contained the wrong date of birth for Michael and a conversation ensued regarding the correct date. Michael appeared to be disengaged from the process. Michael's social worker had visited him twice since the last review (six months ago) but had been unable to visit prior to the review meeting. The foster carer was aware of Michael's feelings and his apprehension about leaving care. She described the review as 'stacking up anxieties' for Michael. During the review the IRO tried to engage Michael in the process, asking 'Have there been any good things that have happened since the last review?'. Michael replied 'Nothing'. It transpired that Michael has 'been down' since the last review due to concerns about his future. The discussion turned to 'progress' with Michael's leaving care plan: Michael had had no contact with a member of the leaving care team, other than a phone call. An application had very recently been made to the housing department for accommodation; the social worker suggested that in the meantime Michael 'will have to look at sharing'. The IRO expressed the following concerns:

• There was no leaving care plan in place.
• Leaving care has been discussed in reviews for the past two years but there were now only two months before Michael is due to leave care and it appeared that little progress has been made.

Michael was informed by the IRO that he had the right to complain if he was not happy with the plans and the preparation. He did not reply. However, the social worker stated that 'He's very good at complaining if he is not happy'. Michael did not make a complaint, and remained withdrawn from the process. The review meeting continued although Michael did not participate and therefore did not have a voice in the decision making.

Research indicates that young people need to have an established relationship with their social worker in order to develop the trust and regular contact necessary to facilitate participation (Boylan, 2005; Holland, 2011; Lefevre, 2010). Furthermore, for Munro, children's experiences should be 'at the centre of actions, decisions or plans' (2010: 19). There is also evidence that the 'rights' agenda has an impact on ensuring that service users have effective relationships with agencies and professionals. For example, Smith (2008) describes how a service user with autism was able to promote changes in the practice of people working with him, following his complaint that:

Social services staff did not take the time to build up a relationship with [the service user] and he kept refusing services offered because he finds new people and new situations frightening. (Local Government Ombudsman, 2005 cited in Smith, 2008: 137)

In Michael's case, the system that was meant to be supporting him and promoting his rights to participation actually excluded him and left him feeling isolated, disempowered and oppressed by the system. Carr notes that:

Exclusionary structures, institutional practices and professional attitudes can still affect the extent to which service users can influence change. It appears that power sharing can be difficult within established mainstream structures, formal consultation mechanisms and traditional ideologies. (Carr 2004: vii)

Empowering practice requires more than a legislative mandate: it requires a commitment to promoting participation and using knowledge and skills in practice to ensure that service users and carers are included as far as possible in decision making. Effective relationships can overcome some of these barriers and encapsulate knowledge of best practice. The following comments indicate how two young people valued their relationship with their social workers:

'Mine (social worker) visits me regular … Well she just comes whenever I want her to really! Like every two, three weeks. Sometimes it can be longer, just depends if she's too busy or what. 'Cos really I think, a lot of social workers are too busy, with the amount of cases they've got. 'Cos they just don't get around to seeing to things, and they don't get things sorted out.' (Lisa)

'My social worker comes to see me after school and we talk about stuff. She tells me about mum and stuff, when I am seeing her and she asks me things about me. She's ace.' (Ellen) (Boylan, 2005)

Lisa recognises that social workers are often very busy. For Michael it may well be that the social worker found it difficult to visit because of her workload and in fact had a good working relationship with the foster carers. However, where Lisa was also positive about her relationship with her social worker, in Michael's case there does not appear to be such a sound basis for a meaningful relationship. Reading Michael's story we can see that there are a number of ways in which social work advocacy may have facilitated his participation, minimised the impact of differential power relations and enabled him to challenge as a 'legitimate strategy' (Smith, 2008: 138) to change how he experienced the provision of services:

- Preparing Michael for his meeting would have enabled him to contribute to the decision-making process.
- Michael would have views and concerns about leaving care. Space for discussion and reflection with Michael would have helped him to articulate his wishes and feelings in this respect.

- Michael needed to feel physically and emotionally safe in order to feel relaxed enough to be able to participate. This could have been facilitated through skills rehearsal prior to the meeting.
- Reviews are adult environments and careful management was needed to minimise the power relations between the adults and Michael.
- There were a number of people involved in Michael's life. Working in partnership with Michael and effective partnership working between the professionals were essential if he was to feel able to participate in the decision making.
- Supporting Michael to meet with other care leavers in order to meet other young people in a similar situation may have encouraged him to organise and articulate his views. This might be in terms of his individual situation and, more systemically, with respect to the provision of services for care leavers.
- Supporting Michael to make a formal complaint, which is an acceptable way of promoting change in social work practice (see Chapter 7).

A feature of the growth of participatory ways of working has been an awareness of the impact of power dynamics and a shift in the power relationships between social work practitioners, social work agencies and service users and carers. Issues of power and oppression are at the heart of debates surrounding effective social work advocacy and service user and carer participation. This adds to the complexity of articulating what is meant by participation and participatory approaches in practice. However, significant contributions have been made from the testimony of the service user and advocacy movements to our understanding of both obstacles and opportunities to meaningful participation and moving the participation agenda forward. Braye (2000: 24) usefully summarises the user literature in this respect and identifies the following features of participatory practice:

- Being clear about the nature and scope of participation.
- Enabling people to participate throughout a decision-making process, rather than only when it suits the professionals concerned.
- Having clear, realistic and agreed goals.
- Ensuring that service users have the choice to participate rather than feeling coerced.
- Ensuring that diverse and marginalised groups are also enabled to participate.
- Ensuring that both individual and collective perspectives are heard.
- Recognising that time, information, resources and training are needed to facilitate meaningful participation.
- Being open to independent advocacy and supporting self-advocacy.
- Ensuring that representation and complaints processes are accessible.
- Being open with accessible structures for dialogue.

Wilson et al. (2011) identify some useful points from service user accounts across three decades that provide an insight into what is needed for effective participation. From their examination of all the accounts, they conclude that social workers need to have good relational skills in their work with service users and be sensitive and respectful in the way that they respond to the concerns of people they are working with. The nature of this relationship is that it is participatory in process and purpose, is supportive, responsive and person-centred, addresses rights, risks and their complex interrelations, and values the experiences and knowledge of service users and how this can enhance the knowledge of social workers (Beresford, 2000: 6). This involves recognising service users as 'experts' about their own lives (Shaping Our Lives, 2007), promoting a culture of participation in social work and acknowledging the social work advocacy role.

Service users and carers across the life course come into contact with powerful individuals and agencies, including social work practitioners. Some experiences will be positive and meaningful, others less so. These interactions have the potential to encourage embryonic participation in planning and decision making to afford service users and carers greater control. They also enable practitioners to learn from service users and both inform and challenge professional understanding of service user experiences, needs and rights. Working alongside service users to explore their views is empowering and facilitates the social work/service user relationship as well as broader goals such as participation in decision making.

Models of participation

There are a number of models of participation which can be used to facilitate exploration of the relationship between rights, participation and social work advocacy. These include: Arnstein, 1969; Shier, 2006; Percy-Smith, 2006; Treseder and Crowley, 2001; Boylan and Dalrymple, 2009. While Arnstein's ladder of citizen participation has been influential and continues to have relevance in thinking about participation, alternative models have since been offered to theorise the mechanisms enabling service users and carers to be involved in decision making.

Shier (2001) developed a model as a tool to help teachers and schools to identify what steps they could take to achieve the best outcomes both for schools and for the students. This model can also be used by social workers to consider what is needed to identify and enhance the participation of service users and carers in individual decision making and in the provision and delivery of services. Shier's model is based on five levels of participation:

- Service users and carers are listened to.
- Service users and carers are supported in expressing their views.
- Service users and carers' views are taken into account.
- Service users and carers are involved in decision-making processes.
- Service users and carers share power and responsibility for decision-making.

In addition, Shier identifies three stages of commitment at each level: openings, opportunities and obligations. The model then provides a logical sequence of fifteen questions as a tool for planning for participation. For Shier there are many pathways to participation and this can be facilitated by making the most of different stages of commitment to the processes that facilitate participation. However, Shier's original framework was criticised for the implication that progression to the highest level should be the desired outcome – a criticism also levelled at Arnstien's ladder. A model by Treseder and Crowley (2001) tries to avoid this by using the concept of a wheel to reflect how varying degrees of power may be applicable to a particular issue at a certain point in time. This means that it is not always necessary or desirable to reach the top level of participation. Shier has responded by noting that a ladder can be a useful tool to complete a task and that a worker will use the ladder to get to the right height to help do this – but it is not always necessary to climb to the top of the ladder in order to complete the job. Shier helpfully uses the analogy of the job of painting a window: a ladder is required to reach the right height to paint efficiently and safely. The ladder may well reach far beyond the top of the window, and at different points in the process the painter will move up a rung or down a rung:

> The Pathways to Participation framework, like the ladder, makes visible the relationships between different levels of participation and the stages within each. In this way Pathways to Participation offers teachers and schools the logical system they need, so that, like the worker on the ladder, they can ask of themselves, 'Are we at the right height for the task in hand?', 'Would it be beneficial to climb higher?', 'What are the potential benefits and risks, if any, of moving up a rung?'. (Shier, 2006: 18)

In Michael's situation, any of the professionals working with him might either individually or collectively find this model helpful in thinking about what the current situation is and reflect on where they want to get to and what needs to be done to get there. The matrix shown in Figure 5.2 helps identify how and where Michael might participate in the decision making about his future, which he has a right to do, as well as helping his social worker and other professionals to understand their advocacy role in this context. For the professionals it provides a framework for each individual person to reflect on their *openings* and how far they are ready to support Michael in expressing his views and take them into account. It may be that Michael does not want to leave the foster carers on the date that he is supposed to 'leave care' and is frightened about the transition. While there may be *opportunities* to find ways to help him to express his views, whether the organisational structures and resources are such that they can be taken into account is a key question to be explored. There are certainly *obligations* for social workers with respect to Pathway Plans for young people, which include the need to document situations where a young person has failed to engage with them and document what has been done to engage the young person (see R (J) Caerphilly County Borough Council [2005] EWHC 586 (admin)). For the people around Michael, if there is consensus between the various professionals involved about the importance of sharing the decision making with him, then the likelihood is that the outcome will

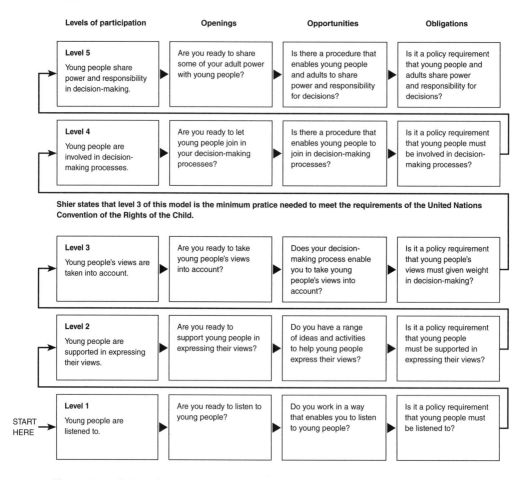

Figure 5.2 Shier's (2006) developed model of participation

be more positive for Michael and for ongoing relationships between him and the professionals in his life.

Pathways to Participation does not suggest that service users like Michael should be coerced to participate in ways or at levels that they do not want, even when openings and opportunities exist. But the starting point is that all service users can participate in some way that is appropriate for them. Furthermore, there is of course more than one pathway that can be taken. Good practice would suggest that a decision on how to participate in decision making should start with the service user – but for the critical reflective practitioner, the matrix can assist consideration in how to share power and responsibility for decisions, while weighing up risks and benefits in order to help service users to be part of the decision making in a supportive environment. There may well be differences in perspective (for example, between Michael and his foster carer, or between Michael and his leaving care worker) and in some instances where the decision making is based on the more controlling aspects of practice.

Shier's model requires an understanding of the organisational culture and what may need to change to facilitate participatory practice. Another approach to participation is to consider four key elements as part of a whole system approach:

- *Culture:* the ethos of the organisation, shared by service users and carers and staff, which demonstrates a commitment to participation.
- *Structure:* the planning, development and resourcing of participation, which can be seen in the infrastructure of the organisation.
- *Practice:* the ways of working, methods for involvement, skills and knowledge that facilitate involvement.
- *Review:* the systems that enable the organisation to the influence and impact of participation. (Moriarty et al., 2007)

While Shier's model is informed by his work with children and young people in schools, the guide to participation produced by Moriarty and her colleagues (2007) for the Social Care Institute for Excellence (SCIE) is focused on the participation of adult service users, including older people, in developing social care. The authors suggest that the four elements outlined above be regarded as pieces of jigsaw which collectively create a framework to systematically examine how service users are being supported to participate in the design, delivery and evaluation of social care services, and in doing so facilitates a holistic and effective approach to participation.

Underpinning models of participation are two broad approaches to participation: consumerist and democratic. Both models are ideologically oppositional with different underpinning philosophical orientations, but they also operate together in practice. Consumerism is rooted in the ideology of the market economy that is the basis of much health and social care provision. A consumerist model reflects the ideology of welfare markets and focuses on the rights of service users and carers to 'choose' services and packages of care. This approach aims to improve the quality of services by being responsive to the needs of service users and offering 'choices'. The challenge for the social work advocate is to try to counter/redress the view held by many service users and carers that there is no choice. Furthermore, the consumerist model does not fundamentally change or challenge the unequal power relationship between service users and carers and social welfare practitioners and providers of services. This perspective has been criticised for supporting the 'managerialist' element of participation (Beresford, 2005; Boylan and Braye, 2006). For service users there is also a level of uncertainty about the consumerist approach because the dominance of professional agendas may overshadow the priorities of service user groups (Boyland and Braye, 2006). Lewis (2009) argues that wider power sharing is unlikely to be achieved through a consumerist approach:

> It has been widely argued that meaningful participation for service users cannot be achieved through a consumerist approach that fails to engage with imbalances of power and divergences of interest between users and providers of services. (Lewis, 2009: 258)

The citizenship or democratic model is a more radical approach aligned to participatory rights through greater empowerment and power sharing. It focuses on promoting full and equal citizenship for service users. This perspective is concerned to ensure that people participate in decision making in the planning, management and review of services. The rationale is that by having more influence on the services that they are using and the organisations that impact on them (including policy development, resource allocation and management of services), people will have more control over their lives (Beresford, 2005).

Partnership working

The term 'partnership' has been a central feature of public policy since the late 1990s and is now a widely used term in health and social care. It is an important concept that suggests sharing, agreement and working together to achieve mutual goals. However, it has also been described as a 'terminological quagmire' (Leathard, 1994), partly because there is no clear or consistent definition and policy and practice is subject to change, dependent on government priorities at a given time. For example, partnerships between *service providers* were dominant in policy at the end of the 1990s; since then partnerships between professionals and service users and carers have also been emphasised. Partnerships may be both formal and informal and involve individuals, groups and communities. They include those between professionals where there is a mutual understanding and respect for each other's perspectives at one end of a continuum, to more unequal relations in partnerships between professionals and service users. For people who have been using services for a long time, or those who do not choose to initiate an intervention with social services, partnership can be difficult and sometimes impossible. Banks (2002) identifies the problems associated with the term 'partnership' and suggests that, as a term, it is 'increasingly losing credibility, as it has become a catch-all for a wide range of concepts and a panacea for a multitude of ills' (2002: 5). Nevertheless, a number of definitions of partnership in relation to social work practice can be identified which assist our understanding of partnership working.

Box 5.2 Useful definitions

[Partnership involves] at least two agents or agencies with at least some sort of common interests or interdependencies; and would probably also require a relationship between them that involves a degree of trust, equality and reciprocity. (Glendenning, 2002: 3)

[Partnership is] a shared commitment, where all partners have a right and an obligation to participate and will be affected equally by the benefits and disadvantages arising from the partnership. (Carnwell and Buchanan, 2009: 7)

Partnership refers to a formal agreement between two or more individuals, groups or organisations to work together to achieve shared goals. There are many types of partnership in social work, between professionals, and between professionals and carers, service users, adults, children and young people. (Dalrymple and Burke, 2009: 261)

As a social work value, partnership means moving away from the traditional, elitist notion of professionalism in which the professional 'knows best' and has the power to decide unilaterally what to do. Partnership involves moving towards a more empowering form of professionalism in which professionals, clients and carers work together to identify: [i] what problems need to be addressed; and [ii] how best to tackle them. In this way, social work should be seen as a shared process, a collective endeavour with people, rather than something we *to* them or for them. (Thompson and Thompson, 2008: 199)

Reflecting on the definitions in Box 5.2, we can see that there are a number of elements which are worth commentary. In terms of thinking about partnership and advocacy in social work, Thompson and Thompson (2008) usefully frame the concept by thinking about partnership as a social work value. Glendenning (2002) refers to the need for trust and respect as well as reciprocity – which indicates a level of mutual benefit and possibly also sharing of risk (Glasby and Dickinson, 2008). Definitions also recognise that there is a formal element to partnerships (for example, in the use of written agreements) and is seen as an empowering way of working in which the relationship enables the partners to identify what the problem is and how to tackle it, and then work together to achieve an outcome that may not have been possible by either party on their own. Implicit in all of the definitions is the notion of relationship.

Working in interdisciplinary teams

The complexity of understanding what is meant by partnership working is compounded by the range of partnerships that social workers may be part of. Within health and social care, partnerships have become a familiar aspect of practice in recommendations from reports on problems within the delivery of services (for example, DH/HO, 2003) and in the bringing together of services in various 'Trusts', strategic partnerships and multi-disciplinary or inter-professional working. Broad partnerships may exist between:

- service providers and service users and carers – the relationship between social workers, other professionals and individual service users, families, groups or carers;
- sectors – public, independent and third sector (including charities, voluntary and community organisations, social enterprises and co-operatives) organisations;
- agencies addressing a particular problem – such as homelessness, domestic violence, substance misuse;
- commissioners of services and service providers.

Generally, partnerships are more formal structures of relationships which combine mutual interests of the partners characterised by commitment to an agreed goal or set of objectives, a shared responsibility for developing common aims, long-term commitment to working together and sharing risks, resources and skills, and an intention that the partnership is mutually beneficial to all parties (Dalrymple and Burke, 2006; Corby et al., 2009). For the social work advocate there is a need to be able to navigate and negotiate the myriad relationships that are part of the process of partnership working in order to respond to the needs of service users and provide more co-ordinated, holistic services and meaningful participation of service user and carers. Critiques of partnership working within service delivery highlight the risks that sources of support may be reduced and service users will find it more difficult to express their views about services, particularly when dissatisfied with them (Glasby and Dickinson, 2008). Therefore the social work advocate needs to be mindful of these difficulties and prepared to question and challenge where necessary.

CASE STUDY

Steve, a white man aged 31, lives on a run-down estate which is characterised by drug misuse and vandalism. The population tends to be transient; however there are a group of residents who have lived there since the estate was first built, and some are involved in the resident's association. There have been long-standing problems in relation to a group of young people who tend to congregate at the local community centre. Steve's eleven-year-old son Bill has started to become involved with this group of young people. The residents association have drawn up a petition and sent it to the local council complaining about the young people and their behaviour.

Steve is arrested and charged following an incident at the local pub where he made an unprovoked attack on the barman, Will, a new barman who is black. As a result of the incident Will suffered facial injuries and was admitted to the local hospital. Steve had been drinking. Steve is known to the police and has previous offences including burglary and aggravated assault. He has ongoing involvement with his probation officer. Steve's home life has been unstable for some time. He is unemployed and separated from his partner Katie with whom he has two children, Bill (age 11) and Paul (age 3). The relationship has been volatile and on occasions Katie has contacted her social worker and moved to a local women's refuge with the children. Steve has contact with Bill and Paul but is not always reliable, and the children are disappointed when he does not arrive as promised.

There are a number of agencies involved in the lives of Steve, Katie, Bill and Paul including health, social work, education and criminal justice, and workers from different agencies including the women's refuge outreach worker who supports Katie and a detached youth worker who has recently started to talk to Bill. Some of these professionals also have contact with members of the resident's association. For the different professionals involved there will be different priorities and obligations, depending on who they view as the service user and on their value base. For example, the social worker, the school and the detached youth worker will all have a different view of Bill alongside different perceptions of each other. The social worker's advocacy role may be to navigate a path between child protection concerns and Bill's expressed views relating to the fact that he likes to see Steve but does not like it when he hits Katie. For the social worker there is a need to understand the roles, expertise, knowledge base and different values of everyone involved if she is to develop working relationships with them. The social worker also needs to ensure that the views of all the family are taken into account and heard in any decision-making processes, including those of Bill and Paul. In this context that would involve the National Probation Service (who are working with Steve), the police, education services (which include teachers and learning mentors), the youth and community service, the health service and voluntary organisations supporting the family.

A number of the professionals involved with Steve, Katie, Bill and Paul will have shared concerns in relation to safeguarding the children. Outcomes are likely to be better for children and young people if they and their families are involved in decision making. This is partly because 'children of sufficient age and understanding often have a clear perception of what needs to be done to ensure their safety and wellbeing' (DH, 2013). However, it is not always easy for children and young people to find their voice in the process, and in practice it has been found that that young people may well need advocacy support if they are to participate in the child protection process in a meaningful way. As a consequence the development of independent advocacy services has been significant and acknowledgement of need for these services in supporting young people is written into government policy:

> Children and families may be supported through their involvement in safe-guarding processes by advice and advocacy services, and they should always be informed of services that exist locally and nationally. Independent advocates provide independent and confidential information, advice, representation and support, and can play a vital role in ensuring that children have appropriate

(Continued)

(Continued)

> information and support to communicate their views in formal settings, such as child protection conferences and court proceedings. (Department of Schools, Children and Families, 2010: para 105)

> The development of working in partnership with parents is usually the most effective route to providing supplementary or substitute care for children. (DH, 1989: 18, principle 7)

> In the process of finding out what is happening to a child, it will be critical to develop a co-operative working relationship, so that parents will feel respected and informed, that staff are being open and honest with them, and that they in turn are confident about providing vital and unique information about their child, themselves and their circumstances. (DH, 2000)

In working at the individual level with service users additional characteristics of the partnership relationship come into play, which are not normally evident in professional partnerships. These include 'praise and encouragement, support and advocacy and enabling choice and equity' (Carnwell and Buchanan, 2009). A key aspect of this relationship is to facilitate the participation of the service user, enable the service user to make informed decisions, express choices, preferences and objections, and make their voice heard. Partnership between the practitioner and service user as active and supportive is one that can go some way to dealing with issues of exclusion and marginalisation that some service user and carers may encounter in their relationships with some social welfare practitioners. This means that the relationship needs to be based on as equal a standing as possible. Clearly in many circumstances this is difficult and the relationship may be far from equal particularly when practitioners are working in the context of compulsory interventions or with involuntary service users. A further tension exists between acting against the wishes of service user and service user autonomy and freedom to make decisions. This means that even when partnerships are successful they may only have a small impact when problems are entrenched and complex. Nevertheless, it is useful for all parties to regularly review the extent to which aspects of the partnership are working and to question if the partnership is not working, why, what needs to be done and whether the terms of the partnership can be renegotiated.

Practitioners seeking to work in partnership will recognise that partnership is fluid and responsive. Social work practitioners will therefore consider partnerships on a number of levels, recognising that partnership working is underpinned by an approach characterised by careful, well considered social work practice. The social work advocacy role in this context is important and underpinned by anti-oppressive social work values and principles. Social work advocates will recognise that the concept of respect is a central feature of the partnership relationship and the importance of understanding differences in power and authority, including differences in professional status and the limits and use of authority. The position and influence of different partners is likely to be unequal: for example, children and young people, vulnerable service users including those experiencing dementia, mental ill health or disability. If partnerships are to work then expectations need to be realistic, giving space to different views about the issues being addressed.

Commentary

For social workers working with service users in decision making and planning, the level and nature of participation may vary depending on the circumstances, and may include promoting participation through:

- Supporting self-advocacy, encouraging service users and carers to speak out, and standing alongside and supporting them in this endeavour.
- Exploring and understanding problems and seeking possible solutions together.
- Working with service users to participate in and influence decision making and planning, for example, influencing assessments of risk and need, shaping services.
- Supporting choice and personal development, developing self-confidence and skills.
- Ensuring that service users and carers voices are listened to, heard, validated and responded to.
- Recognising the need for, and signposting to, independent advocacy.
- Mirroring good participatory practice in your work and critically reflecting on your own and your agencies' participation practice/participation policy.
- Recognising and challenging to kenistic forms of participation and celebrating and sharing examples of effective participation practice.

We are aware from conversations with undergraduate and post-graduate social work students that it is equally important to understand the barriers that prevent service user participation and to recognise that simply 'being at the table' or having a say may not in itself be enough. It is also important to learn from examples of good practice in which participation is regarded as a right located at the heart of social work practice. This may take the form of a social worker fighting for a service user's involvement in decision making, creating a space for service users to express their views and opinions and developing innovative participatory ways of working. Increasingly we have come to understand the complexities of participation and the way in which concepts of participation and voice impact on social work advocacy practice.

A concern for many social workers wishing to promote service user and carer participation is often a lack of opportunity for service users to have a say in decision making, and to engage meaningfully in the delivery, planning and commissioning of services. The nature and terms of the relationship can act as a barrier to effective partnership, particularly in compulsory interventions or when working with involuntary services users who will not have entered into the relationship freely. We have seen earlier in this chapter that position and influence of different (unequal) partners may also constrain social work advocacy, and in some circumstances partnership maybe aspirational, given the power imbalance. Even successful partnerships may only be able to bring partial solutions to entrenched and complex problems.

However, genuine and effective partnerships can lead to strengthened relationships between service users and professionals, inform and enhance decision making, develop confidence and lead to self-advocacy and better outcomes.

Partnership working is central to inter-agency and inter-professional working in health and social care (Boydell, 2000). Policy imperatives driving partnership working regard it as key to the delivery of complex services in health and social care. This requires collaboration between public, private independent and voluntary sector providers to implement national policy directives through local multi-agency arrangements. Inter-professional partnerships are key to the delivery of integrated and effective services. Partnerships are therefore a central feature of local governance.

Summary

- Social work advocacy has an important role in creating a space for participation and partnership working with a range of professionals including those in social work, health, probation and education.
- Meaningful participation requires that the voices of diverse and marginalised groups are heard.
- Partnership working involves working with a range of service users and carers, and professionals.
- Social work advocates play an important role in ensuring that children and vulnerable adults are involved as fully as possible in partnership arrangements.
- Advocacy practice is informed by theories of participation and rooted in anti-oppressive practice.
- Effective relationships can overcome some of the barriers to partnership working.
- Participatory ways of working are informed by an understanding of power relations.

Discussion questions

1 Reflecting on the experiences of Michael in this chapter, what strategies could social workers employ to identify and overcome the barriers to participation that he faced?
2 How do you know when partnerships are working?
3 How could you ensure that the views of all the people in Steve's family (Steve, Katie, Bill and Paul) are heard and taken into account in any decision making and planning?
4 What can we learn from the views of service users and carers about participation and partnership working?

Further reading

Beresford, P. and Carr, S. (2012) *Social Care, Service Users and User Involvement*. London: Jessica Kingsley.

Carnwell, J. and Buchannan, R. (2005) *Effective Practice in Health and Social Care: A Partnership Approach*. Maidenhead: Open University Press.

Gosling, J. and Martin, J. (2012) *Making Partnerships with Service Users and Advocacy Groups Work*. London: Jessica Kingsley.

Kemshall, H. and Littlechild, R. (eds) (2000) *User Involvement And Participation In Social Care Research Informing Practice*. London: Jessica Kingsley.

6

Advocacy Across the Life Course

Overview

- Advocacy and a life course perspective
- Transitions and the life course
- Challenging assumptions and stereotypes
- Commentary
- Summary
- Discussion questions

Advocacy and a life course perspective

Social workers engage with a range of service users and carers across the life course and work with groups of people at different stages of life. The term 'life course' refers to the progression of an individual from conception to death. A 'life course perspective' is way of looking at the whole of an individual's life as offering opportunities for growth, development and change. It is therefore helpful for practitioners to understand the life course as a fluid development over time rather than perceiving service users or carers as fixed in specific, clearly defined developmental stages. A life course perspective recognises the broader parameters of human development and that development is a life-long process which is both multi-dimensional (includes biological, cognitive and social dimensions) and multi-directional (there can be both gains and losses). A person's life is rarely an uncomplicated progression through fixed linear developmental stages; rather, as Marshall (2011: 6) notes, it is 'an individual passage through life, analysed as a sequence of life events from birth to death'. A life course perspective draws attention to the importance of diversity and recognises that our lives are shaped by political, cultural, economic and environmental factors, including adverse environments such as poverty and domestic violence (see Box 6.1). Social workers taking account of the life course often use a narrative or biographical approach when working with service users and carers, focusing on the importance of their stories and experiences about their lives and, importantly, the meanings that they attribute to them. For example, the testimonies of disabled parents about the issues they face 'highlight the importance of public services and spaces, and home and neighbourhood, in shaping their experiences of parenting and family life' (CSCI, 2009: 21).

Box 6.1   Characteristics of the life course

- Change and continuity
- Development is a lifelong process
- Multi-dimensional and multi-directional
- Plasticity
- Gains and losses
- Individual embedded in a context
- Culturally and historically embedded (Sugarman, 2001)

In order to understand the life course social workers draw on a number of disciplines, including sociology, biology and psychology. Each has its own emphasis and underpinning principles. For sociologists there is an emphasis on the interaction between the social and the environment. Bronfenbrenner's (1979) influential ecological theory highlights the way in which interaction between the individual and the environmental is both reciprocal and dynamic. Green (2010: 23) notes that 'life course sociology and life span psychology are both sub divisions of, but draw widely from, different aspects of their parent disciplines' and are both relatively recent disciplines. Life course sociology uses the following mechanisms to understand the shape of people's lives (Mayer, 2003):

- *Institutions:* for example, compulsory education (from the ages of 5 to 16) stipulates when children must attend school and, for state schools, the nature of the curriculum.
- *Trajectories and transitions:* for example, moving from education into employment.
- *Cohort membership:* for example, the 'baby boomers' are generally understood to refer to those people who were born immediately after the Second World War.

Life span psychology focuses on the 'study of individual development (ontogenesis) – a lifelong adaptive process of acquisition, maintenance, transformation and attrition in psychological structures and functions' (Baltes et al., 1999: 472). For social work advocates, understanding theories of human development has to be accompanied by consideration of a broad spectrum of what is normative development.

Social work advocates need to have a more critically informed understanding that many traditional human development theories are normative. This needs to be supported by a critical appreciation of everyday misperceptions around the behaviour, expectations, prejudices and assumptions of people and society. For example, there is a danger that such misperceptions can lead to a belief that

> biology and chronological ageing have an overwhelming influence on what we become and how we live our lives, or alternatively that problems or achievements certain groups of people experience disproportionately, are due more to the inherent individual failings or merits than to societal influences. (Green, 2010: 2)

Thompson and Thompson (2008) also point out that forming a view of a person or group of people based on normative expectations means that the dangers of defining people as abnormal or deviant are heightened, which in turn results in acceptance of misleading stereotypes: for example, child as lacking capacity, young person as troublesome, older person as frail and confused (Green, 2010). The danger in social work practice is that this can translate into uncritical assumptions being made which can have an impact on the relationship between the service user and the social worker. The consequence for service users and carers is that they may experience stigmatisation and exclusion. The critical practitioner will reflect in order to

> uncover unintended assumptions which flavour (and often determine) practice, in order to improve practice by bringing it in line with intended theory. (Fook, 2000: 212)

It is therefore important that as social workers we use our advocacy skills to challenge exclusion, to critically reflect and to recognise the potential for oppressive or discriminatory practice across the life course.

This chapter offers an opportunity for social work advocates to examine personal attitudes and assumptions about the life course. First, however, it will examine the concept of transition in order to understand the notion of a life course perspective rather than perceiving 'stages' of life as unconnected to previous and future aspects of people's lives. This chapter concludes with a reflection on the implications of a life course perspective for social workers undertaking an advocacy role.

Transitions and the life course

In thinking about the life course, the concept of *transition* is identified as a period of change (an event or experience) that occurs as a person progresses through life (Crawford and Walker, 2007: 5). The responses of individual people to the same life event may be different. Whatever the response, however, any change or life transition will involve loss. Even more positive transitions, such as parenthood or grandparenthood, are likely to engender difficult or ambivalent feelings. For Thompson and Thompson a transition is essentially a point of crisis – the word 'crisis' or a 'turning point in someone's life' (2008: 97). They argues that, at the point of crisis, coping methods that a person has previously used become inadequate and new coping mechanisms need to be found. Transitions are therefore a process of learning in life. However, social workers invariably 'intervene' at such points of crisis, so in order to assess a situation and assist service users to manage a particular crisis they need to understand theories of human development, the potential loss the person may be facing at that time and any grief reaction they may be experiencing. Drawing on Erikson's eight stages of development (1987), each stage or life crisis needs to be successfully navigated before moving on to the next stage. If a transition is not successful, then this has a negative impact on one's ability to meet the next transition.

By way of example it is useful to look at youth transitions and transitions faced by older people. Three social transitions have been identified for young people making the transition to adulthood: from full-time education to employment; from family of origin to family of destination; and from residing in the family home to independent living (Coles, 1995). However, experiences will differ according to various factors:

> Everyone has to make the move from child to adult, but different societies at different times organise the move differently. The transition can take days or years, can mean being collected together with people of the same age or being kept apart from them; it can be a time of relative social freedom or oppression. (Frith, 1984: 467)

In relation to the transition from education to employment, Green (2010) points out that the factors impacting on experience of this transition may be historical, structural, geographical or indeed global. She discusses the different experiences of the Baby Boomer and post-1970s generations. In the 1970s, opportunities for employment were many and varied as the UK was an industrialised society with full employment. While opportunities differed with respect to gender and race/ethnicity, most sixteen-year-old male school leavers could easily find employment in factories, on building sites or as apprentices, for example. However, the move of industrial work to developing countries, alongside national and international economic crises and recessions, made it more difficult for young people to obtain full-time jobs straight from school, especially if they had little or no qualifications.

For young people with a learning difficulty the transition to adulthood has been identified as an area that requires particular attention in relation to supporting young people and their families (DH, 2001b). Young people not only have the challenges of growing up faced by their peers, but also challenges that are likely to accompany growing up with a learning disability, such as increased surveillance when compared to non-learning disabled young people and potentially restricted opportunities to form networks with peers (Priestley, 2003). Young people with learning difficulties also experience significant transition when they move from children's services to adult health and care services. A study by the Norah Fry Research Centre (Tarleton and Ward, 2005: 73) note that supporters felt that young people needed their voice to be heard in the transition process, that they needed to be able to say 'This is my life' and 'This is what I want and how I want it'. Supporters and parents in this study expressed concerns that the dreams and aspirations of young people might not come to fruition. Whatever their situation, however, government guidance points out that transition 'should be seen as a process rather than an event' (DH, 2008: 3) for all young people and that forward planning is critical to their successful transition to adulthood (see Box 6.2).

Box 6.2   Characteristics of good transition services

Young people value:

- Continuity (so accounts do not have to be repeated).
- Changes that are less stressful and don't occur at the last minute.
- Maintaining previous links and relationships.
- Making decisions in the context of friends and peer experiences.

Parents value:

- Information on options and processes.
- Planning in good time, leading to reliable arrangements.
- More transparency around funding.
- Good all-round life experiences for the young person (independence, confidence, activities and friendships).
- The young person and their carer should be central to the transition planning and should be kept fully informed and involved in the planning process. They should be given information about legislation and eligibility criteria governing adults services and have realistic expectations of available adult service to meet need.

(DH, 2008: 35)

Older people also face many transitions: positive transitions may include having more time as a result of retirement, becoming a grandparent and taking on different roles and responsibilities. However, this may not be experienced as a positive transition for people who are experiencing poverty, or are in a position of having to undertake a parenting role for grandchildren whose parents have either died or are unable to parent as a result of, for example, their drug or alcohol use. There are other transitions which may be more commonly associated with ageing, such as developing poor health, becoming a carer, losing a partner or needing support from personal social services. As with young people with a learning difficulty, empowerment of older people in decision-making processes is a key element of the social work advocacy role and, for example, older people with high support needs lack visibility and voice (Blood, 2010). There is a need for critical social work practitioners to find ways to support the active participation of older people in decisions about their care, and this is all the more critical in light of the realities of resource constraints which limit choice and increase the danger of proceduralised practice (Beech and Ray, 2009). However, as Beech and Ray point out, 'bringing older people's voices to the forefront of practice can provide empowering experiences for the social work and the older person, offering insights which will be of great value to practitioners in listening to, for example, marginalised groups such as older women with dementia' (2009: 365).

Every time a person faces a transition they face a potential loss. Loss can be experienced in a range of situations other than those discussed above: for example, for children and for their parents following a separation or divorce; for a child moving into local authority care and moving on to other placements; for people of all ages when friends or families move away, or the death of someone significant in their lives; for older people moving into sheltered housing or residential care. Loss is also experienced if people become disabled in any way as their hopes and aspirations are changed through, for example, unemployment or redundancy (which may mean that a person or family loses their home and community), or for refugees and asylum-seeking families who experience the loss of identity, status, position as well as country of origin. Grief can be understood as a reaction to any significant loss.

CASE STUDY

Kevin is a disabled young person with complex health needs. He moved from paediatric to adult health services at sixteen, then at eighteen moved from children's to adult social care. These transitions occurred alongside the transition stages in his education. Since these changes occurred independently of each other, Kevin and his family had to deal with many new agencies and new professionals over a period of three years. Each time they had to tell their story again. During the course of these changes and moves the challenge for practitioners was to ensure that supporting Kevin as he moved into adulthood took account of his needs and aspirations. Local options for Kevin were limited and lack of continuity in provision became apparent as he progressed through the services. The experience for Kevin and his parents was that once he reached the age of sixteen, services seemed to disappear. Government guidance points out that transition 'should be seen as a process rather than an event' (DH, 2008: 3) and that forward planning is crucial to the successful transition of all young people.

Challenging assumptions and stereotypes

Children lack capacity

The assumption that children lack capacity can be analysed in a number of ways. Clearly, as Thompson and Thompson (2008: 87) notes, children are 'qualitatively different from adults'. This goes beyond differences in biological development – it includes development consistent with psychological, social, moral and ontological strands. While children are clearly different from adults, it is also important to understand the influence of societal and cultural expectations on children's lives – expectations of how children should be and behave in an adult world. For social workers to act effectively as advocates with children there is a need to understand child development and the inter-relationship between their development, their immediate family relationships, the community in which they live and wider structural issues.

The disciplines of psychology and sociology have been particularly influential in developing understanding about childhood. Most psychological theories about childhood are underpinned by the concept of human development with childhood as a stage in the lifecycle, characterised by dependency and immaturity. These stage-based theories (for example, Erikson, 1980; Levinson, 1978; Havinghurst, 1972) have been criticised for representing children as developing through the natural process of growing up, focusing on measurement and reaching normative milestones. As a result children are seen as incomplete adults, reinforcing the idea that children lack the capacity to be involved in decision making at certain stages or pre-defined ages (Lansdown, 1997). Children clearly begin their lives in a position of dependency on the caring decisions of adults (Hart, 1997; Alderson, 2000). They should then be assisted by the family and other institutions to become more able to act as their own agents, acknowledging that increasingly making their own decisions is an essential aspect of their development.

Early sociological perspectives on childhood have also been criticised for portraying children as needing to develop as 'complete beings' (Lee, 2001; Thomas, 2000). Children are not aware of the societal norms and conventions of a particular culture when they are born. They become informed about these social conventions through the process of socialisation – children are in essence 'made social' (Thomas, 2000). Lee observes that central to the idea of the socialisation of children is that

> before they can participate fully in social life, before they can say anything worth hearing, they need to be socialised. When children speak, they necessarily speak out of ignorance of social convention. (2001: 89)

These traditional perspectives have reinforced the idea that children lack capacity and their testimonies are not reliable. Therefore the more the dependent a child is the less likely they are to have their views taken seriously, acted upon or listened to.

The discourse of social construction has influenced thinking about the value of children's perspectives and secured greater legitimacy for promoting children's participatory and citizenship rights. Asserting that childhood is a social rather than a biological construct, it reframes childhood as a construct of society constituted by social and historical features, and recognises the significance of varying theoretical understandings and cultural representations (James and Prout, 1997). Rather than being a period in the life course, childhood can therefore be described as a structural feature of societies (Hendrick, 2000). James and Prout's work (1990) challenged concepts of childhood as universal and the image of children as incomplete. Rather, children and young people are 'social actors' in their own right whose voices reflect the reality of their lives. In this way the child is recognised as an individual while childhood is the socially constructed space that children occupy in relation to adults. While this perspective, rightly, is not without its critics (Lavalette and Cunningham, 2002), it has been central in promoting debates about the status of children and young people in an adult world. Understanding children in a particular way enables social workers to elicit what it is like for them to live the lives that they do and gain insight into their world.

Debates about the construction of childhood are also significant in thinking about the issue of children's capacity. This 'new' sociology of childhood has challenged more traditional thinking about childhood and led to the development of participatory ways of working. However, the contribution of psychological perspectives is also relevant to thinking about capacity. For example, there can be ambivalence about the involvement of younger children or disabled children in decision-making processes. This is invariably based on age-based ideas about capacity, or in the case of disabled children assumptions may be made about impairment. While all theories of childhood recognise the evolving capacity of children and young people, children are more likely to be denied rights on the basis of age. However, while children who are physically or mentally immature have relatively little experience, lack knowledge and are likely to be more vulnerable and marginalised, this does not necessarily mean that they cannot have a view about what is happening in their lives and be given the opportunity to participate at some level. The judgement resulting in what is now known as the 'Fraser principle' recognised this point (see Box 6.3). It is now widely used to challenge age-defined thresholds in relation to decision making concerning the lives of young people. It is certainly useful for social workers who work with young people and are involved in multi-disciplinary decision-making processes such as child protection conferences, reviews of young people looked after by the local authority or school exclusions: for example, it can be used to advocate for the participation of young people in decision making. The relationship between the capacity to participate and opportunities to participate is also relevant here. Lansdown (2005) argues that the capacity to participate can be learned if the opportunities are provided.

Box 6.3 The Gillick decision

A ruling by the House of Lords (Gillick v West Norfolk and Wisbech Area Health Authority [1985] 3 All ER 402 HL) was a landmark ruling in challenging an age-defined threshold for young people to consent to medical treatment. This followed the issue of a circular by the Department of Health to doctors, which stated that contraception to young people who were under sixteen could be prescribed at the doctor's discretion and without parental consent or knowledge. Mrs Gillick argued that in doing this doctors would in fact be treating a patient (in this context a young person) without consent, as the right to consent to treatment rested with the parent. Mrs Gillick challenged whether it was lawful for a doctor to give advice and contraception to a person under the age of sixteen without parental consent. The case established what has become known as the 'mature minor principle' or 'Gillick competency'. Lord Scarman stated: 'A minor's capacity to make his or her own decisions depends on the minor having sufficient understanding and intelligence to make decisions and is not to be determined by any judicial fixed age limit'. Therefore a young person under the age of sixteen could consent to treatment if they fully understood the medical treatment being proposed, without the consent of their parents or without their parents being notified.

The implications of the ruling went beyond the scope of consent to medical treatment. It reflects a view that parental authority and rights are not absolute and diminish with the evolving maturity and capacity of the child, and directly challenged the view that an age-defined threshold is sufficient in determining a child's capacity to make a decisions.

Parents with learning difficulties are unable to meet their children's needs

Research by Booth and Booth (2004) indicates that in comparison to other parents (including those with drug and/or alcohol problems, those with a mental illness and parents without disabilities), a smaller proportion of children of families headed by a parent with learning difficulties are returned home to live; a higher proportion are placed out-of-home and outside the family circle; and a higher proportion are freed for adoption than for any other group of parents. They note that 'these outcomes are too easily taken simply as a measure of parenting incapacity when in fact they also demonstrate the hidden effects of temporal discrimination on the workings of the child protection system' (2004: 87).

Stainton (2009) points out that naming the category of people who are currently referred to as having a 'learning difficulty' and identifying who exactly falls into that category is complex and can have an impact on both those who are excluded and those who are included in that category. He points out, for example, that historically being defined as a person who had a learning difficulty led to loss of rights, including, for example, subjection to sterilisation and incarceration. Conversely, however, access services or support is denied to people who are not included within the category of people who are defined as having a learning disability. This means that a critical practitioner needs to be aware of different definitions but also, crucially, to be aware of the impact that this has on people who seek or receive services in order to advocate for services that will meet their needs. Stainton points out that ultimately definitions are social constructs that help social workers understand what is being defined but tell us little about the actual person behind the label. Nevertheless, they are powerful tools that can trigger whether or not services are provided. Furthermore, they influence stereotypical views and assumptions which can similarly have an impact on how services are provided. For example, Ward and Tarleton note that negative stereotypes and assumptions about parents with learning difficulties represent parents 'as incompetent, unable to understand their children's needs or learn skills quickly enough to meet them; in short, they were never going to be "good enough" parents' (2007: 24). We note later in this chapter that this can lead to the removal of children from their parents, although parents with a learning difficulty who are not identified as such until they become parents (and therefore have not previously had previous contact with as social worker) can equally find themselves in a position where their children are removed from their care because they receive support too late.

Medical models of disability have also had an impact on how parents who have learning difficulties are perceived. The medical model focuses on the individual's impairment. The World Health Organization defines disability as 'the restriction or lack (resulting from impairment) of ability to perform an activity in the manner or range considered normal for a human being' (WHO, 1980). This definition has influenced policy, practice and research for some considerable time, although guidance to social workers suggests that practice should be informed by the social model of disability (Pierson and Thomas, 2010). The social model highlights the disabling barriers that are encountered by people with impairments through discriminatory attitudes, environments that are not accessible and 'lack of enabling supports which should be the focus of social policy' (Morris, 2011: 4). Morris notes that 'disability' is the oppression and inequality experienced as a result of these barriers and argues for a vision of society where these barriers are overcome. To date society still fails to ensure that there is provision to include individuals with mental or physical impairments. The Disabled Parent's Network uses an approach based on the social model of disability and which now underpins some more recent government strategies to improve the life chances of disabled people (CSCI, 2009). However, Morris argues that the social model of disability has been corrupted and misused to legitimise changes in welfare reform and adult social care, which in fact will lead to more inequality and discrimination. One way that social workers as advocates can improve the lives of people they are working with is to be aware of and engage in wider political debates about social and economic policy. This involves being up to date with research findings and academic viewpoints and using these to inform knowledge and understanding and actively influence practice.

Research we have referred to above by Booth and Booth (2005) shows that the children of parents with learning difficulties are fifty times more likely to be involved in care proceedings than would be envisaged on the basis of their numbers in the population. These high numbers can, they suggest, be 'too easily mistaken as an indicator of widespread parenting failure on the part of this group of mothers and fathers when it may equally well signify the failure of public policies to address their needs for long-term support' (2005: 1001). Their work makes a number of important points reflecting the reality of the lives of people with learning difficulties, organisational constraints and challenges for practitioners (see Figure 6.1).

Ward and Tarleton (2007) make similar observations from their mapping of support available to parents with learning difficulties and their children. While they identified examples of good practice, they also highlight that the reality of their lives is that parents with learning difficulties who want to look after their children have to overcome a number of obstacles. These arise through the lack of collaboration between adults and children's services and the tensions that exist between balancing the rights of parents and the rights of children. While it is always difficult to balance these rights, this is compounded when parents have a learning difficulty. Nevertheless, it has been noted that parents with learning difficulties also want to ensure that their children are safe and their welfare is promoted, but can only do this if they have access to the support they need (McGraw and Newman 2005). However, Ward and Tarleton (2007) note that there are considerable barriers to overcome before parents with a learning difficulty can demonstrate that they are 'good enough' parents. These include:

- *Negative stereotypes and assumptions about their competence as parents.* It has been argued that notions of competence and independence should be viewed as relational and socially embedded concepts. This means that in the reality of a person's life, competence invariably reflects things that are achieved with others rather than in isolation. A sensible way of working, therefore, is to view competence as something that is distributed within families and social networks rather than something that is just located within a parent or parents (Jenkins, 1998; Priestley, 2003; Booth and Booth, 1998).
- *Fixed ideas about what should happen to their children.* While the Children Act 1989 indicates that children should be supported in their own family wherever possible, the key driver for children and family social work teams is the child protection agenda – which may not always include a concept of providing ongoing support for parents who have learning difficulties. This is compounded by parents' fears that their children might be removed from them, which means that they are less likely to engage with children and family social workers. Social workers then are more likely to have increased concerns.
- *Lack of consistency and clarity about the threshold of 'good' parenting.* Often a number of professionals will be involved with a family over and above social

Parent with a learning difficulty	Practitioner	Organisational issues
Needs to get to know the social worker.	Needs time to establish a meaningful relationship.	Social workers are required to adhere to time scales – the systems create barriers to justice by ignoring the interplay between their learning difficulty and problems with time.
Encounter problems with time: chronological, attention/memory, cognitive processes: sequencing, thinking ahead.	Pressures to complete assessments within pre-determined time scales – therefore even if they understand and want to spend more time they are unable to do this.	
Need support to enable attendance at meetings etc such as prompts (text, phone call), lifts, personalised memory aids.	Parents are best serviced when practitioners have specialist skills and knowledge about working with people who have learning difficulties. Challenge of managing tensions between right to family life and right to protection.	Lack of collaboration between adult and children's services. Structures reinforce working in isolation. A whole family approach is seldom adopted.
Need long-term family support services.	Have to operate within tight time-scales. Operate on a 'fix-it and exit' methodology that leads to an increased likelihood that compulsory intervention will be required once social workers have stopped working with a family which exacerbates the possibility of care proceedings.	Short-term interventions are cheaper. There are no resources for long term support services or a family service ethos.
Can learn to parent but learn more slowly so are seen as lacking the capacity to be able to change.	Have to report back to conference three months after first meeting.	Case conference decision making has little give to accommodate the special needs of parents.
Require specialist training programmes for parenting skills.	Need opportunities to go into the home to teach parents new skills. Need skills to recognise the skills and knowledge that parents have.	Parent training classes fail because they are too generic and not prepared for working with disabled parents who need specialist help.
Find it difficult to understand the system.	Encouraged to use twin tracking approach where the process of placement and adoption go hand in hand. Need skills to explain to parents sensitively what concerns there may be.	Push for permanency places a demand on comprehension and capacity to learn that makes no allowance for disability.

Figure 6.1 Issues for practitioners and organisations when working with parents who have a learning difficulty

workers from adult and from children and family teams. Their professional value bases and standards can be different depending on both personal and professional training and experience. This can be confusing for parents trying to do the best that they can. One mother in Ward and Tarleton's (2007) study was both 'praised' and 'criticised' by different workers because in order to attend college her mother cared for her child one day a week.

- *Late or crisis point referrals.* Some parents only became known to adult services at the point at which they became parents. Since other professionals did not have the skills or training to assess that parents had particular needs at the ante-natal stage, support and referral to adult services often came too late, and in some cases this meant that children were subsequently placed away from their parents. This can be exacerbated in situations where parents failed to reach agency thresholds for community care services and family support services. Services became available at the point at which the children were assessed as being 'at risk' or 'in need'.

A further piece of piece of useful research was undertaken by CSCI in 2009. This was based on a survey of fifty councils and found that society is still failing to recognise the needs of disabled parents and their families. This includes universal services such as education, health and social care services. The report indicates that 'councils are failing to achieve the right balance of interventions to support disabled parents and their families. Extra efforts are required to overcome the new silos that have been created by the separation of adult and children's services so that there is not a disjointed approach to supporting the family. There are a number of actions that need to be taken by councils and other agencies' (2009: 6). Since the separation of adult and children's services a mentality appears to have developed within each department that means information is contained within each department. This has been described as a 'silo' mentality, and has its origins in the free standing grain silos used by farmers. With respect to social services, adult and children's departments a silo culture means that the services operate as independent, self contained, vertical structures where communication occurs within the silo and there is little or no contact with the other silo (or silos if education and health are included). This means that meeting the needs of a family cannot be effective unless information flows freely between departments. The report recommend a number of actions to connect the silos so that they can offer a more meaningful and efficient services. The actions include:

- Joint working and integrated services.
- Information for joint strategic needs assessments.
- More direct payments and individual budget.
- Resourcing support to the family.
- Ongoing support and training for staff.
- Involving disabled parents.

Carla is a young, white, working-class mother who lives with her partner, Leo, and two children on a housing estate in the West Midlands. Their children, Digby (age three) and Simon (age eighteen months) have been described as having 'disturbed behaviour'. Carla and Leo are loving parents whose children were recently allocated a social worker, Rhiannon. Carla and Leo found it difficult to understand why the children had a social worker. However, Carla's sister, Beth, who was very supportive, attended a meeting with Rhiannon (at the request of Carla and Leo) and realised that there were concerns about Carla and Leo's ability to parent – to the extent that Rhiannon was considering care proceedings. When Carla and Leo understood this they became very anxious and subsequently would not be very communicative with Rhiannon when she visited. Until now Carla and Leo had no social worker of their own, so after talking with Rhiannon, Beth made contact with the Adult Learning Disabilities Team and a social worker, Ed, was allocated. Rhiannon realised that Digby and Simon loved their parents but that Carla and Leo did find it difficult to 'juggle' tasks in the home and were much more confident when undertaking one task at a time – such as preparing a meal or supervising Simon. Rhiannon spoke with the local family centre about an outreach service and they started to receive help to support them with daily routines; to start with the outreach worker visited first thing in the morning and again in the evening as these had been the times identified by Beth as particularly stressful for Carla and Leo. Leo's mother always popped in at some point during the day. Rhiannon set up a monthly meeting of everyone working with the family and Ed became their key worker. The professionals were then able to co-ordinate their input to maximise their impact, and Ed's role was to co-ordinate the various supports to Carla and Leo and to facilitate effective communication between all workers and between them and Carla and Leo. He helped them to remember who the different workers were by providing photographs of them.

Ed helped Carla and Leo with the difficult process of telling their story in order to gain more control and meaning. He also continually ensured that they had access to information about all aspects of parenting that they were able to understand. Carla and Leo found this an empowering process, and he helped to bridge the gap between them and Rhiannon by supporting them at meetings and helping them to understand what Rhiannon was asking of them and why. Ed also ensured that the needs of Carla and Leo were addressed not only as parents but also as individuals in their own right.

This strategy enabled Carla and Leo to understand that the help they were getting was genuinely intended to help them to be 'good parents' and they became more confident in their skills. The praise and encouragement of the workers involved was vital here. In this way Carla and Leo were enabled to demonstrate their commitment to be good parents and were allowed the necessary time and support to make the life changes needed to enhance the welfare of Digby and Simon. Central to this was

(Continued)

(Continued)

the co-operation between Ed and Rhiannon (facilitated by a clear policy agreement between adult and children's services), and as a result Carla and Leo were enabled to be parents to the best of their ability, to make use of the support afforded and to share the parenting task with others.

- Rhiannon's advocacy role could have been compromised by her location within the agency and her legal mandates with regard to the welfare of Simon and Digby. However, this did not deter her from undertaking other aspects of the social worker advocacy role in bringing together a team and working closely with Ed to support the family. While ensuring that appropriate 'safeguards' were in place, she also ensured that her assessment was positive and promoted the skills and abilities of Carla and Leo as well as identifying their support needs.
- Ed and Rhiannon worked together to ensure that Carla and Leo understood each worker's role and were clear about what was happening and what their expectations were. They simplified information and presented it clearly to them.
- Ed's advocacy role was to ensure that Carla and Leo had a voice, particularly supporting them in the monthly meetings with professionals: preparing for the meeting in advance, helping them to take part and speaking for them if they wanted this. He also ensured that the meetings were run in a way the enabled their participation.

Both Ed and Rhiannon were aware of current research and government strategies to support disabled parents. Their advocacy role meant that while working in different services and being part of new 'silos' they used their advocacy skills to overcome the barriers and work together to work alongside the whole family in order to understand all of their needs. These skills were enhanced because they were research minded and their practice was therefore informed by both the experiences of parents with learning difficulties and policy directives such as Putting People First (DH, 2007a) and Think Family (Cabinet Office, 2008).

Older people with dementia are unable to participate in decision making

A life course perspective indicates that in order to understand the experiences of people when they are older, especially older people living with dementia, we need to view them in the context of their personal histories, and as unique individuals. A narrative or biographical approach (Sugarman, 2001: 986) enables social workers to pay attention to the personal accounts of the lives of people they are working with, and what it means to them as an individual in terms of their life experiences and how they think about themselves. For social workers there is therefore a need to develop knowledge and understanding about the physical, social and psychological aspects of people's lives as well as the influence of other aspects such as class, race or gender. Challenging the assumptions about the way society perceives ageing is not helped by policy and practice that fails to reflect the diversity of ageing and the various physical, emotional and psychological transitions faced by older people (Ray et al., 2009; Crawford and Walker, 2004). A pivotal role for social workers is to enable people to manage the changes they encounter in their lives and in their relationships. Adams et al. (2009b) note that since the context of people's lives are constantly changing, our understanding of adulthood and ageing is therefore a continual process of growth through critical reflection:

> Maintaining our understanding of how adulthood changes is a crucial ingredient in our social work expertise; we cannot learn about adult development, instead we must continue to explore how adults' lives change as social change affects their life course (2009b: 141).

Stereotypes of old age are generally associated with physical appearance. A biological approach suggests that a feature of growing older is a greater likelihood of ill-health – there is an age-related decline. This approach also suggests that old age is associated with increasing frailty and therefore there is little likelihood of development (Crawford and Walker, 2004). However Phillipson (2008) challenges these assumptions, noting that there are a significant number of people aged over eighty-five who do not, in fact, experience significant health problems. Psychosocial approaches – such as the work of Erikson (1980) – suggest that people move through stages of life, each of which is a dilemma or crisis to be successfully negotiated in order to move through to the next phase. For Erikson the final phase of life involves accepting that life has been fulfilling and that feelings of regret about the choices that have been made lead to despair and eventually a fear of the end of life. However, as stated earlier, ultimately older age is shaped by both experiences and by the meanings that society gives to later life and as such is socially constructed, which leads to the process of stereotyping older age and older people.

The routine nature of assessments in social work can reinforce stereotypes about older people, particularly older service users living in poverty or suffering mental ill-health. Ray et al. (2009) highlight, by way of example, three ways in which assessments can reinforce stereotypes through:

- Focusing on individual dysfunctions and problems reinforces ideas about inevitable dependency.
- Failing to consider the biographical context of an older person fails to take account of the whole of their life experiences.
- Failing to consider the strengths and abilities of older people can portray them as helpless when they are encountering situations of change.

Social work practice is increasingly informed by a critical perspective that challenges the view that experiences associated with growing older are only determined by biological imperatives. Rather, practitioners are now developing an understanding of how key experiences of ageing are constructed, sustained and reinforced by policy, legislation and organisational structures.

A good example of how stereotypical views impact on people's lives can be seen in Maggie's story (see case study below). Expectations of people who have dementia are generally low. There is also a danger that the general views of dementia do not match the lived experiences of individuals like Maggie.

CASE STUDY

Maggie is an 82-year-old retired architect who has Alzheimer's disease. She has lived alone since the death of her lifelong partner, Peter. When she was younger Maggie had always enjoyed activities such as jogging, and for many years was a regular member of the local history society. She would regularly drive to see her son and his family – which took about an hour and was a journey Maggie enjoyed and looked forward to. As her mobility has become more limited, however, Maggie sees less of both her son and her friends. Recently Maggie has started to experience periods of confusion and feels that she cannot think clearly at times. However, at other times Maggie says that she feels fine. Her hobbies are now more focused to activities within the home. She really enjoys cooking, doing puzzles and inviting people to visit her. Maggie has talked to her GP about her dementia and feels that she is managing it well at the moment. However, she is very aware of the reactions and expectations of other people who know about her dementia, which she found frustrating. For example, Maggie is often told that she does not appear to have anything wrong with her. Maggie recently told her son how she was feeling: 'It is strange that some people only seem to think about the dementia – they treat me as though I am stupid. Maybe if the dementia gets worse that might be more relevant, but at the moment it just makes me really cross – and I feel like they are writing me off as a person. They seem to lose sight of the fact that I am still Maggie ... I am still their friend and your Mum, they only seem to see the dementia.'

- Social work advocates have an important role to play in promoting awareness of the way that stereotypical views and assumptions about older people can impact on practice and on the lives of service users and carers.
- Another key role for social workers is to manage and provide support for older people. A strengths-based perspective is useful here rather than highlighting people's difficulties.
- Finally, advocacy is recognised as becoming increasingly important in relation to older people, as social and policy changes have had an impact on family structures, patterns of employment, or the lack of a partner or close relative.

Philipson (2008) points out that crucially social work advocacy is important at particular times, such as the transition into residential care or discharge from hospital,

times when people may feel less autonomous as decisions are taken by professionals and/or carers who may lose sight of the individual person as they struggle to
cope with the demands of the organisation. In such situations the social work
advocate is in a key position to promote relationship-based, individual person-
centred care, rather than a functional approach to personal care, and potentially
specialist advocacy for people, for example, with more advanced dementia and for
whom communication is an issue. Social workers have to be able to work sup-
portively with older people in such situations when they may be feeling frightened,
worried about being able maintain their dignity, and their feeling of self-worth
may be increasingly negative. The challenges for social workers, as we noted above
with Carla and Leo, is that older people with dementia need time to build a relationship with their social worker for the assessment to be meaningful and effective. Beech and Ray (2009: 262) 'challenge the notion that every service user has
needs that will inevitably be short-term.'

Commentary

Thinking about the theoretical concepts in relation to the life course provides a
foundation for us, as critical practitioners, to understand and relate to the people we
work with. While many social workers work with one specific group of people, such
as young people, older people, people with mental health needs, for example, it is
unusual to work with any group of people in isolation. So understanding how the
lives of parents, grandparents or friends impact on the lives of children are important. Equally, Green (2010) points out that understanding how historical events
such as wars, or social events such as advances in technology, impact on older people, as well as considering how stereotypes and assumptions colour people's views
and treatment of older people – either as wise, useful citizens or frail and a drain on
resources – is essential for all professionals who provide services for older people. A
life course perspective draws on a multi-disciplinary understanding, which not only
provides opportunities to critically analyse particular theoretical concepts but also
to use our own personal and professional experiences and biographies to develop
new theory.

The process of taking account of the life course, and recognising that all our lives
are shaped by a number of contextual factors, provides the underpinning knowledge
to inform the social work advocate. Understanding people's lives and, as a result,
taking account of and being sensitive to the telling of their stories and experiences in
developing relationships with them can facilitate voice and involvement in decision
making. For example, listening to the story of a person whose experience throughout
their life has been of being silenced will enable the social worker and the person they
are working with to develop realistic goals and expectations and provides a tool for
planning and intervention for working together.

Drawing on a life course approach facilitates critical anti-oppressive practice
and advocacy. It challenges deficit models, recognises that throughout life there

are opportunities for change and development; it also considers the strengths and resources of service users, and recognises the value and impact of their experiences as told through their accounts of their lives and the meanings they attach to them. Recognising and understanding the service user or carers' story enables practitioners to recognise the relationship between issues affecting services users and carers and broader social/organisational issues. This empowers social workers to respect and value the diversity of people's lives and to challenge assumptions and stereotypes.

Summary

- Life course perspectives consider the whole of life and opportunities for growth.
- Life course recognises how lives are shaped by political, cultural economic and environmental factors.
- The concept of *transition* assists in understanding a life course perspective as a series of changes that occur as a person progresses through life, instead of focusing on stages of life.
- A narrative approach recognises the importance of people's stories when working with service users and carers

Discussion questions

1 Why is thinking about human development across the life course important for social work advocates?
2 How can a critical understanding of life course development support the social work advocacy role?
3 How would you describe personal and professional development in terms of your own life course?
4 Think about your journey into social work. What enabled you in that journey to become a social worker and successful advocate?

Further reading

Department of Health (2008) *Transition: Moving On Well. A Good Practice Guide for Health Professionals and their Partners on Transition Planning for Young People with Complex Health Needs or a Disability.* London: Central Office of Information.
Green, L. (2010) *Understanding the Life Course: Sociological and Psychological Perspectives.* Cambridge: Polity Press.

SCIE (2005) *Helping Parents with Learning Difficulties in their Role as Parents. Research Briefing 14*. London: SCIE.

Sugarman, L. (2001) *Life-Span Development: Frameworks, Accounts and Strategies* (Second Edition). Hove: Psychology Press.

Ward, L. and Tarleton, B. (2007) 'Sinking or swimming? Supporting parents with learning disabilities and their children', *Tizard Learning Disability Review*, 12 (2): 22–32.

7

Representation and Complaints

Overview

- Accountability
- Consumerism and service user involvement
- Complaints and independent advocacy
- Accountability, advocacy and critical reflection
- Commentary
- Summary
- Discussion questions

It is perhaps understandable that no one welcomes a complaint about their work. It suggests that they are not doing their job properly and that someone is dissatisfied about what they are doing. This can be difficult to accept if, for example, they have made a genuine mistake or been working hard, to the best of their ability, possibly without the support that they might want or need (either through supervision or in terms of resources). Social workers are no exception and, by the very nature of their work, they work under intense public scrutiny. The government document *Listening, Responding, Improving* (Department of Health, 2009a) aims to promote a more positive attitude towards complaints. The title of the document demonstrates the importance of respecting what service users have to say about services. It encourages 'a culture that seeks and then uses people's experiences of care to improve quality' (Department of Health, 2009a: 5). This recognises that mistakes can happen however hard health and social care practitioners work to get things right. It also recognises that if services respond to and resolve mistakes quickly, then clearly services can improve for both service users and staff. In particular, the guidance notes the importance of listening to people who have used health and social care services, with an emphasis on learning from their experiences in order to improve services. In many ways this is what advocacy is about: supporting people to have a voice about the services they receive or may need. The importance of listening is exemplified in the thoughts and feelings of people with learning disabilities in relation to their experience of complaining (Box 7.1) and underlines the fact that while it is important to have complaints procedures that are accessible and well supported, these alone will not empower people to complain (Preston-Shoot, 2001; Thurman, 2009). There is also a need to create 'a listening culture that values the views of all people, however they make their views known' (Thurman, 2009: 6). A listening culture is an advocacy culture and social workers have a central role in developing such an ethos, guided by the four principles that inform advocacy practice discussed in Chapter 4:

- Promoting equality, justice and social inclusion.
- Empowering people to speak up for themselves or to have their voices heard in the systems.
- Helping people to become aware of their rights and exercise those rights.
- Enabling people to be involved in and influence decisions being made about their future.

Box 7.1   Feelings and thoughts of people with learning difficulties about the experience of complaining

'Make out you are the important one, but not really.'

'Dusted under the carpet.'

'Staff don't listen.'

'Not allowed to use the complaint procedure.'

'Cannot read the complaint form.'

'Called a trouble-maker.'

'They thought it was trivial but it was important to me.'

(Thurman, 2009)

An open service that welcomes complaints and is prepared to act on them is the ideal being sought by both government guidance and service users. However, it can be difficult for social workers to support service users to make a complaint within systems when a 'powerful blame culture' (Ferguson, 2011: 34) exists in both child and adult protection systems. The government notes that improving the way that complaints are dealt with will make services 'more effective, personal and safe' (Department of Health, 2009a: 4). While this may be the case, the fact remains that professionals are regularly publicly castigated because of their failure to protect and it is more comfortable to retreat to the safe haven of proceduralised practice – becoming a 'static practitioner' (Ferguson, 2011: 39) driven by a fear of pressure from the media and litigation. Issues of accountability then arise and question need to be asked about who the social worker is accountable to and how multiple accountabilities are managed. This chapter will therefore consider the landscape of accountability in social work practice and how social workers can exercise their '"advocacy" responsibilities to advise and assist with a complaint, even if this complaint is against the employing authority' (BASW, 1995: 8).

Accountability

Accountability has been described as 'an integral feature of every day as well as professional life' (Banks, 2009: 32). Banks suggests that 'giving an account' is a key element of the way that we communicate with other people and it is understood and, as such, is part of the way that we construct our identities. Essentially, this means that when we are asked to give an account of what we have or have not done, we may well situate ourselves with our identity as professionals with specific knowledge, values and skills; with our identity as a member of a decision making system that is likely to include other professionals and our own managers; and with our identity as someone who has personal experiences that may impact on how we work. The difficulty is that literature on accountability often focuses on situations where something has gone wrong and the subsequent demand to apportion blame (Banks, 2009). Social workers are expected to be accountable *for* their actions and as such their activity is open to scrutiny. The mechanisms for expressing and ensuring accountability in this respect are what have been identified as 'post-hoc' safeguards. These are the processes for making representation or complaint which provide service users and carers with an opportunity to challenge and instigate a review of a decision, resulting in the organisation having to account for its actions. Target setting, mechanisms to monitor and evaluate performance and inspections are also mechanisms to ensure accountability *for* actions (Braye and Preston-Shoot, 2009a).

Accountability, however, can also be considered in terms of accountability *to* an organisation or group of people. The difficulty for social workers is that accountability is complex (Braye and Preston-Shoot, 1999; Clarke, 2000). Social work can be understood as a process, 'a series of connected contacts between a social work practitioner and the people who the practitioner is trying to help' (Payne 2009b:159). That process takes place within practice settings. However, Payne points out that any process has boundaries which are defined by the context of practice.

He identifies four key boundaries that contribute to the complexity of social work accountabilities:

- *The agency's responsibilities* to its political or managing body (which may have an impact on the priorities and funding of the agency), and to regulators (who set standards of practice).
- *The workers (my) accountability* to the people they are working with and the professional regulatory bodies for professional standards of practice.
- *The different personal identities* of the individuals involved and as part of a family and community.
- *The interests of other stakeholders*, including individuals such as neighbours, and organisations such as the client's employer. (Payne 2009a:170)

Organisations have to provide services within the policy guidance of central and local government while responding to individual demands and competing priorities. There is also financial accountability to funders (central government, charities, the public) and to the regulators of professional practice who set standards, priorities and targets. In addition, there are professional ethical codes of conduct and personal moral codes that social workers are guided by, as well as accountability to service users. These accountabilities are complicated by the fact that while there may be elements of mutuality between accountabilities (Payne 1995), there are also inevitable tensions for social workers between their accountability and obligations as employees and their professional accountability and obligations to codes of ethics and to service users and carers. Accountability in social work codes is also slightly different from the more legal understanding of accountability as these consistently place emphasis on professional competence and the importance of constantly updating knowledge (BASW, 2012; CCW, 2012; General Social Care Council, 2002; Scottish Social Care Council, 2009; HCPC, 2008). There is a link, though, between social work codes and the legal understanding of accountability, since failure to meet professional standards by a social worker may well be a factor contributing to a formal complaint or other legal action (Williams, 2009).

Accountability to service users and carers

Margot, an 83-year-old polish woman who had a mild learning disability, was living in residential accommodation. Her relatives visited regularly and felt worried about the way that she was being treated. They felt that the standard of care was poor and that she was being discriminated against because English was not her first language. They thought about making a complaint but were unsure about what to do and whether this would make things worse for Margot. They decided to talk with their

CASE EXAMPLE

(Continued)

(Continued)

social worker, Lisa, who explained that the residential home had a good reputation and was used a lot by the local authority. Nevertheless, she listened to their concerns and said that she would visit Margot. The social worker had a friend who worked in the home and was a little concerned about the allegations and the position of her friend. However, she also felt that it was essential to take the concerns of the relatives seriously and that an important part of her role was to ensure that all the residents received a good standard of care. Lisa visited Margot and found that Margot was very unhappy. Margot had lost a great deal of weight since Lisa had last seen her. She had not been eating or drinking and told Lisa that the staff often ignored her. Her toenails were very long and this made it difficult for her to walk. This meant that increasingly Margot did little else except sit in a chair. Lisa was concerned and spoke to the GP who then arranged for Margot to be admitted to hospital. Margot was soon back to her normal self after a few weeks, and Lisa worked with Margot and her family to find her a more suitable place to live.

Lisa went on to instigate safeguarding procedures and there was an investigation into what had happened. A case conference decided that Margot had been abused through neglect. The investigating officer upheld the complaint, stating that staff lack of knowledge about Margot's mental capacity was the primary reason for the situation arising. The staff in the home had insufficient knowledge and understanding about mental capacity and had assumed that Margot was exercising choice when she refused food or treatment. It also became apparent that Margot had somehow fallen between learning disability and community health team jurisdictions. Following this incident, staff received training about mental capacity, a review of learning disabilities services was instigated and the home was monitored to ensure that such a situation did occur again.

- Lisa listened to the views of Margot's relatives and although she personally initially believed that the residential accommodation was satisfactory, she subsumed her own ideas and took their concerns seriously
- Lisa listened carefully to Margot and realised that she was unhappy and was also physically in a poor condition.
- Lisa's advocacy here was both issue-based in relation to Margot and systemic in terms of the training and management of staff.

Consumerism and service user involvement

There is a range of legal and policy mandates, professional mandates and service user and carer mandates for involvement (Braye, 2000), and it has been argued that service user involvement is about being accountable to the people who use services (Braye and Preston-Shoot, 1999). Furthermore, of all the accountabilities outlined above, ultimately the most important accountability is to people who use services. However, service users have the least voice, while organisations challenged by mechanisms for redress appear to be in a powerful position and have a choice about whether or not to change (Preston-Shoot, 2001). Contemporary policy and practice recognises the importance of involving service users and carers, and part of the advocacy role of social workers is to ensure that service users and carers have a voice in decisions that affect their lives and in relation to the provision of services.

The development of consumerism means that systems for complaints are viewed as mechanisms to facilitate a view of service users and carers as active participants within the provision of responsive services. The current systems of complaints therefore aim to assist service users as consumers to have issues resolved through 'soft' solutions, while the organisations learn from the process in order to improve the service. Where service users are not happy with such an approach a more formal system is brought into play, with a level of independence factored into the process. From an agency perspective, good practice should be highlighted through these processes, while any recurring complaints can be reviewed and action taken to rectify problems or identify and improve practice. The difficulty is that service providers with limited resources will not want to invest in managing complaints procedures if this has a negative impact on the ability to deliver services. Furthermore, there is obviously a tendency for organisations to be defensive where their staff or systems are criticised (Allsop and Jones, 2008). Nevertheless, enhancing the power of consumers through complaints procedures has resulted in legislation and ongoing examination of complaints systems by government departments to improve the delivery of services (see Box 7.2).

Box 7.2   Legislation and reporting of complaints procedures

Legislating for complaints procedures	Reporting on the operation of complaints procedures
Children Act 1989 (Section 26 (3)) required local authorities to establish procedures to deal with representations, including complaints about 'the discharge by the local authority of any of their functions in respect of services for children in need'.	The Health Service Ombudsman for England (2005), *Making Things Better? A Report on Reform of the NHS Complaints Procedure in England*. London: The Stationery Office.

(Continued)

(Continued)

Legislating for complaints procedures	Reporting on the operation of complaints procedures
Education Act 2002 (Section 29) in Wales requires governing bodies of all maintained schools to establish procedures for dealing with complaints (including from pupils). National Health Service and Community Care Act 1990 gave the Secretary of State power to order Social Services Authorities to establish a complaints procedure.	Department of Health (2007) *Making Experiences Count: A New Approach to Responding to Complaints*. London: The Stationery Office.
	National Audit Office (2008) *Feeding Back? Learning from Complaints Handling in Health and Social Care*. London: The Stationery Office.
Health and Social Care (Community Health and Standards) Act 2003 requires a general complaints procedure to operate.	Healthcare Commission (2009) *Spotlight on Complaints: A Report on Second-stage Complaints about the NHS in England*. London: Healthcare Commission.

A report by the Healthcare Commission in 2009 highlighted the importance of getting 'the customer service aspects of a complaint right at the first time of asking' (2009: 51). It noted that both complaints and feedback from patients were likely become a key mechanism for improving patient care within the NHS and therefore there was a need 'to listen to, and learn from, complaints to ensure that the quality of services meets the increasing expectations of patients and the public' (2009: 51). This is reiterated in the Department of Health guidance published since complaints service for the NHS and complaints about adult social services complaints came under the remit of the Care Quality Commission. This guidance states that by dealing with complaints more effectively, services can get better, 'which will improve things for the people who use them as well as for the staff working in them' (DH, 2009a: 45).

Improving services

Mr Thomas was assessed for a wheelchair following a road traffic accident. He waited a long time for the initial assessment and the service did not explain why there had been such a delay. In the end he hired his own wheelchair. Mr Thomas's social worker talked to him about how to make a complaint and while Mr Thomas was anxious not to 'rock the boat' she supported him to complain to the commissioner of the service and the complaint was investigated. As a result Mr Thomas received compensation and the delivery of his chair was prioritised. Following this complaint, an assessment of other complaints was made, the contracts were reviewed and the service was improved. Mr Thomas and the other people who had complained were given feedback explaining that their actions had resulted in standards being improved.

- The social worker recognised the importance of giving Mr Thomas information about how to make a complaint and the need for him to be supported in that process.
- Case advocacy led to systemic change as the complaints service recognised the need to go beyond the individual issue.
- Services improved as a result of the complaint.

(Adapted from DH, 2009a: 34)

While the impetus for the government guidance to improve complaints processes and enable organisations to learn and improve has its roots in the consumer culture, the mechanisms for accountability within this culture have been described as primarily measures for solving problems rather than any true rebalancing of power relations (Braye and Preston-Shoot, 1999). There is some sense in the consumerist ideology of access, choice, information, representation and redress when service users and carers are viewed as consumers in a market place of provision. However, this culture does not necessarily provide anything more than a few procedural rights for people using health and social services despite the fact that consumerism does attempt to change the balance of power relations between service users and providers.

From service users' perspectives, the mechanisms for making a complaint are far from empowering and can be experienced as a long and difficult process. It can be challenging for complainants to question the explanations given by others, particularly professionals. While holding people to account, disclosure, being given an explanation and having an opportunity for forgiveness through personal interaction with those responsible can be critical elements in resolution (Robinson, 2005). Commentators suggest that while in theory complaints procedures provide the mechanism for independent review, in reality there is not really enough independence for service users to feel confident about the process. Research continues to indicate that complaints procedures are often difficult to access as people often don't know how to complain if they are unhappy or how to suggest an idea for improving things. People who use NHS and social care services have also said they often don't say what they think because they feel inhibited or think services won't listen (Preston-Shoot, 2001; Parliamentary and Health Service Ombudsman, 2012). The results of a recent report have been described as 'stark', since over one third of people who want to complain don't do so. The public lack confidence in the system, processes are long and unwieldy, and lessons from mistakes are not being shared. It is even harder for people who are unwell, vulnerable, or in difficulty.

Even when people do complain, they lack confidence that anything will change as a result. For too many people, the process of complaining is dispiriting and the outcome to their complaint can seem hollow. (Parliamentary and Health Service Ombudsman, 2012: 3)

It is for this reason that the guidance expects organisations to *listen* and *respond* to people making a complaint. However, there are clearly people who need support to manage the mechanisms for complaints and in such instances access to independent advocacy is an option. Complaints processes are never straightforward, and this is recognised in policy and legislation for independent advocacy. The advocacy role of the social worker is to ensure that service users and carers have the information and support that they need. This includes ensuring, if at all possible, that complaints are resolved before they go into any formal mechanisms. If the formal processes are used, then social workers need to know how to contact independent advocates and enable people they are working with to have the support they need.

Complaints and independent advocacy

The statutory right for people to have access to independent advocacy when they make a formal complaint is evidence that it is difficult to make a complaint in relation to health and social care services without support. By its very nature advocacy is oppositional, but often it is about opposing what has gone wrong rather than any particular individual. It has been suggested that a factor which impacts on young people's experiences of complaints procedures, for example, is the managerialism which assumes that services such as advocacy are there to check on the effectiveness of the organisation (Payne, 2000a). What this means for advocates is that if managers behave as though the purpose of advocacy is to check on workers, then those workers are bound to resent and resist the introduction of advocacy in any way. Our own experiences of working as and with independent advocates is that it can take time and patience to explain their role to service providers and ensure clarity about their role. Breaking down such hostility towards independent advocacy is only possible when health and social care professionals understand the role of advocates in relation to service users. If we consider the case of Michael in Chapter 5 we can see that if he did decide to make a complaint then the role of the social worker would have been to ensure that he had the information he needed about how to make the complaint and how to access independent advocacy support in order to do this. Michael's participation in his review was a negative experience, and it would be surprising if he had any faith in achieving a satisfactory outcome from making a complaint. Effective social work advocacy, however, could go some way to reinstating his faith in the process.

The Independent Complaints Advocacy Service (ICAS) supports patients who want to make a complaint about their treatment or care within the NHS. This statutory service was set up by the then Secretary of State (John Reid) in 2003. The original plan was that patient and public involvement in health would be promoted through Patient Forums. ICAS would report trends in complaints to the Forums so that they could take issues to the Trusts in order to improve services. The Forums were dissolved in 2009 when the new complaints regulations (including Adult Social Care) were implemented. Nevertheless, patient and public involvement continues to be emphasised in health and social policy. The introduction of the Patient Advice and Liaison Services (PALS) within the Health Service in 2001 is notable. Evaluation of PALS services demonstrated that they met a clearly expressed need among service users:

- They liked its perceived independence.
- They liked the inside knowledge of PALS staff and their understanding about the NHS.
- PALS could be powerful arbitrators between service users and Trust staff.
- Where PALS worked closely with community and advocacy groups, they facilitated their integration into Trust committees and policy development.

The work of PALS has now become part of Healthwatch, a statutory part of the Care Quality Commission but set up to be independent of it. In the introduction to the Healthwatch transition plan, reference is made to the continuing links the organisation should have with independent advocacy:

> Our plans for Healthwatch will provide people with a single point of contact. They can put people in touch with the right advocacy organisation, or help them find information about the choices they have, they can support people to speak out and they can give those who want to get more involved the opportunity to do so. (Public and Patient Experience and Engagement Team, 2011: 6)

However, it is important to note that although there is statutory advocacy and the aim of Healthwatch is to increase opportunities for service users and carers to have a voice, the role of generic independent advocacy organisations and for formal advocates such as social workers and health care professionals remains key to the success of supporting people to have a voice (see Box 7.3).

Box 7.3   The role of independent advocacy

Disadvantaged groups of people are frequently left out of debate and their ability to exercise choice and control is often lost in an unequal system where the needs of the strongest are heard and the weakest ignored.

The intention of independent advocacy is to see and hear the human side of people and not just the clinical side that looks at what others believe to be the best solution or treatment in any given situation. Some advocacy organisations will be looking to deliver the HNS complaints advocacy service directly, but other advocacy support will be vital to ensure that there is patient engagement with the disadvantaged in our society. Many vulnerable people currently get little choice and control in decision making, and their voices need to be heard so that they receive the services that they need not just as patients but as people.

It has always been the intention of advocacy services to enable each individual to have maximum choice and maximum control in the way their lives are managed. For many with profound learning disabilities, autism, dementia or those experiencing mental ill health, control is not always possible without an advocate to stand by their side and ensure that they are listened to. It is very difficult for them to hold services to account when they rely on those very services for their existence. One only needs to look at the recent account of Winterbourne View in Bristol to see how often services and their regulators fail to keep those very people safe from harm.

The overall purpose of Healthwatch is to give people more say in how care and health services are monitored and delivered. It is vital that advocacy organisations make close links with their local Healthwatch to ensure that the voices of those on the margins of society are included in the provision of Health and social care.

(Advocacy Resource Exchange, 2012)

The need for independent advocacy for children and young people wishing to use formal complaints procedures was highlighted through research and enquiries that identified how many children and young people found complaints procedures difficult to access (Aiers and Kettle, 1998; Wallis and Frost, 1998; Templeton and Kemmis, 1998; Department for Education and Skills, 2003) and hard to use (Children's Rights Development Unit, 1994; Utting, 1997). The need for children and young people to have independent advocacy support was considered a priority following evidence that looked after children and young people in Wales had been unable complain about their abuse (Waterhouse et al., 2000). This resulted in the legislative mandate for advocacy for children and young people making a complaint under the Children Act 1989 (Adoption and Children Act 2002).

Jasper was a twenty-five-year-old young man with learning difficulties who had a melanoma on his eye which required treatment. He had lived with his parents for a number of years but was now about to move into independent accommodation. He told his social worker that he was worried about living on his own because it would mean he would have to go to hospital appointments without the support of his parents. It transpired that while he was able to keep appointments and go to the hospital on his own, Jasper found that when his mother or father were not with him staff were rude, he was not given an explanation about the treatment or why certain things were or were not done. On one occasion he had to wait a long time before he was seen by the consultant. Several people arrived after Jasper but were seen before him. Jasper had not told his parents and said that he was afraid to tell anyone in the hospital as he was worried they would not help him to get better. He explained that there were some very kind staff but they were not always there. Jasper singled out one person as being particularly nasty. His social worker explained that he could make a complaint about the attitude of the staff, the lack of information and poor communication and the fact that he felt he had not been treated with respect. Jasper was initially reluctant, but with his social worker he spoke to PALS, who said they would feed back the information to the senior managers concerned. Jasper was happy with this. However, on his next visit he became very distressed by the attitude of the same member of staff towards him and so he left the hospital without seeing the consultant.

Jasper's social worker suggested that he should make a formal complaint and gave him information about ICAS. She felt that the ICAS service would have the time, knowledge and expertise to support him in this process. A local resolution meeting (LRM) was set up. The independent advocate explained who would be at the meeting and what their roles were before explaining what it would be like. She emphasised to Jasper that it was his meeting and from the Trust's point of view he would be in control of the meeting, explaining that this meant he did not have to talk about things that he did not want to discuss. She also explained that the Trust would expect that by the end of the meeting Jasper would feel satisfied and that as far as possible they would want the issue resolved. The advocate reassured Jasper that his complaint was not unreasonable and that the NHS did invite and welcome complaints so that they could obtain views about the service and information to enable them to improve it. Jasper felt nervous about the meeting.

The advocate went through the response Jasper had received about his complaint and agreed a plan. She emphasised to Jasper that she could say as much or as little as he wished. Jasper explained that he was not always able to say things as clearly as he would like and so he would be happy for the advocate to start the meeting with their plan. She then went through the paperwork with him and agreed the important points that he wanted to highlight as well as clarifying some of the issues and identifying what else might be relevant. She informed Jasper that if he could

(Continued)

(Continued)

explain his experience it would be an opportunity to raise all his concerns. By the time of the meeting Jasper and his advocate were both clear about the key issues that he wanted to discuss and that she would speak for him if he either did not understand something or found it difficult to speak. Jasper wanted to be treated respectfully and to understand what was happening. He also wanted to ensure that what had happened to him did not happen to other people. However, he was concerned about how he would be treated by the people in the meeting as they all worked for the hospital as well. The advocate reminded Jasper that she was independent and reassured him that her role was to ensure that he was not discriminated against either because of his complaint or because he might find himself unable to say what he wanted.

- The advocacy role of the social worker was to inform Jasper of his rights and to ensure that he was treated fairly.
- The social worker listened to Jasper and ensured that his voice was heard.
- The social worker recognised that she might not have the time to support him through the formal process and that the ICAS service had the relevant expertise.
- Ultimately the individual issue raised by Jasper should have a wider systemic impact on how the staff treated patients with a learning difficulty in the future.

It has been argued that there is a problem with the belief that legal access to redress will encourage service users or carers to voice concerns and make organisations accountable for their actions (Preston-Shoot, 2001). Complaints have been described as 'a free form of research' (DH, 2007b: 1) and the advocacy role of social workers, care staff and other professionals is to create a culture that welcomes and uses the opportunities of such research to listen to service users and carers in order to improve services.

Accountability, advocacy and critical reflection

Critical reflective practitioners are always aware of the importance of managing and being accountable for their own social work practice. Thompson notes the importance of being able to take responsibility for our actions 'on the spot' (2010: 250) as opposed to uncritically following instructions. It is a skill to take the time to reflect-in-practice rather than be 'pressed into poor decisions through habitual behaviour or because of, for example, immediate pressures from services users or management' (Pierson, 2011: 434). Equally important is the need to use opportunities made available through routine recording and supervision to take the time to reflect-on-practice in order to learn and develop. Banks (2009) argues that accountability from a critical practice perspective includes the need to pay more attention to routine accountability in everyday situations. She discusses the importance of recording everyday encounters not just because of the need to be able to answer a complaint, explain the course of work to a court or justify a decision to a manager or decision-making meeting but also because, while everyday recordings are likely to be primarily descriptive they are also a tool to

> enable the practitioner to engage in 'reflective practice', to clarify the nature of the situation and her role within it and to reflect on possible courses of action. (Banks, 2009: 34)

Banks uses Fook (2004) to comment that a social worker might well take this a step further in terms of critical reflection through consideration of the political context of social work and possibilities for change. Similarly, using supervision to share thoughts when things have gone wrong or have not gone according to plan provides an opportunity to reflect and learn. While it is natural to want to present one's work in as good a light as possible, this does not then necessarily facilitate learning. However, it is not always possible to find a safe space in the blame culture that currently appears to exist within service provider organisations, so good social work advocates will, on occasions, need self-advocacy skills to ensure that they are able to have a supervisory relationship with a person that feel able to trust:

> Unless workers trust their supervisors and are clear about what information is confidential between the two of them, and what is on record for the organisation, then the potential for reflective learning is diminished. In a climate of blame and defensiveness this can be difficult to achieve, as can any 'safe space' within a team or agency where open dialogue can happen. (Banks, 2009: 35)

The following case example, taken from an analysis by Lymbery and Butler (2004), demonstrates how workers used reflection-in-action to:

- look behind the facts presented to them;
- question certain information;
- share hunches and ideas with colleagues;
- lobby for action from their agency. (Badham and Eadie, 2004: 97)

Reflection in Action

In 1992 the Children's Resource Project was set up. This was a consortium of eleven local authorities across Yorkshire and the North East of England which was managed by The Children's Society, a large national NGO for children and young people. Funding for the project is therefore through statutory agencies, although it is managed by a voluntary agency with a mission to promote children's rights while also providing specialist services. It has a focus on justice and being a force for

CASE EXAMPLE

(Continued)

(Continued)

change. Workers are therefore part of a culture where critical reflection-on-practice underpins their work with an understanding that inequalities and discrimination are not ignored but are recorded with managers.

As a result of supporting young people to make a formal complaint, workers at the Children's Resource Centre began to reflect on the fact that young people living in residential care were more aware of the local authority complaints procedure than young people living in foster care. Young people living in residential care also appeared to be more able to access the complaints system. Through discussions with colleagues it was then possible to make connections and build up a truer representation of the situation: that most complaints were from young people in residential care, who were white, older and able-bodied. They also noted that there were time delays that went over the statutory 28 days stated in the legislation (Children Act 1989). Furthermore, when senior local authority officers responded to complaints they were on an individual basis with little effort made to address the wider systemic issues raised. Collectively it was therefore possible for workers to assess what was happening and find ways to instigate change. In an open organisation committed to values with a justice focus, the culture will enable workers to feel sufficiently supported and confident to voice their fears to managers knowing that this will be taken up by the organisation. In this instance the concerns were taken up by the organisation and the Children's Society funded research that examined five of the local authorities working with the project over five months in 1996–97.

- If the workers had been 'accommodating to the prevailing agency culture' (Badham and Eadie, 2004: 68) they would have missed the wider effects of the issues raised, choosing just to follow procedure.
- As it was, they were reflective practitioners who would therefore consider not just the complaint but the young person's experience of the process.
- The reflective process enabled the advocates to use their combined knowledge to influence systemic change.

Commentary

Accountability to service users and carers is the basis for evaluating practice. A tool for doing this is to make use of representations and complaints procedures, which are also a mechanism for service users and carers to improve the services they receive. However, research has consistently identified failings in the systems of complaints and service users, which means that service users and carers find it difficult to have a voice or make an impact on the delivery of services. In 2005 the 'Making Things Better' report (Health Service Ombudsman for England, 2005) found that people using NHS services found it hard to get a satisfactory response to a complaint and that the NHS did not appear to learn lessons from complaints. A government consultation in 2007 (DH, 2007b) stated that complaints were experienced as inflexible and were not meeting the needs of complainants. This was followed by a National Audit Office report on health and social care services in 2008, where people found that processes for making a complaint were too complex and took too long. A Healthcare Commission Review in 2009 found that a lot of complaints actually related to basic elements of good health care: that is, effective communication with service users, staff attitudes, record keeping, privacy and dignity. There were also problems with how complaints were handled in 19 per cent of cases. Such evidence is worrying reading for anyone who is committed to empowering services users and carers and ensuring that they are involved in decision making. It takes courage to make a complaint, particularly for people who are in receipt of services and dependent on them. When their courage fails them, for whatever reason, then the role of the advocate is even more important.

It is important to remember, though, that social workers also have a key role to play in raising matters of concern. Accountability to service users goes beyond making complaints procedures accessible and being open to change. It also means that social workers have to be vigilant in scrutinising their own organisations. Unfortunately, just as service users and carers find it difficult to make a complaint, social workers also find it difficult to challenge poor practice. Part of the social work advocacy role is to support vulnerable people who do not have a voice, which means challenging bad practice when service users are unable to do this for themselves. Seeing and hearing about bad practice inevitably means that a social worker is in a position to 'whistle-blow', which is probably the most important advocacy role a social worker has:

> Whistle blowing and accountability, in the annals of social work training and education, are located around the tradition of advocacy. (Cox, 1998: 189)

In an organisation where there is a culture of learning and where there is a genuine commitment to improving services, staff will be supported to act as whistle-blowers and highlight ineffective management or bad practice within their own agencies. The Waterhouse Report (2000) highlighted the importance of enabling staff to raise matters of concern, noting that staff should be able to do this without worrying about any possible retaliation from colleagues or managers. However, the fact remains that most social services staff are afraid of the consequences of whistle-blowing (GSCC, 2008). For social workers and the people they are working for, service users and carers, a strong culture of advocacy is required to ensure that services are constantly evaluated and improved. Achieving that accountability requires change, and changing organisational cultures and structures is seldom a pain-free experience. Traditional power relations become unsettled by change and disturb the existing order (Charnley et al., 2009: 206). Reclaiming social work advocacy provides an opportunity for social workers, whose primary accountability is to the service users and carers for whom they are providing a service, to examine their role as professionals. Focusing on accountability to service users and carers does not negate accountability to employers, rather it enables employers to be confident that the services they provide are person-centred and of the highest possible standard.

Summary

- Organisations that are open to listening to service users and carers will ensure that complaints are listened to in order to improve services.
- Social workers have multiple accountabilities but their principal accountability is to service users and carers.
- Consumerism means that systems for complaints are seen as mechanisms to enable service users and carers to be active participants within the provision and delivery of services.
- Being accountable for our actions requires ongoing critical reflection within supportive agency structures.
- Whistle-blowing is situated within the advocacy role.

Discussion questions

1. What do you identify as your primary accountability and why?
2. How do you and how does your organisation promote feedback and complaints from service users?
3. Do you know what is done with that feedback and how service users are informed that their representation has made a difference?
4. How would you describe the culture of your organisation in terms of 'listening, hearing, responding'?

Further reading

Banks, S. (2009) 'Professional values and accountabilities', in R. Adams, L. Dominelli and M. Payne (eds), *Critical Practice in Social Work* (Second Edition). Basingstoke: Palgrave Macmillan.

Department of Health (2009) *Listening, Responding, Improving: A Guide to Better Customer Care*. London: Department of Health.

Hunt, G. (ed.) (1998) *Whistle-blowing in the Social Services*. London: Arnold.

Preston-Shoot, M. (2001) 'A triumph of hope over experience? Modernising accountability: the case of complaints procedures in community care', *Social Policy and Administration*, 35 (6): 701–715.

8

Independent Advocacy

Overview

- History of independent advocacy
- Legal policy mandates for independent advocacy
- The place of independent advocacy in social work practice
- Commentary
- Summary
- Discussion questions

Within the provision of social services an independent advocate ensures that the wishes and feelings of service users and carers are taken into account in relation to decision making and the provision of services and that their rights are protected. The Welsh Assembly Government categorisation of advocacy recognises that there are occasions when both informal and formal advocates are unable to support the people they are working with. In such instances independent or professional advocates have a role. Independent advocates are trained and either paid people or volunteers who are qualified to act as advocates because they have the knowledge and skills to enable them to be effective (Welsh Assembly Government, 2009).

An independent advocate therefore has a specific remit and clearly defined role that differs from the generic advocacy undertaken by professionals or other key adults in the lives of service users. They also have the training and skills to be able to navigate the systems and are free from any conflicts of interest. The role of the independent advocate as a specialist is now clearly established within the provision of services and in policy and legislation for some specific service user groups in particular circumstances. A key role for social workers is to understand when they are unable to advocate for a person they are working with and how to link them to a relevant independent advocacy service when they are unable to act as advocates. This chapter will therefore consider how independent advocacy has become established and its place in social work practice.

History of independent advocacy

While independent advocacy for different service user groups has developed in various ways, generally the growth of independent advocacy services has been informed by the experiences of adult service users through movements which began during the 1960s. Disabled people and survivors of the mental health system are generally acknowledged to be the forerunners of independent advocacy as they found ways to make their voices heard about experiences of poor service provision, discrimination and social inequality. However, the emergence of citizen advocacy in the 1960s is often identified as the starting point for the range of independent advocacy services that exist today for people in different circumstances (see Box 8.1).

Citizen advocacy was developed by Wolf Wolfensberger following a conference of the United Cerebral Palsy Association in the USA in1966. At this conference parents expressed concerns about their children and what would happen to them once their parents were no longer there to support them. Citizen advocacy subsequently developed to support people who are unable to advocate for themselves or who require specific support in order to advocate for themselves. An Advocacy Alliance was formed in 1971, which developed citizen advocacy in the UK. This comprised five mental health charities (MIND, MENCAP, The Spastic Society (changed to 'Scope' in 1994), One-to-One and the Leonard Cheshire Foundation).

Box 8.1   Citizen advocacy

Citizen advocacy essentially involves a one-to-one relationship between a volunteer advocate who is partnered with an individual who is vulnerable and at risk of exclusion and who will therefore find it difficult to challenge professional systems. (Smith and Ing, 1996)

Citizen advocacy is about individual active citizenship, where an ordinary member of the community makes a commitment to the rights of another who is disadvantaged and/or socially excluded (CAIT, 2002: 1).

As such it has been described as 'informal facilitative advocacy' (CAIT, 2002: 1), which is 'different from but complimentary to other forms of advocacy' (2002: 2).

Over the past 50 years there have been many changes in the way that citizen advocates work. This is partly due to the fact that the advocacy task for citizen advocates is becoming more complex. Working with social work managers, for example, in order to challenge health care provision for young disabled people in further education is both a time-consuming and a skilled task. *Valuing People* (Department of Health, 2001b) states that advocacy can transform the lives of people with learning disabilities. As with policy documents for other marginalised groups of people, *Valuing People* effectively validates both citizen and self-advocacy. Citizen advocacy clearly began as an individual form of case advocacy. However, as advocacy services have gathered information about the lives of people with learning difficulties and advocates have developed the knowledge and skills to negotiate with service providers, citizen advocacy services now use opportunities to contribute to policy and therefore have also developed as a systemic approach (Eustace, 2002).

The emergence of the self-advocacy movement for people with learning difficulties also began in the 1960s. Self-advocacy groups initially began in Sweden following a meeting of a parent's organisation in 1968. In the UK the self-advocacy organisation People First was set up by service users and their supporters in 1984. This was the first organised self-advocacy group in the UK, although people with learning difficulties living in long-stay institutions had tried to advocate for their rights long before this (Buchanan and Walmsley, 2006; Traustadottir, 2006). Promoting self-advocacy is seen by many as the ultimate aim for all advocates, whether informal, formal or professional (Brandon, 1995). Furthermore, while it began as a collective way for people with learning difficulties to have their voices heard, it is now recognised as a way of working with any individuals and groups of people who find it difficult to have a voice and be heard in decision making. Effective self-advocacy is an empowering process. However, the ability to advocate for oneself inevitably depends on the particular individual circumstances of a person at a given moment in time, and the ability for people to advocate for themselves may well fluctuate

By the 1980s mental health service users, survivors and their allies in the UK, Canada and Holland had started to introduce advocacy into mental health settings. The advocates were usually volunteers with an understanding of the systems and issues derived from their own experiences as users of mental health services; as such they could be identified as peer advocates. The development of patients' councils was also significant at this point. Built on a successful Dutch model, Patients' Councils brought patients together with hospital managers, planners, policy makers and others to highlight and address concerns. In the UK, patients' councils were developed in acute psychiatric settings such as Ashworth, Broadmoor and Rampton high security hospitals.

Enquiries exposing abuse have had an impact on the understanding of both service providers and policy makers of the need for service users to have access to advocacy support to enable them to have a voice and to be heard. Two notable enquiries are the Blom-Cooper Inquiry into the abuse of patients at Ashworth Hospital (Blom-Cooper, 1992) and the Waterhouse Report (2000) into the abuse of children living away from home in Wales.

The Blom-Cooper Inquiry reported on the systematic abuse of patients at Ashworth Hospital and recommendations in his report included the need to set up a patients' advocacy service which had to be properly resourced, be independent and be staffed by advocates who were adequately trained. The Ashworth Citizen's Advice Bureau Patients Advocacy Service was launched in 1994 which, for its time, was a ground-breaking project. An interesting description of the resources available to this project demonstrates the importance of this service. Staffing consisted of a service manager, deputy, three full-time advocates, two part-time administrators and an office 'resplendent with designer fittings and a set-up budget that was the envy of the voluntary sector' (Bamber, 2007: 83). In today's economic climate such resources are certainly the envy of many independent advocacy services which are primarily located within the voluntary sector.

The Waterhouse Report (2000) highlighted the deficiencies of systems for looking after children and young people who lived away from home. This emphasised the importance of listening to the voices of looked after children and young people. The Report recommended that children making a complaint should have access to advocacy. Another report on safeguards for children in the NHS made the same recommendation (Carlile, 2002). Prior to this, Utting (1997) had reviewed safeguards for children living away from home and concluded that advocacy services were necessary for children and young people wishing to use formal complaints procedures. He endorsed and called for the promotion of collective advocacy or 'in-care' groups run for and by young people in the care system. Utting envisaged that young people in local authority care should have a central role in informing the development of policy and practice. He felt that this could be achieved through the provision of children's rights and advocacy services as well as through the in-care groups. As a result of these reports and enquiries, a number of initiatives in England and Wales led to the development of independent children's advocacy services in both countries.

Finally, it is important to note that the development of service user movements as a reaction to their negative experiences of services is also significant in the development of independent advocacy. During the 1980s, service user groups started to identify and articulate their experiences of using services which had failed to adequately meet their needs. Service users groups were angry about being labelled and marginalised as a consequence of being service users. They made links between these experiences and broader patterns of inequality and discrimination in society. This led to the 'emergence of new participants in social policy: service users and their movements' (Beresford, 2002: 496). Dalrymple and Oliver (2008) note that this analysis indicates why people who experience the effects of social inequality may need someone to speak (act) on their behalf (either informal, formal or professional advocates) or support them to feel able to advocate for themselves (self-advocacy). Independent advocacy has therefore evolved as a response to these experiences to challenge inequality, discrimination and oppression, and through that process to adjust the power relations between service users and providers. The work of service user movements and of carers in campaigning for their right to have a voice has had an impact on both practice and on the process of theory building. It represents the development of transformative practice (Beresford and Croft, 2004) that recognises service users as citizens rather than just recipients of services (Lister, 1998). This approach to service user involvement is a democratic approach and has also been described as a political approach to involvement (Beresford, 2005) because it is focussed on directly promoting change:

> The goals will thus reside in the wider avenues of citizenship in which oppression and exclusion are experienced. They will be chosen by people themselves, rather than enacting professional agendas for meeting need. (Braye, 2000: 19)

However, Beresford and Croft (2004) warn of the dangers of overstating the achievements of service user movements – the impact on user/professional power relations has been limited, for example. Nevertheless, they also observe that they should they have had a significant impact through campaigning for changes in policy and the provision of health and social care services. In particular, it is now recognised in legislation for some service user groups and in policy for many others that access to independent advocacy support needs to be promoted in the range of different situations where decisions are made concerning the lives of individual service users.

Legal and policy mandates for independent advocacy

From the early pioneering work independent advocacy has developed in various ways. Recognition that people find it difficult to complain about services led to the first legal mandates for advocacy support in relation to looked after children and young people making a complaint or representation about their care (Children and Adoption Act 2002) and to adults making a complaint about services (Health Service Ombudsman for England, 2005) as we discussed in Chapter 7. Other groups of people advocacy now have a right to independent advocacy support in certain situations when using mental health services. The Mental Capacity Act 2005 introduced the role of the Independent Mental Capacity Advocate (IMCA) in England and Wales for people who lack capacity. This was introduced as part of a framework of safeguards in relation to decision making where someone lacks the capacity to make decisions themselves. The Act was introduced following concerns expressed about the fact that very little account was taken of the voices of adults who lack capacity in decisions about their care and treatment. Part of the impetus for this legislation was the Bournewood case, which concerned a 49-year-old man with learning difficulties who had been detained in hospital illegally, which highlighted the lack of procedural safeguards for patients who have limited long-term capacity. The Act is an important piece of legislation as it strengthens and protects the rights of people who lack capacity as well as those who want to plan for their future should they lack capacity at some point in their lives.

There are four key principles underpinning the Mental Capacity Act that help understand the advocacy role (see Box 8.2). The act recognises that the majority of people can make many of their own day-to-day decisions and decisions relating to care, however limited their capacity is overall. They may lack capacity with respect to complex decisions for such matters as finance, for example. This means that no one can be said to lack capacity on the basis of a diagnosis or medical condition (such as dementia, for example). The key for all professionals working with people who may lack capacity for a particular decision is to make every effort to communicate and engage the person in decision making.

Box 8.2   Key principles of the Mental Capacity Act 2005

- A person must be assumed to have capacity unless it is established that he lacks capacity.
- A person is not to be treated as unable to make a decision unless all practicable steps to help him to do so have been taken.
- A person is not to be treated as unable to make a decision merely because he makes an unwise decision.
- An act done, or a decision made under this Act for, or on behalf of a person who lacks capacity, must be done, or made in his best interests.
- Before the act is done, or the decision made, regard must be had to whether the purpose for which it is needed can be as effectively achieved in a way that is less restrictive of the person's rights and freedom of action.

The professionals who have to make decisions with respect to the lives of service users who lack capacity (decision makers) have to consult with close relatives, friends or other people who are interested in the welfare of the person, their best interests, their wishes, feelings, beliefs and values with respect to any proposed action. If a person has no one who is able or willing to represent them, or the decision makers cannot contact someone who is appropriate, then the IMCA will represent that person and provide a report for the decision maker. An IMCA must or may be involved when:

- decisions are being made about serious medical treatment, or a move to new accommodation;
- there are adult safeguarding measures being put in place to protect a vulnerable adult;
- there are Deprivation of Liberty Assessments (DOLS) where the person who lacks capacity has no representative, there is a representative but they need support, or the representative is not immediately available.

It is important for social workers to understand the advocacy role of IMCAs as it is slightly different from most other advocacy roles. Enabling the user's service voice to be heard in decision making is still the primary role of an IMCA – ensuring that the views, feelings, wishes, beliefs and values (DH and Office of Public Guardian, 2009) of that person are taken into account in the decision making. However, there is also an investigative role associated with this process, as the IMCA has to assess the situation and find out as much as they can about the views of the service user which, if the person lacks capacity, involves talking with anyone who knows that person well and looking at records. Key to the work of IMCAs is recognition that people often have 'fluctuating capacity' and so, although the role of the IMCA is to assess what the views of the service user were likely to have been, this in part will be informed by what the service user themselves communicate to the IMCA. This means that the role of the IMCA will have elements of instructed advocacy, where the person lacking capacity has been able to convey their wishes and feelings and what is known as 'non-instructed advocacy' (DH and Office of Public Guardian, 2009: 31).

Non-instructed advocacy is a rights-based approach where the advocate will try to represent the views of a service user through asking questions on their behalf about the action that is proposed and look at what options and choices are available. The IMCA also has to ascertain how the decision maker has tried to involve the service user in the planning process in relation to any proposed treatment or change of accommodation. Finally, there is an audit role for the IMCA – which means ensuring that the decision being made is consistent with the principles of the Mental Capacity Act and taken with due regard for the best interest of the service user. No other advocacy role takes a best interest perspective, and it is important that social workers understand this concept. In all other advocacy situations an independent advocate will only be ensuring that the wishes and feelings of the service user are heard and taken into account. Independent advocates never put their own views or what they may feel is in the best interest of the service user. This is the role of other professionals. Indeed, the whole *raison d'être* for independent advocacy is to challenge the view that professionals can make a decision in the 'best interest' of a service user without actually involving that person in the process. Generally, when social workers feel unable to advocate for a service user it is because they have a view about what is in that person's best interest. This is when the social worker who is supported by a culture of advocacy will ensure that the person concerned has access to independent advocacy. However, while the concept of 'best interest' is clearly in the framework of IMCA practice, it is also important to note that their role is primarily rights-based and person-centred.

The role of IMCA

Adam is a 90-year-old man who has lived on his own, in a bungalow that he owns, since his wife died ten years ago. He does not go out and can get muddled at times. Adam has a great sense of humour and enjoys visits about once a month from an old school friend. He was admitted to hospital having been found by a neighbour on the floor in his bathroom suffering from hypothermia. He has been in hospital for two

(Continued)

CASE EXAMPLE

(Continued)

weeks and is now medically fit for discharge. Janine, the social worker and decision maker, says that Adam does not have family or friends who she feels are appropriate to consult. His school friend lives in sheltered accommodation in the next town and is transported to see Adam by a carer. He has a godson who lives abroad but only sends cards for his birthday and at Christmas. An IMCA has therefore become involved because a decision needs to be made about where he goes from hospital. Adam is very independent and wants to go home. He feels that he is able to live at home on his own, which is what he wants to do. He also has neighbours who he trusts and who help him in the house and take him shopping once a week. However, there have been concerns about possible financial abuse by the neighbours following concerns expressed by both the carers agency who visited each morning and his old friend who had told Adam's carer that he did not like the fact that the neighbours looked at his mail without asking him and seemed to be dealing with all his finances. As a result the social worker had started the Safeguarding of Adults process to investigate the situation. The social worker wanted Adam to go to convalescence before returning home. However, Adam was very clear about wanting to return home. The IMCA spoke to Adam, the social worker, staff on the ward, the company who had provided support in the mornings, Adam's friend and his carer and his own GP. The IMCA concluded that it was in Adam's best interests to return home with a significant package of care. Together with actions taken as a result of the Safeguarding Adults Case Conference (which identified the need for locks to be changed on the bungalow and putting in place safeguards to stop the neighbours from being able to withdraw money from his account), the IMCA felt that Adam would be safe in terms of his needs during the day and protected from abuse by his neighbours or other people.

Independent Mental Health Advocates (IMHA) became available for patients who are subject to some elements of the Mental Health Act 1983 when the Mental Health Act 2007 was implemented in 2009. People in England who are subject to compulsory treatment or supervisory community treatment and people who are considering certain types of treatment (for example, neuro-surgery or electro convulsive treatment for young people under the age of eighteen) are entitled to an IMHA. The IMHA has a less specific role than the IMCA and it is an instructed form of advocacy. Access to independent advocacy became a legal right as a response to a campaign to empower and protect people using mental health services. IMHAs therefore help people to understand the Mental Health Act and its impact on them, help them to apply to a tribunal to review their treatment, challenge treatment decisions or make a complaint and support them to make a complaint. Often they support patients on ward rounds and make sure that the professionals involved explain what the treatments are and help them to think about available options, so that they are involved in the decision making about their care. In Wales the Mental Health (Wales) Measure 2010 has a wider remit than the English legislation, so that people who are detained on a short-term basis and those who are receiving treatment on a voluntary or informal basis are also entitled to support from an IMHA.

In Scotland the right for people to have access to independent advocacy occurred with reforms through the Mental Health (Care and Treatment) (Scotland) Act 2003:

Every person with a mental disorder shall have a right of access to independent advocacy; and accordingly it is the duty of

(a)   each local authority, in collaboration with the (or each) relevant health board; and

(b)   each health board, in collaboration with the (or each) relevant local authority,

to secure the availability, to persons in its area who have a mental disorder, of independent advocacy services and to take appropriate steps to ensure that those persons have the opportunity of making use of those services. (Section 259(1))

Interestingly, in Scotland a number of professionals have a duty to advise and inform people about advocacy both under the 2003 Act and in other situations (see Box 8.3).

Box 8.3   Examples of duties to inform people about advocacy in Scotland

Mental Health (Care and Treatment) (Scotland) Act 2003	Mental health officers must advise patients being subjected to short-term detention of their right to advocacy and also must assist the person to access an advocacy service. Hospital managers have a responsibility to ensure people subject to civil or criminal orders receive information about advocacy and are given help when accessing it.
Adult Support and Protection (Scotland Act) 2007	Local authority staff have a duty too tell vulnerable adults about advocacy and how it might be able to help them, and how to contact their local advocacy organisation.
Education (Additional Support for Learning) (Scotland) Act 2009	Local authorities have a duty to tell parents about independent advocacy.
The Patient Rights (Scotland) Act 2011	Health boards have a duty to tell patients about advocacy and how to contact their local advocacy organisation.

In Northern Ireland details about a new statutory right to independent advocacy are still being developed. However, the proposal is to introduce mental capacity legislation.

From social work advocacy to independent advocacy

Johann (age forty) has a diagnosis of schizophrenia and having spent many years in institutional care, he successfully lived in the community for the last ten years supported by the community mental health team. A year ago he met Suzanne, who is also supported by the community mental health team, and they moved in to live together two months ago. He visited his social worker, Harry, in the office each week. However, recently he failed to arrive at the usual time. Harry phoned the flat and Suzanne told him that Johann had been in bed for the last few days and would not speak to her. Harry visited Johann who agreed that it would be best if he was admitted to hospital. When Harry next spoke with Johann on the ward it became apparent that he was unhappy living with Suzanne, who appeared to put demands on him that he could not manage. Harry asked Johann if he wanted to return to the flat, but Harry said that he did not know. However, he had told the consultant that he would be returning home. After discussing the situation together, Johann told Harry that he would prefer to live on his own. Harry explained to Johann that he would need to tell this to the consultant. Johann felt that he could not do this, but Harry then offered to support him. They met the consultant together and Harry explained that Johann had something that he wanted to tell him. Johann told that doctor that he thought Suzanne was detrimental to his health. The consultant talked to him about this decision and agreed that he should not return to the flat. Johann was amazed that someone had listened to him for the first time in his life and told Harry that it made him feel good. From that point Johann started to work towards moving back to live on his own. Together Harry and Johann completed an application for housing. Letters were sent to Harry but he would wait for their weekly meeting to open them with Johann. Eventually Johann was ready to move into his new home, but Harry had to move to a new office at that point and so he contacted a local advocacy service and they met together a few times before Harry left.

- Harry supported Johann to use self-advocacy skills when talking to the consultant.
- Harry advocated for Johann with respect to the housing.
- Harry contacted an independent advocate to ensure that Johann had ongoing advocacy support.

The place of independent advocacy in social work practice

The notion of independence is, as we have seen, a principle of advocacy services recognised in the *Advocacy Charter* (Advocacy Across London, 2002) and *Code of*

Practice (Action for Advocacy, 2006) and standard six of the *National Standards for the Provision of Children's Advocacy Services*:

> The advocacy service is as far as possible, funded and managed in a way that ensures independence from the commissioning body, so that children and young people have confidence that their advocates will act for them and are free from any conflicts of interest. (DH, 2003; Welsh Assembly Government, 2003)

We have noted the potential for independent advocacy to be a tool that can be used to challenge the differential power relations experienced in relationships between users and providers of services. Inevitably, therefore, advocates and service users have considered independence from service providers to be an important principle for successful advocacy practice if people are to be supported to find their voice within the systems.

A guide by the Scottish Independent Advocacy Alliance (SIAA, 2010) for commissioners of independent advocacy services explores the power relations that exist in the provision of services, recognising that professionals are in a powerful position because they are often expected to make judgements that impact on the lives of service users and they control resources. Independent advocates are in a position to challenge the power relations through promoting the right's of service users to be involved in decision making and to have their views valued and listened to with equal importance, however they are expressed (Martin and Franklin, 2010). This does not make advocates better people, rather it means that 'they just stand in a different place and see things from a different perspective' (SIAA, 2010: 21). Different power relations can sometimes make it difficult for service users to participate in decision making because of the service user/social worker power relations and because of the structural power of service providers. This may also make it difficult to share particular issues with a social worker. For service users and carers, the level of independence and distance from the local authority offered by advocates is crucial and will influence how far they feel able to trust and relate to an advocate (Chase, 2008; Crowley and Pithouse, 2008; Oliver and Dalrymple, 2008; Morgan, 2008).

Once of the challenges for advocacy providers, however, is in maintaining their independence. Advocacy services may be delivered by local or national NGOs or directly through local government. Local authorities usually commission advocacy using service-level agreements, which, it has been argued, effectively locates advocacy within service delivery systems despite attempts at creating independence from them. While it is important to actively locate advocacy within services, there is a difficulty that once established they may become integrated into the system they are set up to challenge (Goodley, 2000; Payne, 2000a). Funding for independent advocacy contributes to this problem. While funding for independent advocacy services may be a mix of various sources (local authorities, other statutory sources and NGOs or a combination of funding from a local authority with contribution from an NGO), research of advocacy services for children and young people in England (Oliver, 2008) found that over half of the advocacy services received, all of their funding came from the host local authority. Maintaining independence from that authority in such situations has the potential to be problematic, and for advocacy providers, dependence on funding from local authorities can in reality mean that there is little or no independence (Pithouse and Crowley, 2008). However, Oliver and Sapey (2006) also found that, while some local authorities would view advocacy services as part of their service provision for children and young people, others appeared to be able to protect the independence of advocacy service providers, clearly setting out role and organisational boundaries. Nevertheless, these could be enhanced or constrained by variables such as location of the office, management and supervision arrangements and the culture of participation within the local authority.

The difficulty is exacerbated to some extent by the fact that there are a number of similarities between independent advocacy and social work intervention. Part of the impetus for this book has been to acknowledge the social work advocacy role and highlight how social work intervention incorporates knowledge, skills and values relating to advocacy. Wilks notes that there are common features between the independent advocacy and social work, with many tasks of an independent advocate being 'far from inconsistent with a social work role' (2012: 35). It is important, though, for both independent advocates and social workers to be aware that advocates are *not* alternative social workers. Unfortunately, it may be the case on occasions that for some reason a social worker has not had the time or resources to provide in-depth support. Wilks uses the example of a 35-year-old single parent with a learning difficulty, Trina, who was referred to an advocacy service for people with learning difficulties at the point when social services became involved because of concerns expressed by the school about her ten-year-old son. The independent advocate, Carolyn, was able to support Trina using a range of strategies which brought together formal instrumental advocacy and emotional support and included:

- representation;
- working with Trina to enable her to understand correspondence in order that she could deal with issues herself if they were raised in letters;
- linking Trina into other networks of care and support (which Wilks points out could loosely be termed brokerage);
- working from an empowerment perspective in all her work with Trina.

There was another element to the work here though, which involved supporting Trina to address problems that she had with alcohol that had been the cause of some of her problems. How far this is the role of an independent advocate is debateable. The issue here is that the role of an independent advocate is to be *instructed* by the service user. If Trina asked Carolyn to help her to access a service to help her to manage her alcohol dependency, then this would be a legitimate advocacy role. However, in this instance Carolyn persuaded Trina to see her GP so that she could be referred to a community-based detox programme. The question to be explored is how far this was Carolyn's role as an advocate. Many independent advocates will be in a position that is never afforded a busy statutory social worker – they will have developed a relationship with the service user, who in turn trusts the advocate, who has the time to focus on what it is that the service user really wants and can support them to articulate their wishes and feelings as a result of this. Furthermore, it is possible that Trina did say to Carolyn that she wanted to address her alcohol problems, in which case it could be that Carolyn was signposting her to the right agency, which is not incongruent with the advocacy role.

Commentary

The student reflection below indicates the complexity of social work advocacy and the difficulties in deciding when it is a tricky, if not impossible task to take on the advocacy role, however well intentioned:

> Prior to the meeting ... I asked if the young person would be present. This was met with incredulity and illustrated to me the complex issues that are raised when a child comes into contact with several organizations ... I would have to take on the role of advocate for him in what Jenkins (1995) terms 'passive advocacy' whereby I would speak on his behalf. This turned out to be more complicated than I had imagined as I also wanted to offer my views ... in retrospect I should have contacted the local advocacy service for young people. (Student social worker discussion with one of the authors, 2010)

When independent advocacy services initially became established in the UK they were primarily run by NGOs, and there was no statutory advocacy available. The newly developing services were welcomed and, in relation to advocacy services for children and young people, they were described as 'one of the most beneficial developments of the last decade' (Utting, 1997: 111). However, the challenges facing the development of advocacy as the jigsaw of informal, formal and independent/professional advocacy has emerged means that the process of developing a culture of advocacy within services is far from straightforward. When independent advocacy services were in the early stages of their development, Jenkins (1995) argued that a real advocacy movement for children and young people's rights in the UK needed **PRAISE: P**olitical will; **R**esources financial, human and material; **A**gencies with a power base; **I**nvestment in information and education; **S**upport networks and **E**ngagement with key issues.

Jenkins' model provides a useful framework to consider the future of advocacy in the UK. The *Political will* of the governments in all four nations of the UK to recognise the need for some vulnerable groups of people who use services to have access to independent advocacy is evident in the development of statutory advocacy and locally by local authorities who are prepared to commission advocacy services to support some service users. Resources, however, pose a problem and the paradox here is that recent policies in the UK governments have led to large spending cuts in services, both in statutory and voluntary sector provision. While an understanding that some people should continue to have a strong independent advocate to champion their interests and views and to promote their rights is still current within government rhetoric, cuts in public and voluntary sector funding will make it difficult for many small NGOs to survive. This in turn will mean that *Agencies* providing advocacy will find it difficult to maintain a power base that has the capacity to promote the rights of children and young people in any meaningful way. Nevertheless, there is recognition in all four nations of the UK of the need for independent statutory advocacy with a specific remit to promote the rights and interests of some groups of people. A number of larger national advocacy organisations and NGOs that provide advocacy services have a commitment to ensuring that advocacy remains firmly on the agenda. This is promoted by National Advocacy Consortia, National Standards for Advocacy Services, Quality Performance Marks and Codes of Practice. The difficulty here is that *Investment* in information and education also requires resources. However, there is *Support* within the advocacy sector through the consortia and other overarching organisations that act as a resource and support agencies providing independent advocacy. Support is also provided through the National Advocacy Qualification, which is designed to provide a standard level of advocacy practice. Finally, *Engagement* with key issues is the area that is most significant in terms of promoting the rights of service users to have a voice and participate in decision making. Advocacy has its roots within the NGOs and the service user movement. Both have a history of promoting equality, fairness and social justice. While a culture of advocacy and participation does exist within services, the role of social workers together with independent advocates, advocacy organisations and service user movements is to ensure that this culture remains and becomes stronger as a foundation for the delivery of services in the future.

Summary

- Independent advocacy services have developed as people who use services and their carers have fought for a voice in the decision making that affects their lives.
- There is now recognition that some people should have the right of access to independent advocacy in particular situations, and this is now written into legislation.
- There is a need for social workers to fully understand their role and when they cannot act as advocates for the people they are working with. This requires a sound knowledge and understanding about the independent advocacy sector.
- Social workers need to consider how to promote a culture of advocacy in partnership with advocacy organisations.

Discussion questions

1 What do you know about the advocacy services that are available in your area? Do you understand who they are able to support and how they are organised?
2 Think about a dilemma where your views may be conflicting with the person you are working with. Assess whether an independent advocate would be able to support the service users.
3 Consider your advocacy role and identify how you can develop your role as a formal advocate.

Further reading

Action for Advocacy (2010) *A Manifesto for Independent Advocacy in England and Wales*. London: A4A.

Forbat, L. and Atkinson, D. (2005) 'Advocacy in practice: the troubled position of advocates in adult services', *British Journal of Social Work*, 35 (3): 321–55.

Royal College of Psychiatry (2012) *Independent Advocacy for People with a Mental Disorder. CR171*. London: Royal College of Psychiatry.

SCIE (2009) *At a Glance 12. Personalisation Briefing: Implications for Advocacy Workers*. London: SCIE.

SIAA (2010) *Independent Advocacy: A Guide for Commissioners*. Edinburgh: Scottish Independent Advocacy Alliance.

9

Conclusion: Developing a Culture of Advocacy

Overview

- Good practice in social work advocacy
- Values and social work advocacy
- Advocacy and anti-oppressive practice
- Working with independent advocates
- Commentary
- Summary
- Discussion questions

Good practice in social work advocacy

A culture of advocacy, in its broadest sense, can be described as the behaviours, beliefs and values that inform social workers as advocates and other professionals who recognise advocacy as part of their role. It could be described as a 'way of professional life' for social workers, where the principles of advocacy are imbued in all aspects of their practice. Furthermore, social workers who practice in this way are able to pass on their knowledge and understanding about social work advocacy to newly qualified practitioners so that the culture becomes embedded within everyday practice. In this way a cumulative repository of knowledge and experiences is developed that has an impact on the beliefs, values and attitudes of everyone they work with – in effect institutionalising social work advocacy within the profession. We have argued elsewhere (Boylan and Dalrymple, 2009) that developing a culture of advocacy requires the space for dialogue between the communities of independent advocates and social workers who use advocacy skills in their work. This requires social workers to be familiar with the definitions, knowledge and practice of advocacy, as well as understanding when service users and carers will need support from independent advocates.

The advocacy principles introduced in Chapter 1 are fundamental to effective advocacy practice and are synonymous with traditional social work values. For social workers and for advocates there will always be contradictory and competing values. For example, a social worker's advocacy values may well conflict with the values of their agency and the values of other professionals they are working with. Nevertheless, we argue that practice that is underpinned by the four principles of advocacy ensures that social workers maintain a determination to ensure that the voices of people they are working with are listened to, heard and responded to and that their rights are respected.

The analysis in this chapter will consider specifically the inter-relationship between social work values and advocacy values linking to social justice, challenging oppression and empowerment practice. We will also discuss the capacity of social workers to act as change agents, building partnerships, networking and supporting each other to establish a community of social work advocates. While independent advocates may argue that social work advocacy is not true advocacy, this chapter draws on the arguments developed through the book to demonstrate that social work advocacy remains an essential element of social work practice. Developing a culture of advocacy provides the opportunity for social workers to be activists: dynamic rather than reactive practitioners. Reclaiming advocacy in social work is a step towards ensuring that the experiences of service users are valued and form the bedrock of services which aim to make a difference in the lives of the people who need to use them.

Values and social work advocacy

The significance of values in social work is fundamental, since 'much social work intervention is justified by reference to some value or other – there is simply no avoiding them' (Pierson and Thomas, 2010: 531). While values in social work are not easy to define, it is widely accepted that values refer to 'one or all of religions, moral, political or ideological principles, beliefs or attitudes' (Banks, 1995: 4) and for social workers are 'a set of fundamental moral/ethical principles to which social workers are/should be committed' (1995: 4). A key element of social work training and ongoing reflective practice for social workers is to explore their own value base and engage in critical debate about personal, professional and organisational values – this is key if social workers are to manage the complexity of practice and ethical dilemmas they face on a daily basis (Pierson and Thomas, 2010; Dalrymple and Burke, 2006). Whether or not a social worker feels able to act as an advocate – in either a case or systemic way – may contribute to the ambiguities and the moral dilemmas faced in practice. In order to be clear about the nature and purpose of social work advocacy, a culture is therefore needed that facilitates discussion and debate about the ethical issues and dilemmas that challenge personal beliefs, assumptions and the professional integrity of a social worker taking on an advocacy role. Colleagues, other professionals or service users and carers may have differing views about the key issues and how far it is either feasible or desirable to advocate in a particular case or situation.

Megan is a social worker attached to a team who work with traveller children. She is also a member of the Board of Governors at her local school. During one of the meetings there is a discussion about some traveller children who have recently started to attend the school. One of the committee members expresses concern about the behaviour of the traveller families whose site is close to their property. As the conversation carries on Megan starts to become uncomfortable about the discriminatory comments that are being made and her personal and professional values are challenged by the discussion. She rapidly becomes aware that her values are not shared by the majority of the committee but feels that her personal integrity will be compromised if she does not speak up and convey the values that are important to her relating to social justice, rights and anti-oppressive and anti-discriminatory practice. Megan feels that she has to take on an advocacy role in this situation, although a number of the committee members are also personal friends who she does not want to upset. Megan challenges what she feels is incorrect information about the traveller families and, through speaking up, ensures that their interests are given a voice.

Following this meeting Megan met with the head teacher to discuss training both for the Board of Governors, teaching staff and pupils. Megan also discussed this incident with colleagues in her team and suggested widening the training to other schools and to social workers in other teams.

- There was a conflict of values in this situation at a number of levels: Megan's personal values, her professional values and the values of the majority of the group.
- Megan ensured that her professional integrity was not compromised.
- Megan used her professional skills as a social work advocate to ensure that the traveller families had a voice both within the meeting and, at a macro level, within the school community.
- With all her actions Megan contributed to developing a culture of advocacy.

Advocacy and anti-oppressive practice

We have seen in previous chapters that the practice of advocacy within the context of health and welfare services has its roots in the experience of marginalised groups who, in seeking to have a voice and secure their rights, define advocacy from a radical perspective – in relation to both individual issues and the wider systems. Advocacy can therefore broadly be interpreted as a method for enabling people who have previously been ignored or silenced to come to voice and to ensure that service providers take seriously what they have to say. The definition of advocacy from disabled adult service users illustrates this well. Drawing on their experiences of oppression and powerlessness as a marginalised group, it recognises the impact that such experiences have on their capacity to control their own lives and resonates with the experiences of many other excluded groups:

> When people are denied or unable to gain access to a fair share of what's on offer in society – when they are denied information or opportunities to take part in decisions concerning their lives – when they are dispossessed of insight, dignity, self-confidence – then it becomes necessary in a caring society for more powerful people to act with integrity on their behalf or wherever possible to enable them to move to a point where they can retrieve control for themselves. (Advocacy in Action, 1990)

While the notion of 'more powerful' people acting on behalf of people needing advocacy support is controversial, it also establishes the importance of understanding both the lived experiences of those who feel unable to speak out and the meaning of advocacy relationships. The fact that there is an expressed need for 'more powerful' people to facilitate access to society illustrates how access by the privileged to resources and decision making serves to oppress those who are vulnerable to the authority and power of service providers. Understanding oppressive forms of power relations is key to the transformative practice that is needed to enable the move from feeling 'dispossessed of insight, dignity and self-confidence' towards 'a point where they can retrieve control for themselves' (Advocacy in Action, 1990). Examination of the power relations between service providers and service users enables social work advocates to recognise that if they are to be effective as critical practitioners, challenge oppression and promote empowerment practice, then it is helpful to appreciate the power of dominant discourses. The process of critical reflection and reflexivity enables practitioners to focus on how they 'construct and understand their place, position, purpose, role, practice and power within and in relation to the organisation' (Fook, 2004: 73), which should then contribute to professional development and impact on organisational learning. This initially means recognising the potential for organisations to be oppressive and, within that, acknowledging the responsibility that practitioners have to reflect on their own position. This process inevitably involves ongoing analysis of the relationship between the state, service providers and service users.

Through an exploration of advocacy theory and practice we have seen that advocacy practice is synonymous with the concepts of social justice and rights and as such provides the energy for transformative practice. A rights-based approach has been described as inherently a political approach – one that takes into consideration power, struggle and a vision of a better society as key factors in development. (Chapman, 2005: 7)

This means that the rights of service users can only be realised if there are changes in power relations in individual interactions and within structures and organisations. Service users involved with Advocacy in Action demonstrate that this involves changing who decides what information is shared, who decides whose voice is heard, and what resources will be available in order that they can gain self-esteem and the confidence to advocate for themselves. Our approach to advocacy is a structural model which analyses empowerment from the standpoint of service users. It has been noted that this approach

has the potential to address the place of relationship within advocacy, and, at the same time, through maintaining a focus on anti-oppressive practice, engage with discrimination. (Wilks, 2012: 162)

Underpinning our consideration of social work advocacy in this book has been a focus on relationship practice. In order to be able to develop effective relationships with service users, social work advocates need to be able to critically reflect on the individual issues that particular service users are trying to deal with in their daily lives and the wider systems and structures which can feel oppressive and disempowering. Drawing on the work of a number of commentators we have discussed elsewhere that in relation to advocacy with children and young people empowerment practice operates at three levels (Boylan and Dalrymple, 2009). This can be transferred to advocacy practice with all service user groups. The first level involves the social work advocate enabling service users to share their views and opinions about their situation. For example, in relation to the experiences of looked after children and young people, the social work advocate can play an important advocacy role in facilitating children and young people to explore and share their views and opinions about their situation, their understanding of what is happening. The second level relates to self-awareness. Through dialogue with the social work advocate the child or young person gains greater self-knowledge, an understanding of their own biography, and are then able to reflect on their situation and those of other children and young people in their situation. Essentially, the relationship between the social work advocate and the young person is premised on respect in which the young person feels what they have to say is both valued and taken seriously, which can be experienced as empowering. The third level pertains to systemic advocacy, in which the social work advocate and independent advocates strive towards shaping and informing broader political and social structures, which may lead to changes in legislation, policy and practice.

Working with independent advocates

Despite the fact that the advocacy role of social workers is a traditional part of the social work role, an element of unease remains between the independent advocacy community and social work practitioners. This is partly due to a lack of understanding of each other's role. Independent advocacy is a relative new-comer, particularly with respect to statutory advocacy. It also has its roots in complaints procedures, for example, in situations where service users and carers are dissatisfied with service provision or an individual worker. It is therefore understandable that there is a residual feeling of anxiety by some practitioners who are likely to become defensive about the role of independent advocates. Similarly, independent advocates who are trying to develop their own professional identity may not want to recognise the advocacy role of other professionals. This situation is changing, however, but requires an ongoing culture of mutual dia-logue and preparedness to understand each other's role and to work together when necessary. The starting point here is recognition that the fundamental val-ues underpinning the work of both social workers and of independent advocates are mutual.

The difficulties for social workers in the statutory sector are arguably greater than those in the voluntary sector in relation to the advocacy role. Many professionals working in the voluntary sector consider that their role is primarily defined as that of an advocate. In statutory social work, however, the managerialist and bureaucratic imperatives alongside resource constraints make even the most creative social work difficult.

Commentary

A model of advocacy that brings together the theory and practice of advocacy and recognises the vibrant quality of advocacy practice is that of a bridge. Initially the bridge requires a firm foundation. If we think about this in relation to service users and carers, we can see that social work values and the promotion of service user and carer rights provide a firm foundation for this model. As we have argued in earlier work (Boylan and Dalrymple, 2009: 131), the supporting structures or pil-lars of the bridge are central to its success, they are 'participation, legislation, developing knowledge about the theory of advocacy and developing knowledge about the practice of advocacy'. The alignment of these four pillars alongside a rights perspective form a dynamic culture of advocacy in which the professionals working alongside service users and carers are committed to the knowledge, skills and values that inform advocacy. The bridge joins service users and carers with the services they need and want. However, the flow across the bridge has to be main-tained in both directions through genuine partnership working where service users and carers have a voice in decision making. A good flow enables relationships to develop and dialogue to take place. Ensuring that the flow is constant requires the structure of the bridge to be constantly maintained. The strength of the bridge depends on a commitment by individual practitioners, agencies, local and central government agendas to work together and involve service users and carers in deci-sion making. All these activities ensure that a solid culture of advocacy develops so that the bridge does not collapse.

Local authority services such as health, education and social services may all be committed to the provision of advocacy for particular groups of people. In relation to children and young people, for example, a range of independent organisations may be commissioned to provide advocacy for young people in child protection conferences, for looked after children and young people, and for young people with autistic spectrum disorder in transition planning. In addition, a children's rights and/or participation worker may also be directly employed by the local authority as will independent reviewing officers who have a responsibility to ensure that young people are able to participate meaningfully in their looked after reviews. Social workers are also likely to be committed to promoting children's rights and ensuring that they fully participate in decision making concerning their lives as part of their advocacy role.

However, this may not necessarily mean that a culture of advocacy exists within the authority. For example, as we have already noted, there can be misunderstandings and a degree of suspicion between social workers committed to an advocacy role as part of their professional expertise and the role of independent advocates. Tensions between advocacy organisations with insecure funding and tendering against each other for contracts to provide a service can also contribute to difficult professional relationships and confusion about the advocacy role (Parry et al., 2008; Oliver, 2008). In fact, there may well be several commissioned advocacy services for different service user groups, who are likely to be operating independently, possibly unaware of each other's existence, struggling with limited resources to promote an understanding of their role within a small part of the whole organisational structure. Such pressures do not facilitate a culture of advocacy. A culture will only begin to develop when a space for dialogue is created both within the community of independent advocates and with social workers and other practitioners using advocacy skills within their work. The challenge for both social work advocates and independent advocates is to continue to break down barriers and develop understanding about the role of advocacy in the lives of people using services. In the current political context there is greater need for strong and effective advocacy.

Summary

- Practitioners pass on their knowledge and understanding about social work advocacy so that the culture becomes embedded within everyday practice.
- Social work advocates have a key role in developing a culture of advocacy and being a force for change in promoting equality and social justice.
- Enabling and empowering service users and carers to shape and direct their own lives has become an important aspect of social work practice and reflects the values and principles that underpin the profession.

Discussion questions

1   Why is thinking about a culture of advocacy important for social work advocates?
2   Reflect on the ways in which you are able to contribute to the development of a culture of advocacy.
3   What obstacles have you had to overcome in empowering service users and carers to speak up for themselves and exercise their rights?

References

Action for Advocacy (2006) *A Code of Practice for Advocates*. London: A4A.

Action for Advocacy (2010) *A Manifesto for Independent Advocacy in England and Wales*. London: A4A.

Adams, R. (2002) *Social Policy for Social Work*. Basingstoke: Palgrave.

Adams, R., Dominelli, L. and Payne, M. (2005) 'Transformational social work', in R. Adams, L. Dominelli and M. Payne (eds), *Social Work Futures: Crossing Boundaries, Transforming Practice*. Basingstoke: Palgrave Macmillan, pp. 1–17.

Adams, R., Dominelli, L. and Payne, M. (2009a) *Social Work: Themes, Issues and Critical Debates*, 3rd edn. Basingstoke: Palgrave Macmillan.

Adams, R., Dominelli, L. and Payne, M. (2009b) 'Perspectives on the life course: later life', in R. Adams, L. Dominelli and M. Payne (eds), *Social Work: Themes, Issues and Critical Debates*, 3rd edn. Basingstoke: Palgrave Macmillan, pp. 129–42.

ADSS (Cymru) (Association of Directors of Social Services, Wales) (2005) *Social Work in Wales: A Profession to Value*. Available at: www.adsscymru.org.uk/resource/m_e_Social_Work_in_Wales_-_A_Profession_to_Value.pdf, accessed 9.4.13.

Advocacy 2000 (2002) *Principles and Standards in Independent Advocacy Organisations and Groups*. Edinburgh: Advocacy 2000.

Advocacy Across London (2002) *The Advocacy Charter: Defining and Promoting Key Advocacy Principles*. London: A4A.

Advocacy in Action (1990) *A Model for Consultation*. Nottingham: Advocacy In Action.

Advocacy in Action (1990) *A Model for User Consultation*. Nottingham: Advocacy in Action.

Advocacy Resource Exchange (2012) Healthwatch England [Homepage of Advocacy Resource Exchange], [Online]. Available at: www.advocacyresource.org.uk/HealthWatch, accessed 13.3.13.

Aiers, A. and Kettle, J. (1998) *When Things Go Wrong: Young People's Experience of Getting Access to the Complaints Procedure in Residential Care*. London: National Institute for Social Work.

Alderson, P. (2000) *Young Children's Rights*. London: Jessica Kingsley.

Allan, J. (2003) 'Theorising critical social work', in J. Allan, B. Pease and L. Briskman (eds), *Critical Social Work: An Introduction to Theories and Practices*. Crows Nest, NSW: Allen & Unwin, pp. 32–51.

Allison, A. (2005) 'Embracing diversity and working in partnership', in R. Carnwell and J. Buchanan (eds), *Effective Practice in Health and Social Care a Partnership Approach*. Maidenhead: Open University Press.

Allsop, J. and Jones, K. (2008) 'Withering the citizen, managing the consumer: complaints in healthcare settings', *Social Policy and Society*, 7 (2): 233–43.

Arnstein, S. (1969) 'A ladder of citizen participation in the USA', *Journal of the American Institute of Planners*, 35 (4): 216–24.

Asquith, S., Clarke, C. and Waterhouse, L. (2005) *The Role of the Social Worker in the 21st Century: A Literature Review*. Edinburgh: Scottish Executive Education Department.

Attlee, C. (1920) *The Social Worker*. London: Bell.

Badham, B. and Eadie, T. (2004) 'Social work in the voluntary sector: moving forward while holding on', in M. Lymberry and S. Butler (eds), *Social Work Ideals and Practice Realities*. Basingstoke: Palgrave Macmillan, pp. 85–106.

Baltes, P.B., Straundinger, U.M. and Lindenberger, L. (1999) 'Lifespan psychology theory and application to intellectual functioning', *Annual Review of Psychology*, 50: 471–507.

Bamber, C. (2007) 'Listening to patients in Ashworth time', in D. Pilgrim (ed.), *Inside Ashworth: Professional Accounts of Institutional Life*. Singapore: Radcliffe Publishing, pp. 81–96.

Banks, S. (1995) *Ethics and Values in Social Work*. London: Macmillan.

Banks, S. (2002) *Ethics and Values in Social Work*. Basingstoke: Palgrave.

Banks, S. (2009) 'Professional values and accountabilities', in R. Adams, L. Dominelli and M. Payne (eds), *Critical Practice in Social Work*, 2nd edn. Basingstoke: Palgrave Macmillan, pp. 32–42.

Barclay, P.M. (1982) *The Barclay Report: Social Workers their Role and Tasks*. London: Bedford Square Press.

BASW (1996) *Code of Ethics for Social Work*. Birmingham: BASW.

BASW (2012) *The Code of Ethics for Social Work*. Birmingham: BASW.

Bateman, N. (1995) *Advocacy Skills: A Handbook for Human Service Professionals*. Aldershot: Arena.

Bateman, N. (2000) *Advocacy Skills for Health and Social Care Professionals*. London: Jessica Kingsley.

Beech, C. and Ray, M. (2009) 'Older people', in R. Adams, L. Dominelli and M. Payne (eds), *Critical Practice in Social Work*. Basingstoke: Palgrave Macmillan, pp. 356–67.

Beresford, P. (2000) '"Service users knowledge" and social work theory: conflict or collaboration?' *British Journal of Social Work*, 30 (4): 489–503.

Beresford, P. (2002) 'Service users, social policy and the future of welfare', *Critical Social Policy*, 21 (4): 494–512.

Beresford, P. (2005) 'Service-user involvement in evaluation and research: issues, dilemmas and destinations', in D. Taylor and S. Balloch (eds), *The Politics of Evaluation: Participation and Policy Implementation*. Bristol: Policy Press, pp. 77–86.

Beresford, P. (2007) *The Changing Roles and Tasks of Social Work From Service Users Perspectives*. London: Shaping Our Lives National User Network.

Beresford, P. and Carr, S. (2012) *Social Care, Service Users and User Involvement*. London: Jessica Kingsley.

Beresford, P. and Croft, S. (2004) 'Service users and practitioners reunited: the key component for social work reform', *British Journal of Social Work*, 34(1): 53–68.

Beresford, P., Adshead, L. and Croft, S. (2006) *Palliative Care, Social Work and Service Users: Making Life Possible*. London: Jessica Kingsley.

Beveridge, W. (1942) *Social Insurance and Allied Services*. London: HMSO.

Bicklen, D. (1976) 'Advocacy comes of age', *Exceptional Children*, 46: 308–314.

Biestek, F. (1961) *The Casework Relationship*. London: Unwin University Books.

BILD (n.d) *Factsheet – Human Rights Act*. Kidderminster: British Institute of Learning Disabilities Publications. Available at: www.thh.nhs.uk/documents/_Patients/PatientLeaflets/general/HumanRights-BILD.pdf, accessed 14.4.13.

Blom-Cooper, L. (1992) *Report of the Committee of Inquiry into Complaints at Ashworth Hospital*. London: HMSO.

Blood, I. (2010) *Older People with Higher Support Needs: How Can We Empower Them to Enjoy a Better Life*. York: Joseph Rowntree Foundation.

Bogues, S. (2008) *People Work not Just Paperwork*. Belfast: Northern Ireland Social Care Council.

Booth, T. and Booth, W. (1998) *Growing up with Parents who have Learning Difficulties*. London: Routledge.

Booth, T. and Booth, W. (2005) 'Parents with learning difficulties in the child protection system: experiences and perspectives', *Journal of Intellectual Difficulties*, 9 (2): 109–129.

Booth, W. and Booth, T. (2004) 'A family at risk: multiple perspectives on parenting and child protection', *British Journal of Learning Disabilities*, 32 (1): 9–15.

Boydell, L, (2000) *Partnership Framework: A Model for Health*. Dublin: Ireland: Institute of Public Health.

Boylan, J. (2004) *Looked After Children's Participation in Statutory Reviews and the Role of Advocacy*. Unpublished PhD Thesis, Staffordshire University.

Boylan, J. (2005) *Reviewing Your Review: A Critical analysis of the Role and Impact of Advocacy in Statutory Reviews of Children and Young People Looked After by their Local Authority*. University of Staffordshire. Unpublished Phd Thesis edn.

Boylan, J. and Braye, S. (2006) 'Paid professionalised and proceduralised:can legal and policy frameworks for child advocacy give voice to children and young people?', *Journal of Social Welfare and Family Law*, 28 (3/4): 233–49.

Boylan, J. and Dalrymple, J. (2009) *Understanding Advocacy for Children and Young People*. Maidenhead: Open University Press.

Boylan, J. and Dalrymple, J. (2011) 'Advocacy, social justice and children's rights', *Practice: Social Work in Action*, 23 (1): 19–30.

Brandon, D. (1995) *Advocacy: Power to People with Disabilities*. Birmingham: Venture Press.

Brandon, D. and Brandon, T. (2001) *Advocacy in Social Work*. Birmingham: Venture Press.

Brasnett, M. (1964) *The Story of the Citizens' Advice Bureaux*. London: NCSS.

Braye, S. (2000) 'Participation and involvement in social care: an overview', in H. Kemshall and R. Littlechild (eds), *User Involvement and Participation in Social Care*. London: Jessica Kingsley, pp. 9–28.

Braye, H. and Broadbent, G. (2002) *Legal Materials for Social Workers*. Oxford: Oxford University Press.

Braye, S. and Preston-Shoot, M. (1999) 'Accountability, administrative law and social work practice: redressing or reinforcing the power imbalance?', *Journal of Social Welfare and Family Law*, 21 (3): 235–56.

Braye, S. and Preston-Shoot, M. (2009a) *Practising Social Work Law*, 3rd edn. Basingstoke: Palgrave Macmillan.

Braye, S. and Preston-Shoot, M. (2009b) 'Social work and the law', in R. Adams, L. Dominelli and M. Payne (eds), *Social Work: Themes, Issues and Critical Debates*, 3rd edn. Basingstoke: Palgrave Macmillan, pp. 90–102.

Bronfenbrenner, U. (1979) *The Ecology of Human Development*. Cambridge, MA: Harvard University Press.

Buchanan, A. and Walmsley, J. (2006) 'Self-advocacy in historical perspective', *British Journal of Learning Disabilities*, 34 (3): 133–138.

Bull, D. (1989) 'The social worker's advocacy role: a British quest for a Canadian perspective', *Canadian Social Work Review*, 6 (1): 49–68.

Butler, I. and Williamson, H. (1994) *Children Speak: Children, Trauma and Social Work*. Harlow: Longman.

Cabinet Office Exclusion Unit Task Force (2008) *Think Family: Improving the Life Chances of Families at Risk*. London: Cabinet Office.

Cahill, J. (1996) 'Patient participation: a concept analysis', *Journal of Advanced Nursing*, 24 (3): 561–571.

CAIT (2002) *Comments on the National Standards for Agencies Providing Advocacy for Children and Young People*.

Campbell, J. and Oliver, M. (1996) *Disability Politics: Understanding our Past, Changing our Future*. London: Routledge.

Carers UK (2007) *Real Change, Not Short Change: Time to Deliver for Carers*. Available at: www.carersuk.org/media/k2/attachments/Real_change_not_short_change__time_to_deliver_for_carers.pdf

Carers UK and Sheffield Hallam University (2005) Caring and Older People. Available at: www.carersuk.org/policy_and_practice.

Carlile, L.A. (2002) *Too Serious A Thing: Review of Safeguards for Children and Young People Treated and Cared for by the NHS in Wales*. Cardiff: NafW.

Carnwell, I. and Buchannan, J. (2005) *Effective Practice in Health and Social Care: A Partnership Approach*. Maidenhead: Open University Press.

Carnwell, R. and Buchannan, J. (eds) (2009) *Effective Practice in Health, Social Care and Criminal Justice: A Partnership Approach*. Maidenhead: Open University Press.

Carr, S. (2004) *Has Service User Participation Made a Difference to Social Care Services?* London: SCIE.

Carr, S. (2012) *Personalisation: A Rough Guides*, 3rd edn. London: SCIE.

CCW (2012) *Code of Practice for Social Care Workers and their Employers*. Cardiff: Care Council for Wales.

Central Council for Social Work Education and Training in Social Work (CCETSW) (1995) *Revised Paper 30*. London: CCETSW.

Chambers, P. and Phillips, J. (2009) 'Working across the interface of formal and informal care of older people', in R. Carnwell and J. Buchanan (eds), *Effective Practice in Health, Social Care and Criminal Justice: A Partnership Approach*, 2nd edn. Maidenhead: Open University Press, pp. 96–109.

Chapman, J. (2005) *Rights-based Development: The Challenge of Change and Power*. Advocacy Action Research project, available at: www.gprg.org/pubs/workingpapers/pdfs/gprg-wps-027.pdf, accessed 20.8.13.

Charity Organisation Society (1881) *Occasional Paper*. London: COS.

Charnley, H. Roddam, G. and Wistow, J. (2009) 'Working with service users and carers', in R. Adams, L. Dominelli and M. Payne (eds), *Social Work Themes, Issues and Critical Debates*, 3rd edn. New York: Palgrave Macmillan.

Chase, E. (2008) 'Challenges and complexities of widening access to advocacy services: lessons from an evaluation of voice advocacy service', in C. Oliver and J. Darlymple (ed.), *Developing Advocacy for Children and Young People: Current Issues in Research, Policy and Practice*. London: Jessica Kingsley, pp. 99–115.

Children's Rights Development Unit (1994) *UK Agenda for Children*. London: CRDU.

Clarke, C. (2000) *Social Work Ethics: Politics, Principles and Practice*. Basingstoke: Macmillan.

Coates, J., Gray, M. and Hetherington, T. (2006) 'An "ecospiritiual" perspective: finally a place for indigenous approaches', *British Journal of Social Work Advance Access*, 36: 381–400.

Coles, B. (1995) *Youth and Social Policy: Youth Citizenship and Young Careers*. London: UCL Press.

Coles, J. and Connors, P. (2008) 'Best practice with people with learning difficulties: being seen and heard', in K. Jones, B. Cooper and H. Ferguson (eds), *Best Practice in Social Work: Critical Perspectives*. Basingstoke: Palgrave Macmillan, pp. 198–211.

Corby, B., Young, F. and Coleman, S. (2009) 'Inter-professional communication in child protection', in R. Carnwell and J. Buchannan (eds), *Effective Practice in Health, Social Care and Criminal Justice: A Partnership Approach*. Maidenhead: Open University Press, pp. 64–79.

Coulshed, V.(1991) *Social Work Practice An Introduction*. Basingstoke: BASW/Macmillan.

Coulshed, V. and Orme, J. (1998) *Social Work Practice: An Introduction*. Basingstoke: Macmillan/BASW.

Cox, M. (1998) 'Whistleblowing and training for accountability', in G. Hunt (ed.), *Whistleblowing in the Social Services*. London: Arnold, pp. 5–18.

Crawford, K. and Walker, J. (2004) *Social Work with Older People*, 1st edn. Exeter: Learning Matters Ltd.

Crawford, K. and Walker, J. (2007) *Social Work with Older People*, 2nd edn. Exeter: Learning Matters.

Crisp, B.R., Anderson, M.T., Orme, J. and Lister, P.G. (2005) *Knowledge Review 08: Learning and Teaching in Social Work Education: Textbooks and Frameworks on Assessment*. London: SCIE.

Crowley, A. and Pithouse, A. (2008) 'Advocacy in complaints procedures: the perspectives of young people', in C. Oliver and J. Dalrymple (eds), *Developing Advocacy for Children and Young People*. London: Jessica Kingsley, pp. 150–68.

CSCI (2009) *Supporting Disabled People*. London: Commission for Social Care Inspection.

CWDC (2009) *The Team Around the Child and the Lead Professional; A Guide for Practitioners*. Leeds: Children's Workforce Development Council.

Dalrymple, J. and Burke, B. (2006) *Anti-oppressive Practice: Social Care and the Law*, 2nd edn. Maidenhead: Open University Press.

Dalrymple, J. and Burke, B. (2009) 'Critical intervention', in R. Adams, L. Dominelli, and M. Payne (eds), *Social Work: Themes, Issues and Critical Debates*. Basingstoke: Palgrave Macmillan.

Dalrymple, J. and Oliver, C. (2008) 'Advocacy, participation and voice', in J. Dalrymple and C. Oliver (eds) *Developing Advocacy for Children and Young People: Current Issue in Research, Policy and Practice*. London: Jessica Kingsley, pp. 204–15.

Davies, M. (1994) *The Essential Social Worker*, 3rd edn. Aldershot: Arena.

Davies , M (2000) *The Blackwell Companion To Social Work*. Oxford: Blackwell Publishing.

Davis, A. (2008) *What service users expect from social work*, presentation to the International Conference on Social Work Education, profession and Practice, Tblisi State University, Georgia.

Department for Children, Schools and Families (2009) *Building a Safe, Confident Future. The Final Report of the Social Work Task Force*. London: TSO.

Department for Education (2011) *Children Act 1989 Guidance and Regulations, Volume 2: Care Planning, Placement and Review*. London: The Stationery Office.

Department for Education and Skills (2003) *Get it Sorted: Providing Effective Advocacy Services for Children and Young People Making a Complaint under the Children Act 1989*. Nottingham: DfES Publications.

Department for Education and Skills (2005) *Children's Workforce Strategy. Every Child Matters Change for Children*. HM Government.

Department of Health (1989) *The Care of Children: Principles and Practice in Regulations and Guidance*. London: The Stationery Office.

Department of Health (1998) *Modernising Social Services*. London: The Stationery Office.

Department of Health (2000) *Framework for the Assessment of Children in Need and their Families*. London: The Stationery Office.

Department of Health (2001a) *Nothing About Us Without Us*. London: The Stationery Office.

Department of Health (2001b) *Valuing People: A New Strategy for Learning Disabilities for the 21st Century*. London: The Stationery Office.

Department of Health (2002) *The Single Assessment Process: Guidance for Local Implementation*. London: The Stationery Office.

Department of Health (2003) *The Single Assessment Process: Guidance for Local Implementation*. London: The Stationery Office.

Department of Health (2005) *Independence, Wellbeing and Choice: Our Vision for the Future of Social Care for Adults in England*. Norwich: The Stationery Office.

Department of Health (2007a) *Putting People First: A Shared Commitment and Vision for the Provision of Adult Social Care*. London: Department of Health.

Department of Health (2007b) *Making Experiences Count: A New Approach to Responding to Complaints*. London: The Stationery Office.

Department of Health (2008) *Transition: Moving On Well. A Good Practice Guide for Health Professionals and their Partners on Transition Planning for Young People with Complex Health Needs or a Disability*. London: Central Office of Information.

Department of Health (2009a) *Listening, Responding, Improving: A Guide to Better Customer Care*. London: Department of Health.

Department of Health (2009b) *Valuing People Now: A New Three Year Strategy for People with Learning Difficulties. 'Making it Happen for Everyone'*. London: Central Office of Information.

Department of Health (2009c) *Safeguarding Adults: Report on the Consultation on the Review of No Secrets*. London: Department of Health.

Department of Health (2010a) *Local Authority Circular (LAC): A Vision for Adult Care*.

Department of Health (2010b) *Prioritising need in the Context of Putting People First: A Whole System Approach to Eligibility for Social Care*. Guidance on eligibility for adult social care, England 2010. London: The Stationery Office. Available at: www.dh.gov.uk/en/Publications andstatistics/Publications/PublicationsPolicy AndGuidance/DH_113154, accessed 9.4.13.

Department of Health (2013) *Working Together to Safeguard Children: A Guide to Interagency Working*. London: HMSO.

Department of Health and Home Office (2000) *No Secrets: Guidance on Developing and Implementing Multi-agency Policies and Procedures to Protect Vulnerable Adults from Abuse*. London: Department of Health.

Department of Health and Home office (2003) *The Victoria Climbie Inquiry: Report of an Inquiry by Lord Laming*. London: The Stationery Office.

Department of Health and Office of Public Guardian (2009) *Making Decisions: The Independent Mental Capacity Advocate (IMCA) Service*. London: Department of Health.

Department of Health, Social Services and Public Safety (2011) *Developing Advocacy Services – A Guide for Commissioners*. Dublin: DHSSPS.

DfES and Department of Health (2006) *Options for Excellence: Building the Social Care Workforce for the Future*. London: Central Office of Information.

DfES and Department for Skills and Families (2009) *Building a Safe, Confident Future*. London: Central Office of Information.

Dickens, J. (2011) 'The definition of social work in the United Kingdom 2000–2010', *International Journal of Social Welfare*, 21: 34–43.

Dominelli, L. (2009) *Introduction to Social Work*. Cambridge: Policy Press.

Donnison, D. (2009) *Speaking to Power: Advocacy for Health and Social Care*. Bristol: Policy Press.

DSCF (2010) *Working Together to Safeguard Children and Guide to Interagency Cooperation*. London: HMSO.

Elsley, S. (2010) *'Advocacy Makes You Feel Brave': Advocacy Support for Children and Young People in Scotland*. Edinburgh: The Scottish Government. Available at: www.scotland.gov. uk/Publications/2010/01/07144331/0, accessed 13.4.13.

Erikson, E. (1980) *The Life Course Completed*. New York: Norton.

Erikson, E. (1987) *A Way of Looking at Things: Selected Papers from 1930–1986*. London: Norton.

Eustace, A. (2002) *Speaking Up*. Community Care Available at: www.communitycare.co.uk/ Articles/2002/01/10/34601/speaking- up.html, accessed 1.8.13.

Ferguson, H. (2011) *Child Protection Practice*. Basingstoke: Palgrave Macmillan.

Flekkoy M.G. (1998) 'Child advocacy in Norway', *Children and Society*, 4, 2: 307–18.

Flekkoy, M.G. and Kaufman, N.H. (1997) *The Participation Rights of the Child: Rights and Responsibilities in Family and Society*. London: Jessica Kingsley.

Folgheraiter, F. (2004) *Relational Social Work: Toward Networking and Societal Practices*. London: Jessica Kingsley.

Folgheraiter, F. (2007) 'Relational social work: principles and practices', *Social Policy and Society*, 6 (2): 265–74.

Folgheraiter, F. (2012) *The Mystery of Social Work: A Critical Analysis of the Global Definition and New Suggestions According to the Relational Theory*. Trento: Edizioni Erickson.

Fook, J. (ed.) (2000) 'Deconstructing and reconstructing professional expertise', in B. Fawcett, B. Featherstone and A. Rossiter (eds), *Practice and Research in Social Work: Postmodern Perspectives*. London: Routledge, pp. 105–20.

Fook, J. (2002) *Social Work Critical Theory and Practice*. London: Sage.

Fook, J. (2004) 'Critical reflection and organisational learning and change: a case study', in N. Gould and M. Baldwin (eds), *Social Work, Critical Reflection and the Learning Organisation*. Aldershot: Ashgate, pp. 57–73.

Forbat, L. and Atkinson, D. (2005) 'Advocacy in practice: the troubled position of advocates in adult services', *British Journal of Social Work*, 35 (3): 321–55.

Frith, S. (1984) *The Sociology of Youth*. Ormskirk: Causeway Press.

Glasby, J. and Dickinson, H. (2008) *Partnership Working in Health and Social Care*. Bristol: Policy Press.

Glasby, J. and Littlechild, R. (2009) *Direct Payments and Personal Budgets: Putting Personalisation into Practice*, 2nd edn. Bristol: Policy Press.

Glendenning, C. (2002) 'Partnerships between health and social services: developing a framework for evaluation', *Policy and Politics*, 30 (1): 115–127.

Goodley, D. (2000) *Self-advocacy in the Lives of People with Learning Difficulties*. Buckingham: Open University Press.

Gosling, J. and Martin, J. (2012) *Making Partnerships Work with Service Users and Advocacy Groups*. London: Jessica Kingsley.

Green, L. (2010) *Understanding the Life Course: Sociological and Psychological Perspectives*. Cambridge: Polity Press.

GSCC (2002) *Codes of Practice for Social Care Workers and Employers*. London: General Social Care Council.

GSCC (2008) *Social Work at its Best: A Statement of Social Work Roles and Tasks for the 21st Century*. London: General Social Care Council.

Hallett, C., Murray, C. and Punch, S. (2003) 'Young people and welfare: negotiating pathways', in C. Hallett and A. Prout (eds), *Hearing the Voices of Children: Social Policy for a New Century*. London: Routledge Falmer, pp. 123–38.

Hare, I. (2004) 'Defining social work for the 21st century: the International Federation of Social Workers revised definition of social work', *International Journal of Social Work*, 47: 407–24.

Hart, R. (1992) *Innocenti Essays No. 4. Children's Participation: From Tokenism to Citizenship*. Florence: UNICEF International Child Development Centre.

Hart, R. (1997) *Children's Participation: The Theory and Practice of Involving Young Citizens in Community Development and Environmental Care*. London: Earthscan.

Havinghurst, J. (1972) *Developmental Tasks and Education*, 3rd edn. New York: David Mckay.

Haynes, K. and Mickelson, J.S. (1997) *Affecting Change: Social Workers in the Political Arena*. New York: Longman.

Health Care Board (2012) *Transforming your Care: From Vision to Action*. Belfast: Department of Health, Social Care and Public Safety.

HCPC (2008) *Standards of Conduct, Performance and Ethics*. London: Health and Care Professions Council.

HCPC (2012) *Standards of Proficiency*. London: Health and Care Professionals Council.

Health Service Ombudsman for England (2005) *Making Things Better? A Report on Reform of the NHS Complaints Procedure in England*. London: The Stationery Office.

Healthcare Commission (2009) *Spotlight on Complaints: A Report on Second-stage Complaints about the NHS in England*. London: Healthcare Commission.

Henderson, R. and Pochin, M. (2001) *A Right Result? Advocacy Justice and Empowerment*. Bristol: The Policy Press.

Hendrick, H. (2000) 'The child as a social actor in historical sources: problems of identification and interpretation', in P. Christensen and A. James (eds), *Research with Children, Perspectives and Practices*. London: Falmer, pp. 36–61.

Herbert, M.D. and Mould, J.W. (1992) 'The advocacy role in public child welfare', *Child Welfare*, 71 (2): 114–30.

Hodgson, D. (1995) 'Advocating self-advocacy: partnership to promote the rights of young people with learning disabilities', in J. Dalrymple and J. Hough (eds), *Having a Voice and Exploration Of Children's Rights and Advocacy*. Birmingham: Venture Press, pp. 123–34.

Holland, S. (2011) *Child and Family Assessments in Social Work Practice*. London: Sage.

Holloway, M. (2005) 'Planning', in R. Adams, L. Dominelli and M. Payne (eds), *Social Work Futures: Crossing Boundaries, Transforming Practice*. Basingstoke: Palgrave Macmillan, pp. 54–67.

Horner, N. (2009) *What is Social Work?* 3rd edn. Exeter: Learning Matters.

Humphreys, C., Berridge, D., Butler, I. and Ruddick, R. (2003) 'Making research count: the development of a knowledge based practice', *Research Policy and Planning*, 21 (1): 41–50.

Hunt, G. (ed.) (1998) *Whistle-blowing in the Social Services*. London: Arnold.

Hutchins, A. and Taylor, I. (2007) 'Defining the profession? Exploring an international definition of social work in the China context', *International Journal of Social Welfare*, 16: 382–90.

International Federation of Social Workers (IFSW) and International Association of Schools of Social Work (IASSW) (2001) *International Definition of Social Work*. IFSW/IASSW.

James, A. and Prout, A. (1990) 'Re-presenting childhood: time and transition in the study of childhood' in A. Prout and A. James (eds), *Constructing and Reconstructing Childhood: Contemporary Issues in the Sociological Study of Childhood*. Basingstoke: Falmer, pp. 216–38.

James, A. and Prout, A. (1997) 'A new paradigm for the sociology of childhood', in A. James and A. Prout (eds), *Constructing and Reconstructing Childhood: Contemporary Issues in the Sociology of Childhood*. London: Falmer, pp. 7–32.

Jenkins, P. (1995) 'Advocacy and the UN Convention on the Rights of the Child', in J. Dalrymple and J. Hough (eds), *Having A Voice: An Exploration of Children's Rights and Advocacy*. Birmingham: Venture Press, pp. 31–52.

Jenkins, R. (1998) *Questions of Competence: Culture, Classification and Intellectual Disability*. Cambridge: Cambridge University Press.

Jordon, B. (2004) 'Emancipatory social work? Opportunity or oxymoron?', *British Journal of Social Work*, 34 (1): 5–19.

Kemshall, H. and Littlechild, R. (eds) (2000) *User Involvement And Participation In Social Care Research Informing Practice*. London: Jessica Kingsley.

Kennedy, S. (1990) 'Politics, poverty and power', *Social Work Today*, 14 June, pp. 16–17.

Kerr, B., Gordon, J., Macdonald, C. and Stalker, K. (2005) *Effective Social Work with Older People*. Edinburgh: Scottish Executive.

Kirby, P., Lanyon, C., Cronin, K. and Sinclair, R. (2003) *Building a Culture of Participation: Research Report*. London: Department for Education and Skills.

Kutchins, H. and Kutchins, S. (1978) 'Advocacy and social work', in G.H. Weber and G.J. McCall (eds), *Social Scientists as Advocates: Views from the Applied Professions*. Beverley Hills, CA: Sage, p. 13.

Lansdown, G. (1997) 'The case for a children's rights commissioner', *Children First*, (Winter): 17–21.

Lansdown, G. (2005) *The Evolving Capacities of the Child*. Florence: Innocenti Research Centre, UNICEF.

Lavalette, M. and Cunningham, S. (2002) 'The sociology of childhood', in B. Goldson, M. Lavalette and J. McKechnie (eds), *Children, Welfare and the State*. London: Sage, p. 9–28.

Leathard, A. (1994) 'Interprofessional developments in Britain: an overview', in A. Leathard (ed.), *Going Inter-Professional for Health and Welfare*. London: Routledge, pp. 3–37.

Lee, N. (2001) *Childhood and Society*. Maidenhead: Open University Press.

Lee, S. (2007) *Making Decisions: The Independent Mental Capacity Advocacy Service*. London: Mental Capacity Implementation Programme.

Lefevre, M. (2010) *Communicating with Children and Young People: Making a Difference*. Bristol: Policy Press.

Leung, J.C.B. (2007) 'An international definition of social work for China', *International Journal of Social Welfare*, 16: 391–7.

Levinson, D. (1978) *The Seasons of a Man's Life*. New York: Ballantine.

Lewis, E. (2009) 'Politics of recognition: what can a human rights perspective contribute to understanding service users experiences of involvement in mental health services', *Journal of Social Policy and Society*, 8 (2): 257–74.

Lister, R. (1998) 'Citizenship on the margins: citizenship, social work and social action', *European Journal of Social Work*, 1 (1): 5–18.

Litzelfelner, P. and Petr, C.G. (1997) 'Case advocacy in child welfare', *Social Work*, 42 (4): 392–402.

Local Government Ombudsman (2005) *Customer Service Survey, 2005*. Office of the Local Government Ombudsman.

Lynn, E. (1999) 'Value bases in social work education', *British Journal of Social Work*, 29: 939–53.

Lymbery, M. (2004) 'Responding to crisis: the changing nature of welfare organisations', in M. Lymbery and S. Butler (eds), *Social Work Ideals and Practice Realities*. Basingstoke: Palgrave Macmillan.

Macintosh, A. (2004) *Using Information and Communication Technologies to Enhance Citizen Engagement in the Policy Process, in Promises and Problems of e-democracy: Challenges of Online Citizen Engagement*. Paris: OECD.

Marshall, V. (2011) 'A life course perspective in IT work', *Journal of Applied Gerontology*, 30 (2): 185–98.

Martin, K. and Franklin, A. (2010) 'Disabled children and participation in the UK: reality or rhetoric?', in B. Percy-Smith and N. Thomas (eds), *A Handbook of Children and Young People's Participation: Perspectives from Theory and Practice*. Abingdon: Routledge, pp. 97–104.

Mayer, K.U. (2003) 'The sociology of the life course and life span psychology', in M. Stuandinger and U. Lindenberger (eds), *Understanding Human Development: Dialogues with the Life Span*. New York: Springer, pp. 93–117.

McGraw, S. and Newman, T. (2005) *What Works for Parents with Learning Disabilities?* Ilford: Barnardos.

McLoughlin, J., McLoughlin, R. and Stewart, W. (1979) 'Advocacy for parents of the handicapped: a professional responsibility and challenge', *Learning Disability Quarterly*, 2 (3): 51–7.

McNeil, F., Batchelor, S., Burnett, R. and Knox, J. (2005) *Reducing Re-offending – Key Practice Skills*. Glasgow: SWIA & Glasgow School of Social Work.

Mickelsen, J.S. (1995) 'Advocacy', in R.L. Edwards (ed.), *Encyclopedia of Social Work*, Vol 1 (19th ed). Washington, DC: NASW Press, pp. 95–100.

Miller, C. (2004) *Producing Welfare: A Modern Agenda*. Basingstoke: Palgrave Macmillan.

Mordy, M. and Crutchfield, J. (2004) 'User involvement in supported housing', *Housing Care and Support*, 7 (1): 7–10.

Morgan, R. (2008) *Children's Views on Advocacy: A Report by the Children's Rights Director for England*. London: Ofsted.

Moriarty, J., Rapaport, P., Beresford, P., Branfield, F., Forrest, V., Manthorpe, J., Martineau, S., Cornes, M., Butt, J., Iliffe, S., Taylor, B. and Keady, J. (2007) *The Participation of Adult Service Users, Including Older People, in Developing Social Care*. London: SCIE.

Morris, J. (2011) *Rethinking Disability Policy*. York: Joseph Rowntree Foundation.

Munro, E. (2010) *The Munro Review of Child Protection. Part 1: A Systems Analysis*. London: The Stationery Office.

Munro, E. (2011) *The Munro View of Child Protection. Final Report: A Child-centred System*. Norwich: The Stationery Office.

Murray, C. and Hallett, C. (2000) 'Young people's participation in decisions affecting their welfare', *Childhood*, 7 (1): 11–25.

National Audit Office (2008) *Feeding Back? Learning from Complaints Handling in Health and Social Care*. London: The Stationery Office.

Newman, J. and Yeates, N. (eds) (2008) *Social Justice: Welfare, Crime and Society*. Maidenhead: Open University Press.

Northern Ireland Social Care Council (2008) *The Roles and Tasks of Social Workers in Northern Ireland in the 21st Century*. Belfast: NISCC.

Nua Research Services (2001) *The Information Process in Citizen Information Centres: Analysis and Assessment*. Dublin: Comhairle.

Oliver, C. (2008) 'Setting the scene: funding, patterns of advocacy provision and children's access to advocacy services', in C. Oliver and J. Dalrymple (eds), *Developing Advocacy for Children and Young People: Current Issues in Research, Policy and Practice*. London: Jessica Kingsley, pp. 26–44.

Oliver, C. and Dalrymple, J. (eds) (2008) *Developing Advocacy for Children and Young People: Current Issues in Research, Policy and Practice*. London: Jessica Kingsley.

Oliver, C., Knight, A. and Candappa, M. (2006) *Advocacy for Looked After Children and Children in Need: Achievements And Challenges*. London: Thomas Coram Research Unit.

Oliver, C., Knight, A. and Candappa, M. (2005) *Advocacy for Looked After Children and Children in Need: Findings of a Telephone Survey of Advocacy Services*. London: University of London.

Oliver, M. and Sapey, B. (1999) *Social Work with Disabled People*. Basingstoke: Macmillan.

Oliver, M. and Sapey, B. (2006) *Social Work with Disabled People*, 3rd edn. Basingstoke: Palgrave Macmillan.

Parker, J. and Bradley, G. (2010) *Social Work Practice: Assessment, Planning, Intervention and Review*, 3rd edn. Exeter: Learning Matters.

Parliamentary and Health Service Ombudsman (2012) *Responsive and Accountable? The Ombudsman's View of Complaint Handling by Government Departments and Public Organisations 2011–2012*. London: The Stationery Office.

Parry, O., Pithouse, A., Anglim, C. and Batchelor, C. (2008) '"The tip of the iceberg": children's complaints and advocacy in Wales - an insider view from complaints officers', *British Journal of Social Work*, 38 (1): 5–19.

Parton, N. (2000) 'Some thoughts on the relationship between theory and practice', *British Journal of Social Work*, 30 (1): 449–63.

Payne, M. (1991) *Modern Social Work Theory*. London: Macmillan.

Payne, M. (1995) *Social Work and Community Care*. Basingstoke: Macmillan.

Payne, M. (1996a) *Modern Social Work Theory*, 2nd edn. Basingstoke: Palgrave.

Payne, M. (1996b) *What is Professional Social Work?* Birmingham: Venture Press.

Payne, M. (1997) *Modern Social Work Theory*, 2nd edn. Basingstoke: Macmillan.

Payne, M. (2000a) *Anti-bureaucratic Social Work*. Birmingham: Venture Press.

Payne, M. (2000b) *Teamwork in Multiprofessional Care*. Basingstoke: Macmillan.

Payne, M. (2005) *Modern Social Work Theory*, 3rd edn. Basingstoke: Palgrave Macmillan.

Payne, M. (2006) *What is Professional Social Work?* Birmingham: Venture Press.

Payne, M. (2009a) 'Adult services and health-related work', in R. Adams, L. Dominelli and M. Payne (eds), *Social Work: Themes, Issues and Critical Debates*, 3rd edn. Basingstoke: Palgrave Macmillan, pp. 320–37.

Payne, M. (2009b) 'Understanding social work process', in R. Adams, L. Dominelli and M. Payne (eds), *Social Work: Themes, Issues and Critical Debates*, 3rd edn. Basingstoke: Palgrave Macmillan, pp. 159–74.

Percy-Smith, B. (2006) 'From consultation to social learning in community participation with young people', *Children, Youth and Environments*, 16 (2): 153–179.

Phillips, J., Bernard, M. and Chittenden, M. (2002) *Juggling Work and Care: The Experiences of the Working Carers of Older Adults*. Bristol: Policy Press.

Phillipson, C. (2008) 'The frailty of older age', in M. Davies (ed.), *Blackwell Companion to Social Work*, 3rd edn. Oxford: Blackwell Publishing, pp. 49–54.

Pierson, J. (2011) *Understanding Social Work*. Maidenhead: Open University.

Pierson, J. and Thomas, M. (2010) *Dictionary of Social Work: The Definitive A–Z of Social Work and Social Care*. Maidenhead: Open University Press.

Pithouse, A. and Crowley, A. (2008) 'Complaints and children's advocacy in Wales: getting behind the rhetoric', in C. Oliver and J. Dalrymple (eds), *Developing Advocacy for Children and Young People: Current Issues in Research, Policy and Practice*. London: Jessica Kingsley, pp. 132–49.

Pithouse, A. and Parry, O. (2005) 'Children's advocacy in Wales: organisational challenges for those who commission and deliver advocacy for looked after children', *Adoption and Fostering*, 29 (4): 45–56.

Preston-Shoot, M. (2001) 'A triumph of hope over experience? Modernising accountability: the case of complaints procedures in community care', *Social Policy and Administration*, 35 (6): 701–15.

Preston-Shoot, M. and Wigley, V. (2005) 'Mapping the needs of children in need', *British Journal of Social Work*, 35 (1): 255–75.

Priestley, M. (2003) *Disability: A Life Course Approach*. Cambridge: Polity Press.

Prout, A. (2005) *The Future Of Childhood: Towards the Inter-Disciplinary Study of Children*. Falmer: Routledge.

Public and Patient Experience and Engagement Team (2011) *Healthwatch Transition Plan*. London: Department of Health.

Ray, M., Bernard, M. and Phillips, J. (2009) *Critical Issues in Social Work with Older People*. Basingstoke: Palgrave Macmillan.

Ray, M. and Chambers, P. (2009) Social work with older people and social gerontology: distant relations or natural allies? *Generations Review*, 7–14.

Reamer, F. (1998) *Ethical Standards in Social Work: A Critical Review of the NASW Code of Ethics*. Washington, DC: NASW Press.

Rees, S. and Wallace, A. (1982) *Verdicts in Social Work*. London: Edward Arnold.

Rimmer, J. (1980) *Troubles Shared: The Story of a Settlement 1889–1979*. Birmingham: Phlogiston.

Ritchie, A. and Woodward, R. (2009) 'Changing lives: critical reflections on the social work change programme for Scotland', *Critical Social Policy*, 29 (3): 510–532.

Robinson, J. (2005) 'Complaints and forgiveness: the healing process', *British Journal of Midwifery*, 13 (4): 243.

Rogowski, S. (2010) *Social Work: The Rise and Fall of a Profession?* Bristol: Policy Press.

Royal College of Psychiatry (2012) *Independent Advocacy for People with a Mental Disorder*. CR171. London: Royal College of Psychiatry.

Ruch, G (2005) 'Relationship-based and reflective practice in contemporary child care social work', *Child and Family Social Work*, 4 (2): 111–24.

Ruch, G., Turney, D. and Ward, A. (eds) (2010) *Relationship-based Social Work: Getting to the Heart of Practice*. London: Jessica Kingsley.

Samuel, J. (2002) 'What is people-centred advocacy?', *PLA Notes*, 43: 9–12.

Sayce, L. (2000) *From Psychiatric Patient to Citizen: Overcoming Discrimination and Exclusion*. Basingstoke: Macmillan.

Schneider, R.L. and Lester, L. (2000) *Social Work Advocacy: A New Framework for Action*. Belmont, CA: Brooks/Cole.

SCIE (2005) *Helping Parents with Learning Difficulties in their Role as Parents. Research Briefing 14*. London: SCIE.

SCIE (2009) *At a Glance 12. Personalisation Briefing: Implications for Advocacy Workers*. London: SCIE.

SCIE (2010) *Facts about FACS 2010: A Guide to Fair Access to Care Services*. London: SCIE.

SIAA (2008) *Principles and Standards for Independent Advocacy*. Edinburgh: Scottish Independent Advocacy Alliance.

SIAA (2010) *Independent Advocacy: A Guide for Commissioners*. Edinburgh: Scottish Independent Advocacy Alliance.

Scottish Executive (2001) *Independent Advocacy: A Guide for Commissioners*. Edinburgh: Scottish Executive.

Scottish Executive (2006) *Changing Lives: Report of the 21st Century Social Work Review*. Edinburgh: Scottish Executive.

Shaping Our Lives, National User (2007) *Shaping Our Lives: What People Think of Social Care Services They Use*. York: Joseph Rowntree Foundation.

Shardlow, S.M., Myers, S., Berry, A., Davis, C., Eckersley, T., Lawson, J., McLaughlin, H. and Rimmer, A. (2005) *Teaching and Assessing Assessment in Social Work Education within English Higher Education: Practice Survey Results and Analysis*. Salford: Salford Centre for Social Work Research.

Sheafor, B. and Horejsi, C.T. (2003) *Techniques and Guidelines for Social Work Practice*. Boston, MA: Allyn & Bacon.

Shier, H. (2001) 'Pathways to participation: openings, opportunities and obligations', *Children and Society*, 15 (4): 107–117.

Shier, H. (2006) 'Pathways to participation revisited', *Middle Schooling Review*, 1 (2): 14–19.

Smale, G., Tusab, G. and Statham, D. (2000) *Social Work and Social Problems*. Basingstoke: Palgrave.

Smeeton, J. (2012) 'Child protection social work', in M. Daives (ed.), *Practice in Social Work with Children and Families*. Basingstoke: Palgrave Macmillan, pp. 155–69.

Smith, J. and Ing, P. (1996) *Combating Social Exclusion: Advocacy and the Needs of Service Users*. Stoke-on-Trent: Housing and Community Research Unit.

Smith, R. (2008) *Social Work and Power*. Basingstoke: Palgrave Macmillan.

Sneddon, H. (2012) 'The challenging nature of research in child protection', in M. Davies (ed.), *Social Work with Children and Families*. Basingstoke: Palgrave Macmillan, pp. 137–54.

SSI/SWSG (1991) *Quality Standards, Assessment and Care Management*. London: DHSS.

SSSC (2009) *Codes of Practice for Social Workers and Employers*. Dundee: Scottish Social Services Council.

Stainton, T. (2009) 'Learning disability', in R. Adams, L. Dominelli and M. Payne (eds), *Critical Practice in Social Work*, 2nd edn. Basingstoke: Palgrave Macmillan, pp. 346–55.

Sugarman, L. (2001) *Lifespan Development: Frameworks, Accounts and Strategies*, 2nd edn. Hove: Psychology Press.

Tarleton, B. and Ward, L. (2005) 'Changes and choices: finding out what information young people with learning disabilities, their parents and supporters need at transition', *British Journal of Learning Disabilities*, 33: 70–6.

Taylor, H., Beckett, C. and McKeigue, B. (2008) 'Judgements of Solomon: anxieties and defences of social workers involved in care proceedings', *Child and Family Social Work*, 13: 23–31.

TCSW (2012) *Professional Capabilities Framework for Social Workers in England*. London: The College of Social Work.

Templeton, J. and Kemmis, J. (1998) *How Do Young People and Children Get Their Voices Heard? Feedback from Young People and the VCC Services in London*. London: Voice for the Child in Care.

Thomas, N. (2000) *Children, Family and the State*. Basingstoke: Macmillan.

Thompson, N. (2000) *Theory and Practice in Human Services*. Buckingham: Open University Press.

Thompson, N. (2006) *Anti-discriminatory Practice*, 4th edn. Basingstoke: Macmillan.

Thompson, N. (2010) *Theorising Social Work Practice*. Basingstoke: Palgrave Macmillan.

Thompson, N. and Thompson, S. (2008) *The Social Work Companion*. Basingstoke: Palgrave Macmillan.

Thurman, S., (2009) *Making Complaints Work for People with Learning Difficulties*. Kidderminster: BILD.

Timms, N. (1964) *Social Casework*. London: Routledge & Kegan Paul.

Timms, J. (1995) Children's Representation. London: Sweet and Maxwell .

Topss UK Partnership (2002) *National Occupational Standards for Social Work*. Leeds: Topss England.

Towler, K. (2012) *Missing Voices: A Review of Independent Professional Advocacy Service for Looked After Children and Young People, Care Leavers and Children in Need Wales*. Cardiff: Children's Commissioner for Wales.

Townsley, R., Marriott, A. and Ward, L. (2009) *Access to Independent Advocacy: An Evidence Review*. Bristol: Office for Disability Issues, University of Bristol.

Traustadottir, R. (2006) 'Learning about self-advocacy from life-history: a case study form the United States', *British Journal of Learning Disabilities*, 34 (3): 175–80.

Treseder, P. and Crowley, A (2001) *Taking the Initiative: Promoting Young People's Participation in Decision Making in Wales*. London: Carnegie Young People's Initiative.

Trevithick, P. (2005) *Social Work Skills: A Practice Handbook*. Maidenhead: Open University Press.

Trevithick, P. (2012) *Social Work Skills and Knowledge: A Practice Handbook*, 3rd edn. Maidenhead: McGraw Hill.

UCAN (2001) *Annual Report, April 2000–March 2001*. Cardiff: UCAN Productions.

UCAN (2005) *Annual Report, April 2004–March 2005*. Cardiff: UCAN Productions.

Utting, W. (1997) *People Like Us: Report of the Review of the Safeguards For Children Living Away From Home*. London: The Stationery Office.

Wallis, L. and Frost, N. (1998) *Cause for Complaint: The Complaints Procedure for Young People in Care*. London: The Children's Society.

Ward, L. and Tarleton, B. (2007) 'Sinking or swimming? Supporting parents with learning disabilities and their children', *Tizard Learning Disability Review*, 12 (2): 22–32.

Warren, J. (2007) *Service User and Carer Participation in Social Work*. Exeter: Learning Matters.

Waterhouse, R., Clough, M. and Le Fleming, M. (2000) *Lost in Care: The Waterhouse Report*. Report of the Tribunal of Inquiry into the abuse of children in the former county council areas of Gwynedd and Clwyd since 1974. Cardiff: Children in Wales.

Weafer, J. (2003) *The Jigsaw of Advocacy: Finding a Voice*. Dublin: Comhairle.

Welbourn, P. (2011) 'Twenty-first century social work: the influence of political context on public service provision in social work education and service delivery', *European Journal of Social Work*, 14 (3): 403–420.

Welsh Assembly Government (2003) *National Standards for the Provision of Children's Advocacy Services*. Cardiff: Welsh Assembly Government.

Welsh Assembly Government (2007) *Fulfilled Lives, Supportive Communities: A Strategy for Social Service in Wales over the Next Decade*. Cardiff: Welsh Assembly Government.

Welsh Assembly Government (2008) *Service Framework for the Future Provision of Advocacy for Children in Wales*. Cardiff: Welsh Assembly Government.

Welsh Assembly Government (2009) *A Guide to the Model of Delivering Advocacy Services to Children and Young People*. Cardiff: Welsh Assembly Government.

Welsh Assembly Government (2011) *Sustainable Social Services for Wales: A Framework for Action*. Cardiff: Welsh Assembly Government.

Whelan, R. (2001a) *Helping the Poor: Friendly Visiting, Dole Charities and Dole Queues*. London: Civitas.

Wilks, T. (2012) *Advocacy and Social Work Practice*. Maidenhead: Open University Press.

Williams, P. (2009) *Social Work with People with Learning Difficulties*, 2nd edn. Exeter: Learning Matters.

Williams, P. and Shoultz, B. (1982) *We Can Speak for Ourselves*. Boston: MA: Brookline Books.

Wilson, K., Ruch, G., Lymbery, M. and Cooper, A. (2011) *Social Work: An Introduction to Contemporary Practice*, 2nd edn. Harlow: Pearson Education.

Wolfensberger, W. (1974) *A Multi-Component Advocacy Protection Scheme*. Canadian Association for the Mentally Retarded.

Wolfensberger, W. and O'Brien, J. (1977) *Citizen Advocacy Programme Evaluation*. London: CAPE.

Woodroofe, K. (1962) *From Charity to Social Work*. London: George, Allen & Unwin.

Woodrow, P. (1997) 'Nurse advocacy: is it in the patient's best interests?', *British Journal of Nursing*, 6 (4): 225–9.

World Health Organization (WHO) (1980) *International Classification of Impairments, Disabilities and Handicaps* (ICIDH). Geneva: WHO.

Wyllie, J. (2002) *Hear Me Now: Respecting Children's Rights*. Cardiff: UCAN Productions.

Young, D. (1992) 'Organising principles for international advocacy organisations', *Voluntas International Journal of Voluntary and Nonprofit Organisations*, 3 (1):1–28.

Younghusband, E. (1959) *Report of the Working Party on Social Workers in the Local Authority Health and Welfare Services*. London: HMSO.

Younghusband, E. (1978) *Social Work in Britain, 1950–1975*. London: George Allen and Unwin.

Index

Page references to Figures or Tables will be in *italics*, while references to Notes will have the letter 'n' following the page number.